Illustrated Borland® C++

Norman E. Smith, CDP

Wordware Publishing, Inc.

Library of Congress Cataloging-in-Publication Data

Smith, Norman E. (Norman Earl), 1952-
Illustrated Borland C++ / prepared by Norman E. Smith : prepared for Wordware Publishing.
p. cm.
Includes index.
ISBN 1-55622-295-5 : $24.95
1. C (Computer program language) 2. Turbo C (Computer program).
I. Wordware Publishing, Inc. II. Title.
QA76.73.C15S58 1992
005.26'2--dc20 92-24853
CIP

1506 Capital Avenue
Plano, Texas 75074

Printed in the United States of America

ISBN 1-55622-295-5

10 9 8 7 6 5 4 3 2 1
9211

All inquiries for volume purchases of this book should be addressed to Wordware Publishing, Inc., at the above address. Telephone inquiries may be made by calling:

(214) 423-0090

Contents

Contents

Contents

Number	*Title*	*Page*
83	STRCAT( ) and STRNCAT( )	294
84	STRCHR	297
85	STRCMP( ) and STRNCMP( )	300
86	STRCPY( ) and STRNCPY( )	303
87	STREAM I/O	306
88	STRINGS	311
89	STRLEN	315
90	STRUCT	318
91	STRUPR( ) and STRLWR( )	322
92	SWITCH	324
93	TYPEDEF	328
94	UNGETC( )	331
95	UNION	334
96	VARIABLES	337
97	VIRTUAL FUNCTIONS	340
98	VOID	344
99	WHILE	347
100	WHILE( ){ }	348
101	WINDOW MENU	351

Learning Sequence

Learning Sequence

Learning Sequence

Module 1
ABOUT THIS BOOK

INTRODUCTION

This book describes the programming language Borland C++. The Borland C++ package, a product of Borland, Inc., is one of the most popular C and C++ compilers for the IBM PC and compatible computer systems. This book covers the elements of C++ including object oriented programming extensions that make C++ unique among traditional high level programming languages. The book is designed as both a tutorial and reference. Novice C users can follow the prescribed learning sequence to learn the language. Experienced C users will find the numerous examples and alphabetical organization a valuable reference and aid to extracting the most from Borland C++.

WHAT IS C

Brian Kernighan and Dennis Ritchie of Bell Labs developed C in the early 1970s in an effort to create a portable language for implementing the Unix operating system. Much of the "shorthand" syntax of C came about because typical terminals of the day were slow (10 or 11 character per second) Teletype ASR-33s.

C was implemented on a PDP-11 minicomputer. Many of C's commands map one-to-one to PDP-11 Assembly Language instructions. This closeness between the high-level language, C, and the Assembly Language instructions accounts for much of the efficiency in the code that C compilers generate. It also puts C into the low-level language category along with Forth. Low level in this context denotes close to the hardware. In fact, many people consider C to be a high-level Assembly Language.

Today's C is very portable among computers of different architectures and vendors. Much of this portability can be attributed to the efforts of the ANSI Standards Committee X3.159, which produced the document *American National Standard for Information Systems-Programming Language C, X3.159-1989*. This document standardizes the language. The original defacto C standard was *The C Programming Language* by Kernighan and Ritchie. It left much open to interpretation by the language implementor. Standard libraries were not even addressed. The result was that every C compiler contained unique commands and function libraries guaranteed to be incompatible. This has changed through the efforts of the ANSI C committee.

C++ is C with extensions to support object oriented programming. It was developed by Bjarne Stroustrop of AT&T Bell Labs in 1986 as a means of making complex programs easier to write and maintain. The name C++ is a combination of the old name 'C' and the increment operator '++,' indicating an incremental development of C. The name shows that C++ extends C rather than being a completely new language.

C++ Version 1.2 was the initial AT&T release. The AT&T implemented C++ as the *cfront* translator. C++ 1.2 has been available both as ports of cfront and as C++ compilers for a variety of computers including PCs.

The current AT&T version of C++ is 2.1. It is available both in translator form (cfront) and compiler form (Borland C++ and others). C++ Version 2.1 adds several features to C++. Some of the primary new features include:

- Multiple inheritance
- Explicit support for abstract classes
- Pointers to class members
- Additional operator overloading

These are significant enhancements over previous C++ standards.

WHAT IS OOP

Object Oriented Programming or OOP is a software development technique that has gained popularity because of potential gains in programmer productivity over conventional software development methodologies. C, Fortran, and Basic are procedural programming languages in contrast. There are several characteristics of an object oriented language, which include:

- Information hiding
- Data encapsulation or abstraction
- Inheritance

An object is a self-contained unit or module of data and code. All data and procedures related to the object are defined within it. So, procedures (called methods in OOP terminology) are tied to the data. This is in contrast with procedural languages that pass data to procedures. A 'message' identifying a method to execute is passed to the object.

The advantages of OOP fall into two broad categories, increased programmer productivity and decreased maintenance costs. Well-chosen classes and objects may be reused in other applications. Reused code has already been tested, so it should need little testing when used in a new program. Objects help partition complex problems into simpler ones that are easier to implement.

Application testing time is generally shorter because objects are small and contain independent code and local data segments that are verified with less effort than in conventional programs. When a bug does occur, a particular object is usually implicated. This makes isolating and correcting the bug easier.

Data abstraction is a large benefit to OOP. Data is declared local to an object. It can be either private or public. Use whatever combination of data forms required to describe the problem. Hiding data from other parts of a program makes it possible to totally change the data structure of an object without affecting the operation of the program. This is significant!

There is a price to pay for all that the object oriented programming brings the developer, however. A different way of thinking about and approaching problems is required. Choosing the correct classes of objects has a great deal to do with how much OOP helps a project. Learning this comes only with doing. Data abstraction takes time to become accustomed to, also. These all contribute to the steep learning curve to making effective use of OOP.

WHY BORLAND C++

There are many reasons for choosing Borland C++ as a programming language. It is suitable both as a learning tool and as a serious programming language. The advantages of Borland C++ include:

- Borland C++ is very fast, both in compile time and execution speed.
- The Borland Integrated Development Environment provides an extremely efficient program development environment. Editing files, compiling programs, testing programs, and debugging programs is well integrated and very convenient. Mouse support is included.
- The Borland Assembler and Borland Debugger are included in the professional package. Both are integrated directly into existing Borland C++ menus without user configuration.
- Borland C++ is really two compilers built into one. Full ANSI C is supported for existing C programs. The AT&T C++ 2.0 language specification is supported for Object Oriented Programming. This combination of being able to compile both C and C++ code provides the programmer with the opportunity to gradually make the switch from normal ANSI C to C++ and its object oriented capabilities.

- Both extended and expanded memory is automatically detected and used if present.

WRITING STYLE

Knowledge about the writing conventions followed in this book is helpful in reading the text.

- Borland C++ identifiers and reserved words are set in italic type.
- Keys you type or press are set in bold type.
- All steps performed in the Hands-On Activities are numbered.
- Two-key combinations are a combination of a shift key and a letter. The shift keys are Alt, Ctrl, and Shift. For example, "Press **Ctrl-C** to exit." means press the 'C' key while holding the Ctrl key down. The word "Press" indicates a key or key combination should be pressed to continue.

ORGANIZATION

This book is organized alphabetically by subject topic for use as a reference. If you are learning C++, do not attempt to learn the language by reading the book in numerical order. Rather, follow the Recommended Learning Sequence (or) page number specified in the front of the book.

The book contains modules instead of chapters. Each module covers a single C++ related topic. It consists of a description of the topic or feature, applications, and detailed usage examples. The description serves as a formal definition of the topic to be covered. Applications discuss potential uses of the C++ commands. Usage, along with examples of the command are given in the Hands-On Activity section. A module may include other sections if necessary to fully explain a given topic.

Continue the learning sequence with Module 2.

Module 2

SAMPLE SESSION

DESCRIPTION

This module guides you through a sample Borland C++ session. The Programmer's Platform is introduced and a simple C++ program written. The steps include starting the compiler, editing the C++ program, running it, and saving your work. This module serves as an introduction to Borland C++ Programmer's Platform operation. It provides the beginner a place to start learning how to use Borland C++ and is probably all experienced programmers need to begin using the package.

APPLICATIONS

Most program development in Borland C++ is done from within the Integrated Development Environment. The built-in menu system provides access to Borland C++'s program development features. The built-in text editor is quite powerful and is convenient to use. After the program is entered into the editor, it can be compiled and executed via Programmer's Platform menu selection. The built-in debugger is also invoked from the menu system. Be sure to save your work frequently to reduce the risk of losing your work in case of power failure.

The Integrated Development Environment provides a fast and convenient means to exercise the full program development cycle from within a single program environment. This speeds program development time significantly over conventional compilers that require you to load a text editor to edit source code, load the compiler to compile the program, run the linker to create a .EXE file, and run the program to test. Reloading the editor, compiler, linker, etc. for every source code change takes a great deal of time.

After completing development of a Borland C++ program, it can be compiled to disk for later use. Borland C++ provides the facilities to develop large C and C++ programs using Project and Make files to define all of the modules to the compiler. A module is devoted to Project Files and Make Files.

HANDS-ON ACTIVITY

This session demonstrates some of the features of the Borland C++ Programmer's Platform. Specifically the multifile text editor, running a program, saving the program, and exiting back to DOS. The editor uses most of the WordStar™ key bindings. You will feel right at home if you are already comfortable using the WordStar™ control key layout. The special PC keyboard keys, such as PgUp and PgDn operate as expected. Context sensitive help is also available at any time by pressing F1.

STARTING BORLAND C++ The following instructions assume that Borland C++ is installed and functional on your computer, that power is on, and DOS is loaded.

1. Change to the directory that you plan to use for exercises in this book. (The directory \EXERCISE is suggested.) Type **CD \EXERCISE** now.
2. Type **BC** at the DOS prompt and press **Enter**. The following display appears on the screen.

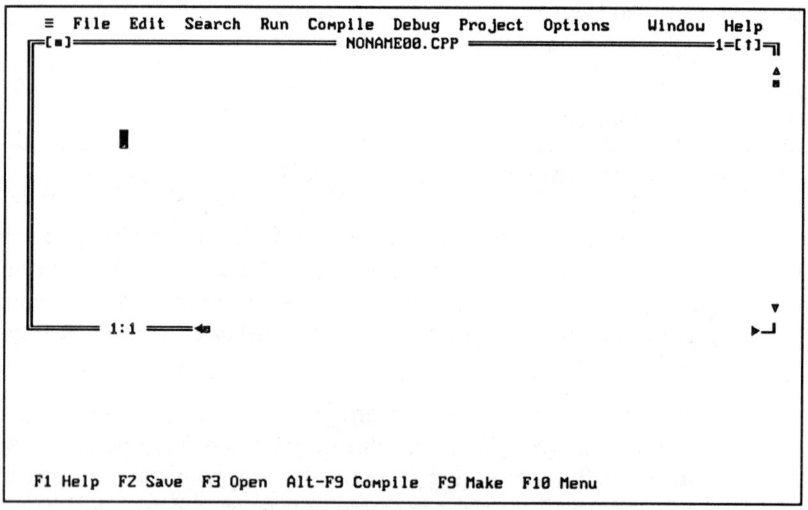

The opening Programmer's Platform screen begins with an empty default file named NONAME00.CPP. After the initial session, Borland C++ remembers the last filename edited and automatically loads that file into the editor the next time BC executes.

Notice that there are eleven pull-down menus available. These are:

≡	Miscellaneous information about Borland C++ and interface to external programs such as Borland and Borland Debugger. (Turbo Assembler and Turbo Debugger are optional programs included with the Professional version of Borland C++.)
File	File related operations such as opening and saving a file.
Edit	Cutting and pasting operations.
Search	Find, find and replace, etc.
Run	Compile and run the file currently loaded in the text editor. Some debugging such as setting/clearing trace points can be performed from this menu.
Compile	This menu item compiles a source file to an object file or a .EXE file. The filename in the editor is used for the default filenames to compile and link.
Debug	Debug provides access to interactive debugging. Variables can be examined/set/cleared, and you can watch variables change during execution.
Project	This menu item controls Borland C++'s handling of large programs that are in multiple source files. All of the files of the program are specified in a .PRJ file. The project file tells Borland C++ which source files to compile to build the program.
Options	Borland C++ has a multitude of options. Default options are set during installation. The user can change any option at any time via this menu. Some of the things that can be changed are code optimizations, C++ compile options, and which math library to include.
Window	The Programmer's Platform is a window based environment. The Window menu is used to manipulate the screen windows. Window operations include zoom, arranging windows on the screen, and closing windows.
Help	Borland C++ includes a context sensitive help capability. Select **Help** or press **F1** to bring up a help window. Once help is invoked, any help can be accessed.

The Programmer's Platform pull-down menus can be accessed several ways.

- Press **F10**, then move the cursor to the desired menu item and press **Enter**.
- Click the mouse cursor on the desired menu item.
- Press **Alt** and the first character of the menu item. For example, press **Alt-F** to pull down the File menu.

NOTE Remember that a shifted command sequence, such as Alt-Ctrl-, or Shift- followed by a character, is activated by holding the specified shift key down while you press the character. Ctrl-X means hold the Ctrl key down while pressing X.

NOTE Borland C++ automatically generates two cursors when it finds a mouse driver installed. The mouse cursor is a large inverse video block that moves when the mouse is moved. The editing cursor is an underline. The editing cursor can be moved with the mouse by positioning the mouse cursor in the editing window and clicking the left button.

The Alt-character method of accessing menu items is used for the remainder of this book for consistency. Using a mouse with Borland C++ increases productivity significantly.

EDITING A FILE The Programmer's Platform begins in the edit window. You may begin typing source code at this point.

NOTE If you make a typing mistake, press Backspace to erase the error. Type the correction and continue entering source code. Borland C++ is case sensitive, so "this" and "This" and "THIS" are all different to the compiler.

3. Type **#include <iostream.h>** and press **Enter**.

```
 ≡ File  Edit  Search  Run  Compile  Debug  Project  Options    Window  Help
[■]══════════════════════ NONAME00.CPP ══════════════════════1=[↑]
#include <iostream.h>
```

Most C++ programs begin with one or more *#include* statements. This *#include* is a preprocessor directive that causes the file IOSTREAM.H to be loaded during compilation. Files listed with *#include* statements usually end with .H in C and .HPP for C++ and are referred to as "header files." Borland C++ uses the .H extension for all of its system header files.

4. Type **main( )** and press **Enter**.

```
 ≡ File  Edit  Search  Run  Compile  Debug  Project  Options    Window  Help
[■]══════════════════════ NONAME00.CPP ══════════════════════1=[↑]
#include <iostream.h>
main()
```

Every C++ program must include one function named main. This is the starting point for execution when the program is run.

5. Type { and press **Enter.**

```
  ≡ File  Edit  Search  Run  Compile  Debug  Project  Options    Window  Help
╔[■]═══════════════════════ NONAME00.CPP ═══════════════════════════1=[↑]═╗
║#include <iostream.h>                                                    ▲
║main()                                                                   ■
║{
```

C++ is a block structured language. Blocks of source code are identified with an opening { and a closing }. Every function must have at least one brace pair.

6. Type **cout << "This is my first C++ program.\n";** and press **Enter.**

```
  ≡ File  Edit  Search  Run  Compile  Debug  Project  Options    Window  Help
╔[■]═══════════════════════ NONAME00.CPP ═══════════════════════════1=[↑]═╗
║#include <iostream.h>                                                    ▲
║main()                                                                   ■
║{
║        cout << "This is my first C++ program\n";
║
```

There are several important notes about this line of code. First, a built-in C++ function, cout, is called to print a line of output to the console and is defined in iostream.h. The '<<' statement is pronounced 'put to' because the parameter on the right is being put to the object on the left. Notice the *\n* toward the end of the line. This tells cout to skip to a new line at that point. There are several special characters that are made up of a "\" followed by a character. Each has a specific meaning.

Character	*Meaning*
\n	Newline
\t	Tab
\0	Null
\v	Vertical Tab
\b	Backspace
\r	Carriage Return
\f	Form Feed
\a	BEL Character (beep)
\\	Backslash
\?	Question Mark
\'	Single Quote
\"	Double Quote
\ooo	Octal Number, where ooo are three octal digits
\xhh	Hex number, where hh is two hex digits

The final point is that statements in C and C++ end with a ";". Preprocessor commands are not directly processed by the compiler and do not use the ";".

7. Type } and press **Enter.**

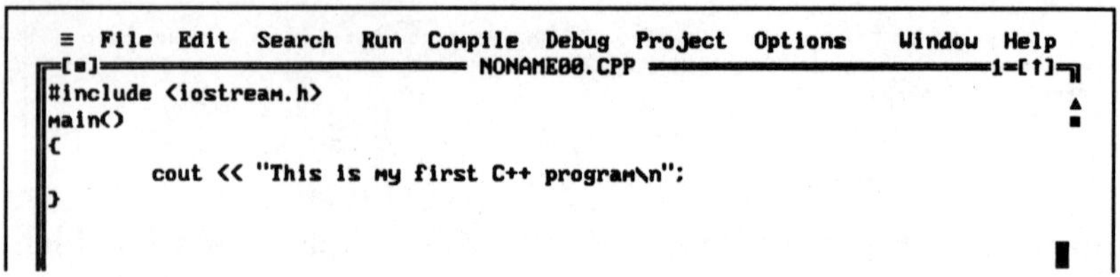

You have now entered a complete C++ program. The closing } marks the end of the function main to the compiler.

SAVING YOUR WORK It is important to save your work frequently to guard against accidental loss of code. Save the sample program before going on.

8. Press **Alt-F** to activate the File menu.

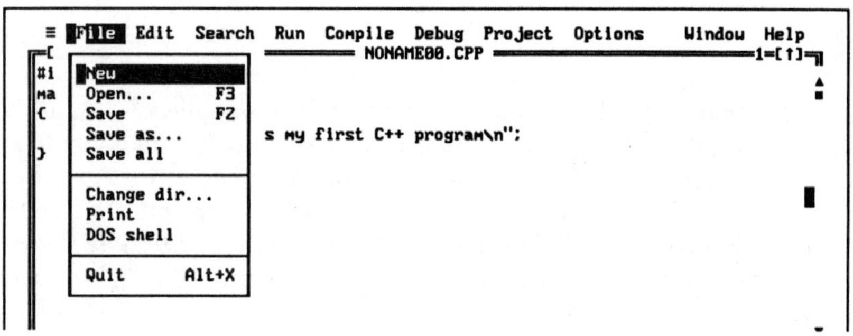

9. Move the menu cursor to Save as... by pressing **Down Arrow** three times.

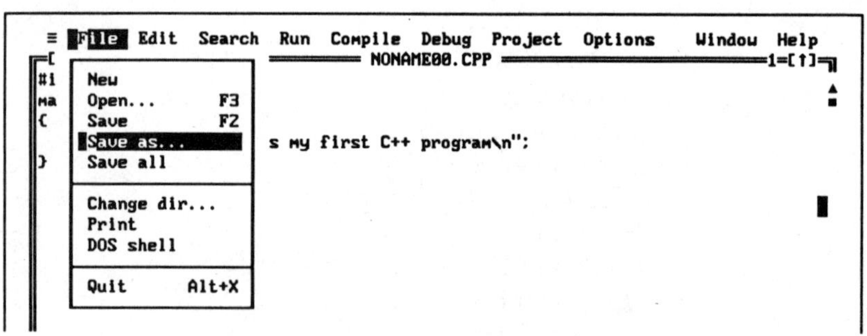

10. Press **Enter** to activate the Save as... selection.

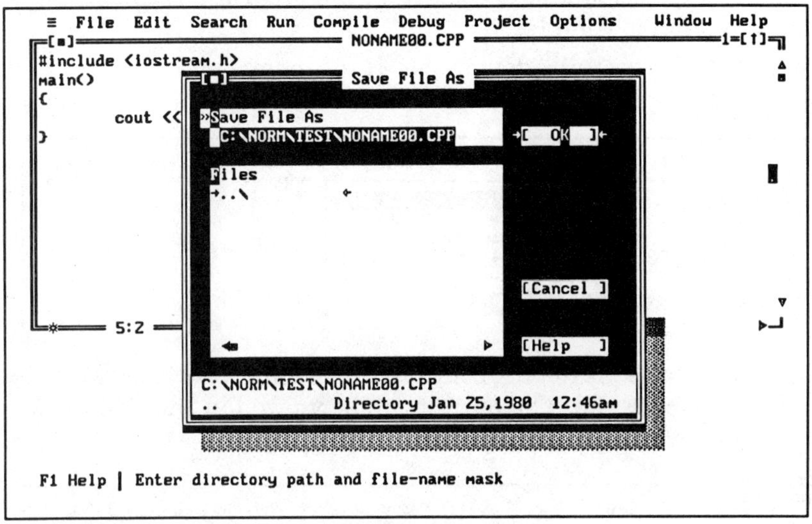

11. Type **mod2.cpp** and press **Enter** to save the program.

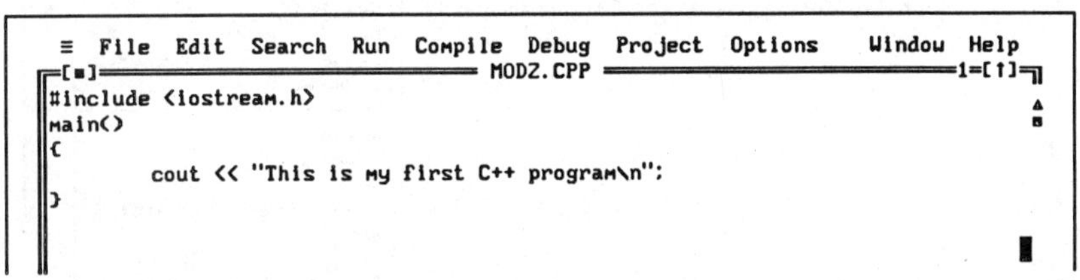

After mod2.cpp has been saved, the Programmer's Platform returns to the Edit window.

NOTE The following list of symbols are used commonly in the example programs. All will be described in detail later in this book.

Command	*Meaning*
//	Comment to end of line
<<	Write string to screen
{ ... }	Grouping characters
/*	Begin multiline comment
*/	End multiline comment
*	Pointer to a variable
&	Address of a variable

RUNNING A PROGRAM Running a program is a matter of pulling down the *Run* menu. Compilation and execution of the program in the editor begins when the selection is completed.

12. Press **Alt-R** to pull down the Run menu and **Enter** to begin compilation.

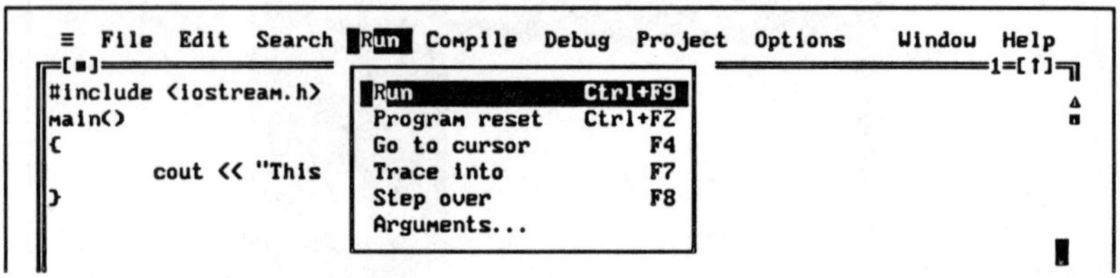

A compile window opens during compilation to show progress. Module1.cpp is compiled and executed. The output can be viewed in the Output window.

13. Press **Alt-W** to pull down the Window menu.

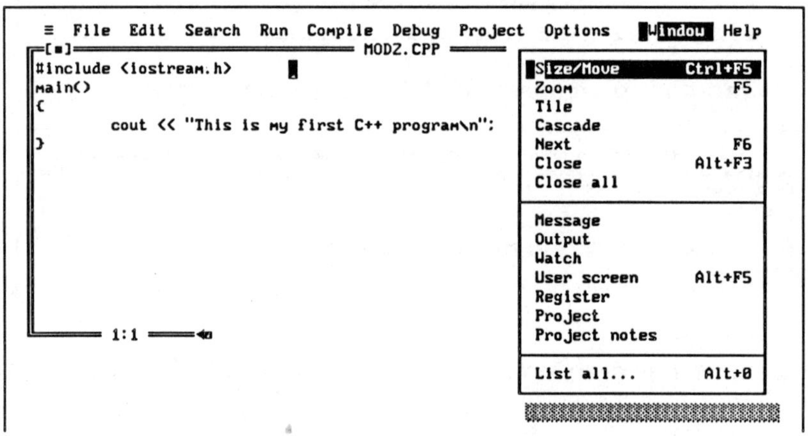

14. Move the menu cursor down to Output and press **Enter** to view the output when you execute the sample program.

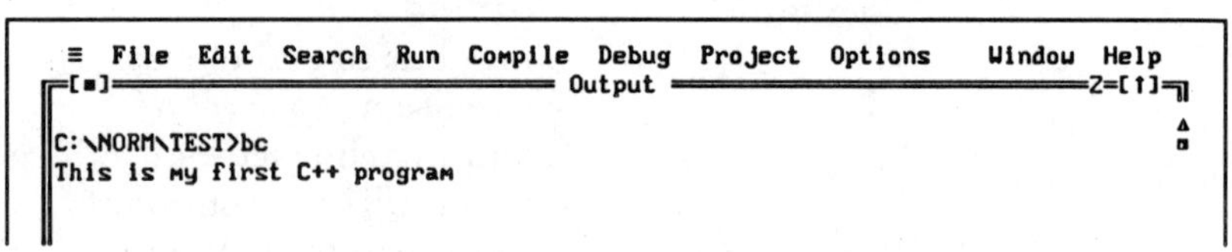

Congratulations! You have successfully entered and executed a C++ program using Borland C++'s Integrated Development Environment. All that remains is exiting back to DOS.

15. Press **Alt-X** to exit Borland C++ and return to the DOS prompt.
16. Continue the learning sequence with Module 3.

Module 3

≡ MENU

DESCRIPTION

This module describes the Borland Programmer's Platform ≡ menu. Each of the options is discussed in detail. The ≡ menu provides the interface to optional external Borland packages and desktop housekeeping functions.

APPLICATIONS

Use the ≡ menu to access external programs.

There are eight menu items in the ≡ pull-down menu.

- Clear desktop
- Repaint desktop
- GREP
- Borland Assembler
- Borland Debugger
- Borland Profiler
- Resource Compiler
- Import Librarian

This menu is pulled down by pressing the F10 key, then moving the cursor to the ≡ character at the far left of the menu bar and pressing Enter. Menu entries are selected by moving the highlight bar to the desired entry and pressing Enter.

Clear desktop and Repaint desktop manipulate the Programmer's Platform desktop windows. The desktop can be corrupted by writing directly to video memory in a C++ program.

GREP invokes the GREP regular expression search program that Borland includes with Borland C++. This is a powerful tool for finding strings in a source file. More than one file can be searched at a time.

Borland Assembler, Borland Debugger, and Borland Profiler are optional Borland products and are beyond the scope of this book.

Resource Compiler and Import Librarian are tools associated with developing Windows programs.

HANDS-ON ACTIVITY

This session shows how to select and invoke options of the ≡ menu. When Borland C++ starts, the Programmer's Platform desktop windows will be restored just as you left them at the end of the last session. Thus, the File window will contain MOD2.CPP assuming you just completed Module 2, the Sample Session.

1. Start Borland C++ by typing **BC** and pressing **Enter** at the DOS prompt.
2. Press **F10** to activate the menu bar at the top of the screen.

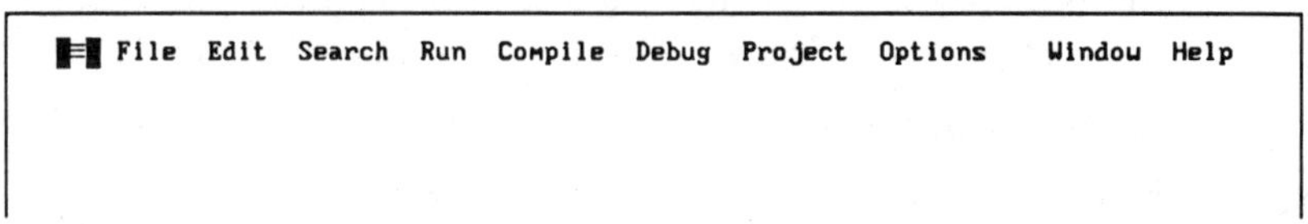

3. Move the cursor to the leftmost entry, the ≡ character, by pressing **Left Arrow** as many times as necessary to position the cursor. Then, press **Enter**.

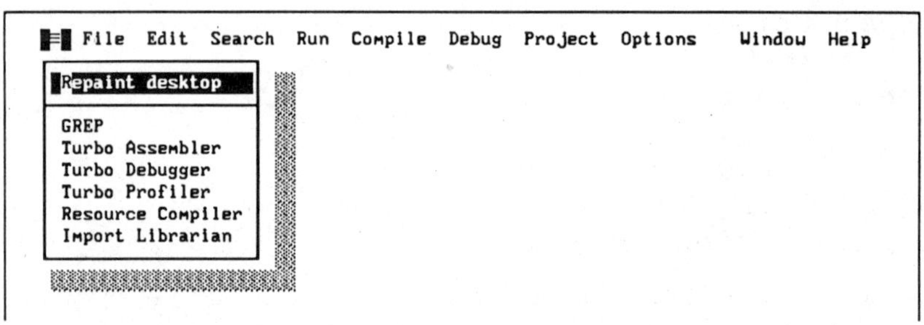

4. Press **Down Arrow** once to position the selection bar on the entry labeled GREP and press **Enter**. This command searches all files with an extension of .C for the string "void."

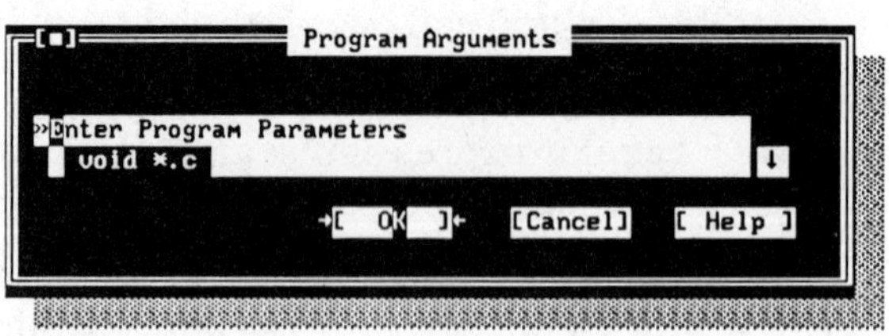

5. Press **Esc** to close the window and return to the window that was active previously, the Edit window in this example.

REPAINT DESKTOP The Programmer's Platform provides a way to refresh the screen in case a window becomes corrupted while testing code. This example demonstrates its operation.

6. Press **F10** to activate the Main menu selection bar.
7. Move the cursor to the leftmost entry, the ≡ character by pressing **Left Arrow** as many times as necessary to position the cursor. Then, press **Enter**.
8. Press **Down Arrow** to position the selection bar on Repaint desktop.

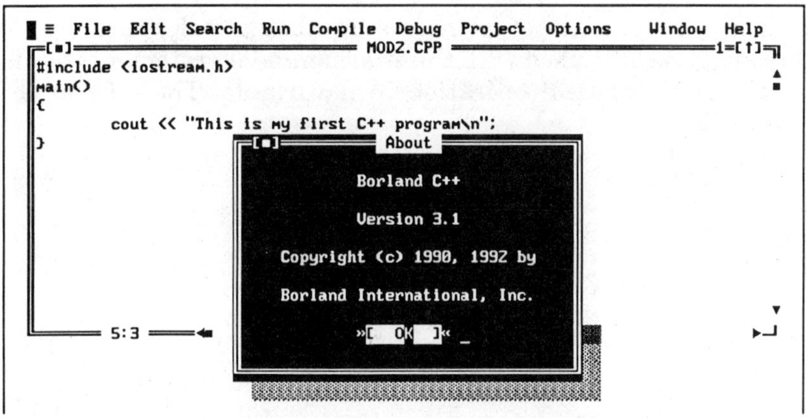

9. Press **Enter**. The currently open windows on the screen are redrawn and the session resumes in the active window.
10. Press **Alt-X** to return to DOS.
11. Continue the learning sequence with Module 42.

Module 4

ARITHMETIC

DESCRIPTION

C++ provides a number of primitive mathematical operators. These operators are generally used with the '=' assignment statement to place the results of a mathematical operation in a variable. The C++ arithmetic operators are:

Operator	*Name*	*Type*
+	Add	Binary
–	Subtract	Binary
*	Multiply	Binary
/	Divide	Binary
%	Modulo	Binary
++	Increment	Unary
– –	Decrement	Unary
+	Plus	Unary
–	Negative	Unary

The binary operators require two operands:

```
x = operand_1 + operand_2;
```

Unary operators require only one operand:

```
x++;
```

Operands may be variables, constants, or function results. The operand types are automatically cast by the compiler depending on the operation and the data types involved. The casting attempts to keep the maximum precision.

C++ follows a set hierarchy of precedence in evaluating expressions using mathematical operators. The order of precedence is *, /, &, +, then – for the binary operators. The precedence order can be modified using parentheses.

APPLICATIONS

Use the mathematical operators to calculate formulas required for an application. A set of math functions such as cos( ) and abs( ) are available in supplied libraries. The binary operators are the most commonly used.

BINARY OPERATORS Arithmetic operators can be combined with parentheses for grouping to calculate complicated formula results. A simple example of this is converting temperatures between Celsius and Fahrenheit.

```
f_temp = c_temp * 1.8 + 32;
c_temp = (f_temp - 32) * (5/9);
```

Binary operators require two operators, one before and one following the operator. This style of notation is called infix because the operator is in between the operands.

UNARY OPERATORS The unary operators are associated with a single operand. + and – are sign designators. A negative number is represented with a leading '–'. –42 is a negative number. +27 is a positive number. The compiler determines whether + and – are sign operators or addition and subtraction by the usage context.

> **NOTE** Putting spaces around + and – to mean addition and subtraction is good coding practice. Likewise, use no space after + and – to mean a positive and negative number. The visual difference helps the programmer determine the intended usage.

The increment (++) and decrement (– –) operators are unique. Where the operator falls in relation to the operand can vary and modifies its operation. Increment adds one to the operand then stores the result back in the operand. Decrement subtracts one from the operand then updates its value. Increment and decrement may be either pre- or postoperations.

Usage	*Meaning*	
++x;	x = x + 1;	// preincrement
x++;	x = x + 1;	// postincrement
– –y;	y = y – 1;	// predecrement
y– –;	y = y – 1;	// postdecrement

Preincrement and decrement operators perform the addition or subtraction before using the variable in an expression. For example,

```
ch = string[++i];
```

i is incremented before being used as the array index. string[0] cannot be referenced by this statement.

Postincrement and decrement operators do the addition or subtraction after the operand is used in the expression. For example:

```
ch = string[i++];
```

This expression moves the character referenced by string[i] to ch before incrementing i. i points to the next character in the array after the statement is completed. ++ and – – can be used in calculations but are confusing to the programmer and should be avoided.

HANDS-ON ACTIVITY

The sample program illustrates arithmetic operators and the casting that is done by the compiler.

1. Start Borland C++.
2. Press **Alt-FN** to pull down the File menu and create a new file.
3. Type the following code into the NONAME00.CPP edit window:

```
#include <iostream.h>
#include <stdio.h>
#include <string.h>
#include <conio.h>

void main()
{
      int   f_temp;
      float c_temp;

      int value;

      clrscr();
      cout << "Module 4\n\n";
      cout << "This module demonstrates arithmetic operators\n";
      cout << "Enter a temperature: ";
      cin  >> value;
      cout << "\nvalue     is: " << value << "\n";

      cout << "That was Fahrenheit, so convert to Celsius...\n";
      c_temp = (value - 32) * (5.0/9.0);
      cout << "Celsius: " << c_temp << "\n\n";
      cout << "Oops, it was really Celsius, ";
      cout << "make it Fahrenheit...\n";
      f_temp = value * 1.8 + 32;
      cout << "Fahrenheit : " << f_temp << "\n";

      cout << "Press any key to exit";
      do {;} while(!kbhit());
}
```

4. Press **Alt-RR** to compile and run the sample program.

```
Module 4

This module demonstrates arithmetic operators
Enter a temperature:
```

5. Type **45** and press **Enter**. The following is displayed:

```
Module 4

This module demonstrates arithmetic operators
Enter a temperature: 45

That was Fahrenheit, so convert to Celsius...
Celsius: 7.222222
Oops, it was really Celsius, make it Fahrenheit...
Fahrenheit : 113
Press any key to exit
```

6. Press any key to exit the sample program and return to Borland C++.

Notice in the code the conversion calculation to Celsius:

```
c_temp = (value - 32) * (5.0/9.0);
```

It uses 5.0 and 9.0 instead of 5 and 9 to force the compiler to treat the division as floating point instead of integer. Integer division will cause c_temp to always be zero! The Celsius result is printed with 6 decimal positions because c_temp is declared a floating point variable. The Fahrenheit value printed as an integer because f_temp was declared integer.

Parentheses are used in the Celsius calculation to modify the evaluation order. No parentheses would have resulted in the following evaluation order:

a = 32 * 5
b = a / 9
c = value – b

7. Continue the learning sequence with Module 92.

Module 5
ARRAYS

DESCRIPTION

A variable defined with multiple occurrences is an array. Any data type may be used as an array. Define an array by adding the number of occurrences enclosed in [ ] to a normal variable definition. For example:

```
char string[80];
int  counters[9];
```

string defines a character array named string. string may contain up to 80 bytes of memory (79 characters plus a NULL string terminator). *counters* allocates nine ints.

C and C++ support multiple-dimensioned arrays. Each [ ] pair represents an array dimension:

```
char lines[10][80];
long matrix[3][3];
char constant[] = "This is a constant string";
```

lines could represent 10 lines of 80 characters each. lines allocates 800 bytes of memory. *matrix* is a two-dimensional matrix of integers. The first dimension is the row and the second dimension is the column. An array may have an implied length. This is illustrated by *constant*.

Arrays have the following special rules:

- The last character in a character string is 0.
- Addressing starts with [0].
- No bounds checking is done by the compiler.

A convention in C and C++ is that the last character in a character string is zero. Zero is the character NULL. It is not printable and signals the end of the string. All of the C++ string functions make this assumption. For example, the function strlen( ) matches each character in the string to NULL and returns the length based on where the NULL is detected.

Array addressing is zero based. That is, the first byte of an array is [0]. The second byte is [1] and so forth.

```
char junk[10] = "012345678";
```

junk[0] is '0.' junk[5] is '5.' The last subscript is junk[9]. C++ will not prevent subscripting past the end of an array. Bounds checking when a program runs requires several extra instructions per array access. The lack of array run-time bounds checking is one of the reasons C has enjoyed a reputation for speed over the years. Borland C++ allows run-time bounds checking as an optional feature. Bounds checking is selected from the Option menu.

APPLICATIONS

Use arrays when multiple occurrences of a variable are required. Each value in an array is tied to the address of the start of the array, then referenced relative to the start. That is why the first value is [0]; the array start + 0. Entry [1] is the array start + 1.

The most common application of arrays is defining character strings. There is a set of built-in functions to manipulate character string (see Module 83). Arrays can also be manipulated via pointers. Pointers are discussed in Module 69.

HANDS-ON ACTIVITY

Usage of arrays is illustrated in the sample program.

1. Type **BC** and press **Enter** to start up the compiler.
2. Press **Alt-FN** to pull down the File menu and create a new file.
3. Type the following code into the NONAME00.CPP edit window:

```
#include <iostream.h>
#include <stdio.h>
#include <string.h>
#include <conio.h>

void main()
{
     char digits[] = "012345";
     char string[80];
     int  matrix[3][3];
     int  i;

     cout << "\nModule 5\n";
     cout << "Index through digits: ";
     for(i=0;i<8;i++){
          printf("%d ",digits[i]);
     }
     cout << "\n Digits[6] is 0 for end of string\n";
     cout << "Next, use string copy to copy contents of";
     cout << " digits to string,\n then display string: ";
```

```
        strcpy(string,digits);
        cout << string;
        cout << "Load values into matrix...\n";
        for(i=0;i<9;i++){
              matrix[0][i] = i;
        }
        cout << "matrix now contains 0-8\n";
        printf("%d %d %d \n%d %d %d  \n%d %d %d\n",
              matrix[0][0],matrix[0][1],matrix[0][2],
              matrix[1][0],matrix[1][1],matrix[1][2],
              matrix[2][0],matrix[2][1],matrix[2][2]);

        cout << "\nPress Any Key To Exit\n";
        do{;} while (!kbhit());
}
```

4. Press **Alt-RR** to compile the program, then run it.
5. Press **Alt-F5** to view the user screen.

```
C:\NORM\TEST>bc

Module 5
index through digits: 48 49 50 51 52 53 0 0
 Digits[6] is 0 for end of string
Next, user string copy to copy contents of digits to string,
 then display string: 012345load values into matrix...
matrix now contains 0-8
0 1 2
3 4 5
6 7 8

Press Any Key To Exit

_
```

6. Press **Alt-X** to exit Borland C++ and return to the DOS prompt.
7. Continue the learning sequence with Module 61.

Module 6

ASSIGNMENT OPERATORS

DESCRIPTION

The C++ assignment operators move a value into a variable. The source of the value can be one of several sources:

Another variable	i = x;
A constant	i = 27;
A function call	i = strlen(string);
An arithmetic operation	i = x * 2;
Data initialization	int i = 0;

The assignment operators are all a variation of '='. Do not confuse = with ==. = is the assignment operator and == tests two expressions for equality.

APPLICATIONS

The = operator can be combined with several other arithmetic operators to form a shorthand assignment statement. The C++ assignment operators are:

Operator	*Name*
=	Assignment or equal
+=	Plus equal
–=	Minus equal
*=	Times equal
/=	Divide equal
>>=	Right shift equal
<<=	Left shift equal
&=	Bitwise and equal
^=	Bitwise or equal
|=	Bitwise xor equal

Be sure to include a blank before the compound assignment operators. The blank prevents ambiguous conditions such as:

```
x*=addr;
```

The compiler doesn't know whether this statement should be

```
x *=addr;
```

or

```
x* =addr;
```

Compound assignments combine data movement with another operator. All of the operators listed after '=' in the list are compound operators. Sample usage for the compound operators are:

<table>
<tr><th>Operator</th><th>Usage</th><th>Same As</th></tr>
<tr><td>Assignment or equal</td><td>x = 1;</td><td></td></tr>
<tr><td>Plus equal</td><td>x += 27;</td><td>x = x + 27;</td></tr>
<tr><td>Minus equal</td><td>x –= 27;</td><td>x = x – 27;</td></tr>
<tr><td>Times equal</td><td>x *= 42;</td><td>x = x * 42;</td></tr>
<tr><td>Divide equal</td><td>x /= 42;</td><td>x = x / 42;</td></tr>
<tr><td>Right shift equal</td><td>x >>= 8;</td><td>x = x >> 8;</td></tr>
<tr><td>Left shift equal</td><td>x <<= 8;</td><td>x = x << 8;</td></tr>
<tr><td>Bitwise and equal</td><td>x &= 64;</td><td>x = x & 64;</td></tr>
<tr><td>Bitwise or equal</td><td>x |= 64;</td><td>x = x | 64;</td></tr>
<tr><td>Bitwise xor equal</td><td>x ^= 64;</td><td>x = x ^ 64;</td></tr>
</table>

HANDS-ON ACTIVITY

The sample program illustrates several of the assignment operators.

1. Type **BC** and press **Enter** to start up the compiler.
2. Press **Alt-FN** to pull down the File menu and create a new file.
3. Type the following code into the NONAME00.CPP edit window:

```
#include <iostream.h>
#include <stdio.h>
#include <string.h>
#include <conio.h>

void main()
{
     int X = 0;
     int value;

     cout << "Module 6\n\n";
     cout << "This module demonstrates assignment operators\n";
     cout << "Enter a number: ";
     cin  >> value;
     cout << "\nvalue      is: " << value << "\n";
     cout << "X           is: " << X     << "\n";
     X += value;
     cout << "X += value  is: " << X     << "\n";
```

```
        X -= 2;
        cout << "X -= 2     is: " << X     << "\n";
        X = strlen("ABCDEF");
        cout << "X = function : " << X     << "\n";
        X *= value * 2;
        cout << "X *= math  is: " << X     << "\n";

        cout << "Press any key to exit";
        do {;} while(!kbhit());
}
```

4. Press **Alt-RR** to compile and run the sample program.

```
Module 6

This module demonstrates assignment operators
Enter a number:
```

5. Type **27** and press **Enter**. The following is displayed:

```
Module 6

This module demonstrates assignment operators
Enter a number: 27
value      is: 27
X          is: 0
X += value is: 27
X -= 2     is: 25
X = function : 6
X *= math  is: 324
Press any key to exit
```

6. Press any key to exit the sample program and return to Borland C++.
7. Continue the learning sequence with Module 4.

Module 7
BITWISE EXPRESSIONS

DESCRIPTION

Bitwise operators manipulate data items as bit patterns or binary values. These operators work with integer values. The C++ bitwise operators are:

Operator	*Type*
~	One's complement
|	Logical OR
&	Logical AND
^	Logical Exclusive OR
<<	Logical Shift Left
>>	Logical Shift Right

These may be used as an expression in a conditional or with assignment operators.

```
if(1 & 3){ ... }
mask = truth << 2;
mask >>= 4;
```

The if statement uses the logical and of 1 and 3 to determine truth. Next, the contents of truth are shifted two bits to the left and assigned to mask. The final example shifts the contents of mask four bits to the right and places the result back into mask.

One's complement (~) transforms all of the 1 bits to 0 and the 0 bits to 1. The effect is negation of the value with sign extension. The following syntax is used for this operator:

```
result = ~1;
```

yields:

```
11111111 11111110 binary
```

The contents of result becomes –1.

Logical OR (|) performs a bitwise ORing of two values. If either bit in a given position is on (1), then the result is 1 for that bit position.

Value 1	*Value 2*	*Result*
0	0	0
0	1	1
1	0	1
1	1	1

Assume value1 contains 0xC5 and value2 contains 0x0F. The following statement ORs and assigns the result to number:

```
number = value1 | value2;
```

The contents of number is 0xCF:

```
value1     1100 0101      C5
value2     0000 1111      0F
number     1100 1111      CF
```

Logical AND (&) does a logical *and* operation on two values. The result bit is turned on (1) only if both bits are 1 in the operators.

Value 1	*Value 2*	*Result*
0	0	0
0	1	0
1	0	0
1	1	1

The syntax for assigning the logical and of two values to a variable is:

```
number = value1 & value2;
```

If value1 is 0xC5 and value2 is 0x0F, the result of the above statement is:

```
value1     1100 0101      C5
value2     0000 1111      0F
number     0000 0101      05
```

Logical Exclusive OR (^) turns the result bit on only if one of the bits in the values is on.

Value 1	*Value 2*	*Result*
0	0	0
0	1	1
1	0	1
1	1	0

The syntax for the exclusive or of two values to a variable is:

```
number = value1 ^ value2;
```

If value1 is 0xC5 and value2 is 0x0F, the result of the above statement is:

```
value1     1100 0101      C5
value2     0000 1111      0F
number     1100 1010      CA
```

Logical Shift Left (<<) shifts the contents of each bit the number of places to the left specified by the modifier. The syntax is:

```
result = value << 1;
```

The modifier is 1 in this statement. If value contains 0x01, then result will be 0x02. The bit patterns are:

value	0000 0001	01
result	0000 0010	02

The left shift operator has the effect of multiplying the operator by a power of two.

Left Shift	*Multiply*
value << 1	value * 2
value << 2	value * 4
value << 3	value * 8
value << 4	value * 16

Logical Shift Right (>>) shifts the contents of each bit the number of places to the right specified by the modifier. The syntax is:

```
result = value >> 2;
```

The modifier is 2 in this statement; the contents of value will be shifted two bit positions to the right. If value contains 0x81, then result will be 0x20. The bit patterns are:

value	1000 0001	81
result	0010 0000	20

Bits shifted past the starting point are lost. The right shift operator has the effect of dividing the operator by a power of two.

Right Shift	*Multiply*
value >> 1	value / 2
value >> 2	value / 4
value >> 3	value / 8
value >> 4	value / 16

APPLICATIONS

Use the bitwise operators to manipulate bit values such as setting up hardware registers in a chip.

HANDS-ON ACTIVITY

The sample program illustrates bitwise operators.

1. Type **BC** and press **Enter** to start up the compiler.

2. Create a window for the new file by pressing **Alt-FN**.
3. Type the following code into the NONAME00.CPP edit window:

```
#include <iostream.h>
#include <stdio.h>
#include <string.h>
#include <conio.h>

void main()
{
      int value1;
      int value2;
      int result;

      clrscr();
      cout << "Module 7\n\n";
      cout << "Bitwise operators\n";
      cout << "Type a number: ";
      cin  >> value1;
      cout << "Multiply by 4 by shifting...\n";
      value1 = value1 << 2;
      cout << "\nvalue1 is: " << value1 << "\n";
      cout << "Set value1 to 0xC5 and value2 to 0x0F\n";
      value1 = 0xC5;
      value2 = 0x0F;
      cout << "value1 & value2 is: ";
      result = value1 & value2;
      cout << result << "\n";

      value1 = 0xC5;
      value2 = 0x0F;
      cout << "value1 | value2 is: ";
      result = value1 | value2;
      cout << result << "\n\n";

      cout << "Press any key to exit";
      do {;} while(!kbhit());
}
```

4. Press **Ctrl-F9** to compile and run the program.

```
Module 7
Bitwise operators

Type a number:
```

5. Type **99** and press **Enter**.

```
Module 7
Bitwise operators

Type a number: 99
Multiply by 4 by shifting...

value1 is: 396
Set value1 to 0xC5 and value2 to 0x0F
value1 & value2 is: 5
value1 | value2 is: 207

Press any key to exit
```

6. Press any key to exit the sample program and return to Borland C++.
7. Continue the learning sequence with Module 80.

Module 8

BORLAND C++ FUNCTION LIBRARIES

DESCRIPTION

Borland C++ includes function libraries like any other C compiler. These libraries maintain high compatibility with Borland C. Even in cases where Borland C++ replaces C functionality, the old libraries are still available. This section describes the Borland C++ function libraries.

Each function library has a corresponding header (.h) file. The Borland C++ function library header files are:

- alloc.h
- assert.h
- bcd.h
- bios.h
- complex.h
- conio.h
- constrea.h
- ctype.h
- dir.h
- direct.h
- dirent.h
- dos.h
- errno.h
- fcntl.h
- float.h
- fstream.h
- generic.h
- graphics.h
- io.h
- iomanip.h
- iostream.h
- limits.h
- locale.h
- malloc.h
- math.h
- mem.h
- memory.h
- new.h
- process.h
- search.h
- setjmp.h
- share.h
- signal.h
- stdarg.h
- stddef.h
- stdio.h
- stdiostr.h
- stdlib.h
- string.h
- strstrea.h
- time.h
- utime.h
- values.h
- varargs.h

Each header file is described below. A list of the functions/values in each header file is included. Header files related to streams do not include the list of methods because that information is covered in Module 87.

C programs usually require:

```
#include <stdio.h>
```

at the beginning of every program. C++ is a little different. Most C++ programs use <iostream.h> instead. Existing C programs should rarely require changes to include statements. However, you should follow the new conventions for C++ programs.

The Borland Linker does not handle resolving multiple references to the same header file by different modules. This is handled by defining a symbol that is the filename with two leading and one trailing underscore. The following line is found in stdio.h:

```
#ifndef __stdio.h_
#define __stdio.h_
        ...
        (code for stdio.h)
        ...
#endif
```

The net effect is that the contents of the header file is compiled only once, no matter how many #include statements show up in the source code. You should follow this convention to prevent duplicate symbol errors when linking multimodule programs.

alloc.h This header file contains prototypes and variables for memory management functions.

assert.h This header file defines the assert debugging macro.

bcd.h Overloaded functions and operators that perform Binary Coded Decimal arithmetic are included in this header file. bcd.h is also part of Borland C. The overloaded operators include +, –, *, /, ==, !=, >=, <=, >, <, +=, –=, *=, and /=.

bios.h This header file provides the interface to the BIOS interrupt routines.

complex.h C++ adds a set of routines to operate on complex values. Most are overloaded versions of functions from math.h. Also see math.h and float.h header files.

conio.h This header file contains function prototypes for console I/O for the PC ports.

ctype.h The prototypes for the character manipulation function such as isalpha and tolower are in ctype.h.

dir.h The structures and prototypes for manipulating path names and file management routines. These functions are at a higher level than the ones in bios.h.

direct.h This header file defines structures and prototypes for dealing with path names and directories.

dirent.h The fuctions and structures for POSIX directory operators are in this header file.

dos.h Interface to DOS interrupt routines. DOS interrupts to manipulate disk drives at the device level and time and date functions are in this header.

errno.h System error return values along with the definition of 'errno' can be found here.

fcntl.h Constant symbols associated with opening a file are in fcntl.h.

float.h Function prototypes for floating point routines are in this header file.

fstream.h This header file contains class definitions and data structures for file I/O in C++. It is derived from iostream and automatically includes iostream.h.

generic.h Contains macro definitions to "fake" generic class definitions. It is obsolete and will not be included in future versions of C++.

graphics.h Borland supplies a large number of graphics routines with Borland C++. graphics.h contains prototypes for these routines.

io.h File handling and low-level I/O functions prototypes are included in this header file.

iomanip.h Stream I/O redirection function prototypes.

iostream.h Stream I/O class function prototypes.

limits.h This header file contains variables and constants that relate to range values of Borland C++.

locale.h The Borland C++ specific environment variables reside in this header file.

malloc.h The memory management functions and variables are in this header file.

math.h This header file contains function prototypes for a variety of math operations including algebraic and trigonometric functions and constants. Additional header files that contain math related prototypes are complex.h and float.h.

mem.h The memory manipulation function prototypes can be found in this include file.

memory.h This header file contains the memory manipulation fuctions.

new.h The operators new and newhandler are accessed in this header file.

process.h Structures and function prototypes for process management such as spawning a new process are in process.h.

search.h This header file contains the fuctions for searching and sorting.

setjmp.h The prototypes for functions setjmp and longjmp are contained in setjmp.h.

share.h This header file contains file sharing mode flags associated with sopen.

signal.h ANSI C specifies that signal.h be included. It defines constants used by signal and raise.

stdarg.h Macros used by functions such as printf that use a variable number of arguments are defined in stdarg.h.

stddef.h Miscellaneous macros are contained in this header file.

stdio.h The prototypes for 'standard' I/O functions are contained in this header file. The logical file descriptors for stdio, stdin, and stderr are defined here. The C++ version of stdio.h implements this capability via streams. stdio.h maintains compatibility with C programs. stdio.h is automatically included when iostreamio.h is referenced.

stdarg.h Macros used by functions such as printf that use a variable number of arguments are defined in stdarg.h.

stddef.h Miscellaneous macros are contained in this header file.

stdiostr.h C++ stream I/O classes used with stdio type file structures reside in this header file.

stdlib.h Conversion, sort, and other miscellaneous function prototypes are defined in stdlib.h.

string.h The C string function prototypes are included in this header file.

strstrea.h This header file contains the declarations for the stdiobuf and stdiostream classes. These classes are obsolete; use fstream.h instead for new code.

time.h This header file provided an interface to MS-DOS time functions.

utime.h The utime function and the utimbuf struct that is returned is defined in this header file.

values.h Borland C++ symbols and variables are included in this header file.

varargs.h This header file contains the definitions for accessing parameters in functions that accept a variable number of arguments.

APPLICATIONS

The Borland C++ function libraries are used to reference system level code. The function libraries generally contain function prototypes, variables, and data structures. The program interface is the .h header files identified earlier in this module.

Continue the learning sequence with Module 63.

Module 9
BREAK

DESCRIPTION

The break statement is a "branch to the end" of the command. It can be used with the *switch, do, while,* and *for* statements. break has no operands:

```
break;
```

break takes the place of goto in structured programming constructs.

APPLICATIONS

Use *break* to exit a switch, do, while, or for statement. The switch branches to the case that matches the expression. Execution begins at the case and continues until either the end of the switch or a break command is encountered. Execution branches to the end of the switch at the break command.

```
switch(expression){
case ONE:
        statements;
case TWO:
        more_statements;
        break;
case THREE:
        three_statements;
        break;
default:
        otherwise_statements;
}
```

If *expression* evaluates to ONE, execution starts at *statements,* falls through the TWO case, executes *more_statements,* then encounters the break to exit the switch.

```
for(i=0;i<end;i++){
        ch = string[i];
        if(ch == 0){
```

```
                break;
            }
            destination[i] = ch;
        }
```

The for loop executes until i >= end. If ch is zero, the break command executes and the branch is taken out of the loop.

```
        do{
            ch = getch();
            string[i++] = ch;
            if(ch == Q){ break; }
        }while(ch);
```

The do loop reads a character, then stores it in string. The break statement branches out of the loop when ch is 'Q.'

```
        while(keep_going){
            exit_flag = some_function();
            if(exit_flag){ break; }
            keep_going--;
        }
```

The while loop executes until keep_going is zero. If exit_flag is TRUE, the break statement branches out of the loop.

HANDS-ON ACTIVITY

The sample program illustrates the use of break to exit control structures.

1. Type **BC** and press **Enter** to start up the compiler.
2. Press **Alt-FN** to pull down the File menu and create a new file.
3. Type the following code into the NONAME00.CPP edit window:

```
#include <iostream.h>
#include <stdio.h>
#include <string.h>
#include <conio.h>

#define TWO         '2'
#define THREE             '3'
#define FOUR              '4'

void main()
{
      int  i;
      char value;
      char ch;
```

```
        clrscr();
        cout << "Module 9\n";
        cout << "The break statements\n";

        cout << "Enter a digit: ";
        cin  >> value;

        switch(value){
        case '1':
              cout << "The digit is ONE\n";
              cout << "Branching to the end of the switch..";
              break;
        case TWO:
              cout << "The digit is a 2\n";
              cout << "Taking the break branch..";
              break;
        case THREE:
              cout << "Three falls through to FOUR\n";
        case FOUR:
              cout << "This could be either 3 or 4\n";
              cout << "break is next to skip the default case";
              break;
        default:
              cout << "The default case is here.";
        }
        cout << "\nAt the end of the switch statement\n\n";

        cout << "Test break in a for loop\n";
        cout << "Type lower case alpha characters: ";
        for(i=0;i<40;i++){
              ch = getch();
              if(ch == 'q'){ break; }
              cout << ch;
        }
        cout << "\nq for quit gets to end of for loop\n\n";

        cout << "Press any key to exit";
        do {;} while(!kbhit());
}
```

4. Press **Alt-RR** to compile and run the sample program.

```
Module 9

The break statements
Enter a digit:
```

5. Type **2** and press **Enter**. The following is displayed:

```
Module 9

The break statements
Enter a digit:
The digit is a 2
Taking the break branch..
At the end of the switch statement

Test break in a for loop
Type lower case alpha characters:
```

The break statement was used at the end of case TWO to branch out of the switch statement.

6. Type **abcdefgq**. The following is displayed:

```
Module 9

The break statements
Enter a digit:
The digit is a 2
Taking the break branch..
At the end of the switch statement

Test break in a for loop
Type lower case alpha characters: abcdefg
q for quit gets to end of for loop

Press any key to exit
```

The for loop reads and displays up to 40 characters from the keyboard. When a 'q' is entered, the break statement is executed and the loop exited.

7. Press any key to exit the sample program and return to Borland C++.

The sample program shows two of the four uses for the break statement. break usage is identical in all of the looping constructs. break is also illustrated in the FOR, DO, and WHILE modules.

8. Continue the learning sequence with Module 25.

Module 10
CASE

DESCRIPTION

The case statement is a component of the switch statement described in Module 92. The general usage of case in a switch statement is:

```
switch(expression){
case 1:
        statements_case1;
case 2:
        statements_case2;
        break;
case 3:
case 4:
case 5:
        statements_case3_4_5;
        break;
default:
        statements_default;
}
```

The syntax for the case portion is:

```
case value:
```

Where value is an integer number. The value is compared with the result of evaluating the switch expression to determine which case to execute. Program flow jumps to the appropriate case, then continues until either a break or the end of the switch statement. This allows multiple cases to have common processing, as with cases 3, 4, and 5 in the example.

APPLICATIONS

Use a case statement for each condition that requires separate processing in a switch statement. Think of a switch as a nested if and each case logically replaces the conditional portion of an if in the nested construct. The case value is an integer number.

HANDS-ON ACTIVITY

The sample program illustrates the case component of the switch statement.

1. Type **BC** and press **Enter** to start up the compiler.
2. Press **Alt-FN** to pull down the File menu and create a new file.
3. Type the following code into the NONAME00.CPP edit window:

```
#include <iostream.h>
#include <stdio.h>
#include <string.h>
#include <conio.h>

#define COMMA                '\,'
#define PERIOD               '\.'
#define QUESTION             '\?'
#define SEMICOLON            '\;'
#define COLON                '\:'
#define EXCLAMATION          '\!'

void main()
{
     char value;

     clrscr();
     cout << "Module 10\n\n";
     cout << "The case statement\n";

     cout << "Enter a punctuation character: ";
     cin  >> value;

     switch(value){
     case PERIOD:
          cout << "The character is a period.";
          break;
     case COMMA:
          cout << "The character is a comma,";
          break;
     case EXCLAMATION:
          cout << "Excitement: an exclamation point!";
          break;
     case QUESTION:
          cout << "The character is a question mark?";
          break;
     case SEMI_COLON:
          cout << "The character is a semicolon;";
          break;
```

```
        case COLON:
              cout << "The character is a colon:";
              break;
        default:
              cout << "The character was other punctuation";
        }
        cout << "\n\n";
        cout << "Press any key to exit";
        do {;} while(!kbhit());
  }
```

4. Press **Alt-RR** to compile and run the sample program.

```
Module 10

The case statement
Enter a punctuation character:
```

5. Type **!** and press **Enter**. The following is displayed:

```
Module 10

The case statement
Enter a punctuation character: !
Excitement: an exclamation point!

Press any key to exit
```

6. Press any key to exit the sample program and return to Borland C++.
7. Continue the learning sequence with Module 9.

Module 11
CASTS

DESCRIPTION

C and C++ both provide a way to explicitly perform data type conversions. This is called casting. A cast expression is a type name enclosed in parentheses, followed by an operand.

```
(long) any_non_long_variable
```

This statement converts the value of *any_non_long_variable* to a long. Casts are used to modify the return value of a function or to store a value into a variable of another type.

APPLICATIONS

Explicit casts are sometimes necessary when a value must be as a type other than its current form. Two general situations are discussed that happen occasionally in advanced C++ programs. The first is changing the variable type for a function call. This frequently happens when using the malloc( ) system function to allocate memory. The malloc( ) function normally returns a void pointer to the allocated memory. If memory for a structure is allocated, the result will be stored in a pointer to that structure. The void pointer return of malloc( ) must be cast into the proper structure pointer. For example:

```
struct Dict{
      char name[32];
      int  len;
      int  status;
};

struct Dict *an_entry;

an_entry = (struct Dict*) malloc(sizeof struct Dict);
```

A dictionary structure consisting of name, length, and status is defined by the struct statement. A pointer to the Dict structure is defined by an_entry.

The void pointer returned by malloc( ) is converted to a Dict pointer before being stored in an_entry. This situation happens frequently with malloc( ).

The second use for casts is slightly more obscure. This case occurs when a single data structure is used to store mixed variable types. Assume that a program uses a LIFO stack structure for storing temporary values rather than variables. There are valid reasons to follow this approach in certain cases. The reasons are beyond this discussion. The stack is defined as an array of long integers:

```
long stack[32];
```

A function named push( ) is used to add a new value onto the top of stack. The function prototype for push( ) is:

```
void push(long);
```

Any call to push( ) must pass a parameter of type long. The following call casts a Dict pointer to long:

```
push((long) an_entry);
```

This call converts the Dict pointer from the previous example to long. push( ) obeys and uses the pointer as a long and stores the value on the stack data structure. The primary caution is that the result of the cast is large enough to hold the value.

Continue the learning sequence with Module 71.

Module 12

CHAR

DESCRIPTION

The *char* operator sets aside a single byte of storage for a variable to be used as a character. Character variables are generally defined as arrays to hold character strings. char variables may be signed or unsigned. This is the reason built-in character functions deal with 7-bit values. The normal ASCII character set is in the range of 0-127. A character variable must be defined as unsigned to access the extended PC character set. Examples of character variables include:

```
char ch;
char string[80];
unsigned char extended_char;
char message[] = "This is a message";
```

The variable ch is a single byte that can hold a 7-bit ASCII character. string is a character array that can hold up to 79 characters plus the trailing NULL. The unsigned character extended_char can hold characters whose value is between 0 and 255. The final example is an initialized array whose length is determined by the compiler based on the constant initialization value. Detailed discussions about arrays in general and C's set of character string manipulation functions are covered in separate modules.

The character constants recognized by C++ are:

Character	*Description*
\a	Bell
\b	Backspace
\f	Form feed
\n	Newline
\r	Carriage return
\t	Horizontal tab
\v	Vertical tab
\\	Backslash
\?	Question mark
\'	Single quote
\"	Double quote

\0	Null
\nnn	Octal number
\xnn	Hexadecimal number

APPLICATIONS

Use char variables when the values to be represented are ASCII characters. A normal ASCII character (0-127) is treated as a signed value. Extended PC characters (128-255) must be defined as unsigned. Character values can be used in arithmetic operations. Converting an ASCII digit to integer can be done by subtracting 48 from it.

```
int  value;
char digit = '9';
value = digit - 48;
```

The integer variable value contains 9. Converting an integer digit to its ASCII representation is simply a matter of adding 48.

HANDS-ON ACTIVITY

The sample session illustrates several uses of the char data type. The program prints the complete character set from 0 to 255 in two separate loops. One loop uses signed char variables and one loop uses an unsigned char to print the characters greater than 128.

1. Type **BC** and press **Enter** to start up the compiler.
2. Press **Alt-FN** to pull down the File menu and create a new file.
3. Type the following code into the NONAME00.CPP edit window:

```
#include <iostream.h>

void main()
{
      int  i;
      char ch;
      unsigned char trash;
      char string1[80] = "String 1 test";
      char string2[80] = "String 2";

      cout << "Module 12\n";
      cout << "This module uses char\n\n";
      cout << "Step 1 - Copy String 1 to String 2\n";
      cout << "  String 1: " << string1 << "\n";
      cout << "  String 2: " << string2 << "\n";
      cout << "  Do the copy...\n";
      ch = 1;          // Init ch to dummy value
      for(i=0;ch>0;i++){
```

```
            ch = string1[i];
            string2[i] = ch;
        }
        cout << "  String 1: " << string1 << "\n";
        cout << "  String 2: " << string2 << "\n";

        cout << "\nStep 2 - Display extended characters.\n";
        for(i=128;i<256;i++){
            trash = i;
            cout << trash;
        }

        cout << "\n\nStep 3 - Display the ASCII character\n";
        cout << "          set in reverse order\n";
        for(i=127;i>=0;i--){
            ch = i;
            cout << ch;
        }
}
```

4. Press **Alt-RR** to compile the program, then run it.
5. Press **Alt-F5** to view the user screen.
6. Press **Alt-X** to exit Borland C++ and return to the DOS prompt.
7. Continue the learning sequence with Module 60.

Module 13
CIN, >>

DESCRIPTION

Using Stream I/O is a little different from using the file-based I/O functions. Overloaded operators are used instead. The operator >>, when used with a stream descriptor in front and a variable after it, performs the "get from" operation rather than the right shift operation >> normally performs. cin may be redirected on the command line to read from a file instead of the keyboard. The syntax is:

```
#include <iostream.h>
cin >> variable;
```

Typical usage is:

```
#include <iostream.h>
     ...
char string[80];
     ...
cin >> string;
```

>> reads a value from cin into the variable named string. Multiple "get from" operators may be used to read multiple variables from the input line.

```
cin >> variable_1 >> variable_2;
```

White space is considered the field separator by >>. The >> operator is overloaded for all standard C++ data types. The input will be converted according to the data type of the variables used in the statement. If *variable_1* is a character array and *variable_2* is an integer, the correct data conversion is done automatically in both cases.

Input from cin using >> is buffered, so the program will not get individual characters until Enter is pressed.

APPLICATIONS

Use >> to read a field from the standard input (cin) stream. An advantage of using >> is convenience. The compiler automatically opens stdin. The programmer does not have to explicitly open or close the stream nor specify the error handling code associated with opening a stream.

Command line I/O redirection also works for >>. Files specified on the command line with a leading < are read rather than the keyboard. For example:

```
C:\> ANY_PROG <FILE.INP
```

This command runs ANY_PROG and redirects stdin to be FILE.INP. >> reads from FILE.INP rather than the keyboard.

HANDS-ON ACTIVITY

This program uses >> to read variables from the keyboard.

1. Start Borland C++ and open a new file window.
2. Type the following code in the file window:

```
#include <iostream.h>
#include <stdio.h>
#include <string.h>
#include <conio.h>

void main()
{
     int  integer;
     char word[80];

     clrscr();
     cout << "Module 13\n";
     cout << "This module uses >>\n\n";
     cout << "Type a word: ";
     cin  >> word;
     cout << "The word is: " << word << "\n";

     cout << "Type a number then a word: ";
     cin  >> integer >> word;
     cout << "\nThe word is    : " << word << "\n";
     cout << "The integer is: " << integer << "\n";

     cout << "\nPress any key to exit";
     do {;} while(!kbhit());
}
```

3. Press **Ctrl-F9** to run the program.

```
Module 13
This module uses >>

Type a word:
```

4. Type **stuff**, then press **Enter**. The following is displayed:

```
Module 13
This module uses >>

Type a word: stuff
The word is: stuff
Type a number then a word:
```

The characters typed on the keyboard are buffered and automatically echoed to the screen. The characters are not available to >> until the Enter key is pressed.

5. Type **42 trash**, then press **Enter**.

```
Module 13
This module uses >>

Type a word: stuff
The word is: stuff
Type a number then a word: 42 trash

The word is    : trash
The integer is: 42

Press any key to exit
```

cin is buffered. White space is used to delimit fields. You could have typed "stuff 42 trash" all on one line and all of the reads would be read in.

6. Press any key to exit the sample program and return to Borland C++.
7. Press **Alt-X** to exit Borland C++ and return to DOS.
8. Continue the learning sequence with Module 23.

Module 14

CLASS

DESCRIPTION

Classes are central to Object Oriented Programming (OOP) and C++. This module discusses classes and the C++ *class* keyword.

A class is an abstract idea that can be represented with data structures and functions. Functions associated with a class are called methods.

In nonprogramming terms, a class is a dog or cat or boy or girl. Spot is the name of a particular dog and Fluff is the name of a particular cat. Spot and Fluff are objects of the class dog and cat. You can view a class as a cookie cutter and objects as the cookies they form.

From a programming point of view a class is an abstract idea or concept. Stacks or queues are examples of classes. Number_stack is a particular instance of a stack and thus an object. Print_queue is an object of class queue.

A class combines data and procedures into a single programming unit. This is encapsulation. Data and procedures are tied together logically. The parts that make up a class can be protected from the rest of the program to varying degrees. The programmer has control over the protection of individual entries in the class definition. The types of protection available within a class are:

- Public
- Private
- Protected

PUBLIC Public items can be accessed from anywhere in the program without restrictions. Class methods are usually public. As a general rule, data should not be declared public.

PRIVATE Items within a class marked as private can only be accessed by methods defined as part of the class. Data is most often defined as private.

PROTECTED Items declared protected can be referenced directly within the class or in any class that inherits the class.

The general syntax for the *class* keyword is:

```
class ClassName{
protection:
     data_structures;
protection:
     methods;
}
```

Where: *class* is the keyword to start a class definition.

ClassName is the name of the class being defined.

protection declares access protection, usually private for data and public for methods.

data_structures are any normal C++ data structures.

methods are the functions that have access to the data defined in the class.

The basic class definition is started with the keyword *class,* followed by the data structures, followed by function definitions for its methods. In C++, a *struct* is a special form of class that has no methods.

The class definition for cstr follows. cstr defines a class to manipulate counted strings. Data declared for a class is private by default. Portions or all of the data may be declared public. *len* and *string* can be accessed only by methods declared for cstr or friends. (Friend functions are discussed in the module on methods.)

```
class cstr{
     int  len;                           // Private data
     char string[100];
public:                                  // Interface portion
     cstr();                             // Constructor
     ~cstr();                            // Destructor
     void append(cstr*,cstr*);           // Method
     virtual move_string(cstr*, cstr*);  // Virtual function
     int length(cstr*) {return len};     // Inline function
     cstr& operator+(cstr& arg);         // Overloaded operator
}
```

The various other pieces of the class definition are discussed in separate modules.

APPLICATIONS

Use class to define a C++ class. A class definition is made up of multiple parts. The two broadest categories of items in a class definition are data structures and methods. The data structures usually come first. Data in a class definition is private by default. Methods for the class are sometimes referred to as the program interface. Part or all of the class data can also be declared protected or public.

Methods in the class statement are really function prototypes. These are generally public to allow normal functions to call them. The division between data structures and methods is the keyword public. Methods are discussed in Module 62.

Even though data structures are defined first, followed by the method declarations by convention, changing the order will not cause compiler errors. Likewise, public, protected, and private may be used multiple times and in any order in a class definition.

This discussion has mentioned public, protected, and private modifiers several times. These modifiers define the access to functions or classes by functions outside the current class. The protection of the various class components can be specified as the programmer feels necessary.

The public modifier causes the data or method to be accessible to any other function in the program. In general, data is not public and methods are public.

Protected items can be accessed by the class and any derived classes. The protection can be increased in derived classes, but cannot be decreased. A class item declared protected in a class cannot be made public later in derived classes. Making a public item protected or private in a derived class is allowed.

Private affords an item the most protection from external functions. Private data and methods can only be referenced within the scope of the current class. This is information hiding, which is a primary benefit of object oriented programming.

HANDS-ON ACTIVITY

This sample program defines and manipulates a simple class.

1. Type **BC** then press **Enter** to start up the compiler from the DOS prompt.
2. Press **Alt-FN** to pull down the File menu and create a new file.
3. Type the following code into the edit window (You can save some time by not typing the comments.):

```
#include <iostream.h>
#include <stdio.h>
#include <string.h>
#include <conio.h>

class Cstring
{
      char* string;                  // ptr to a string
      int len;                       // actual memory used
public:
                  /*
                  | CONSTRUCTOR AND DESTRUCTOR
                  */
      Cstring(char*);
      ~Cstring() { };
                  /*
                  | METHODS
                  */
      void type();
};
// ****************************************************
//                Cstring METHOD DEFINITIONS
// ****************************************************
Cstring::Cstring(char *svalue)
{
      string  = new char [80];
      strcpy(string,svalue);
      len     = strlen(svalue);
}
// ****************************************************
void Cstring::type()
{
      char *temp_string;
      char ch;
                  /*
                  |  Do for each character in the string
                  */
      temp_string = string;
      for(int i=0;i<len;i++){
            ch = *temp_string++;
            cout << ch;
      }
}

void main()
{
      char  string1[80] = "";
```

```
        clrscr();
        cout << "Module 14\n";
        cout << "This module defines a class\n\n";
        cout << "Type a string: ";
        gets(string1);
        Cstring the_string(string1);// define object
        the_string.type();

        cout << "\nPress any key to exit\n";
        do {;} while(!kbhit());
}
```

4. Press **Alt-RR** to compile and run the sample program.

```
Module 14
This module defines a class

Type a string:
```

5. Type **Man is only truly great when he acts from his passions.** and press **Enter**. The following is displayed:

```
Module 14
This module defines a class

Type a string: Man is only truly great when he acts from his passions.
Man is only truly great when he acts from his passions.

Press any key to exit
```

6. Press any key to exit the sample program and return to Borland C++.
7. Press **Alt-X** to exit Borland C++ and return to DOS.

This module contains a simple but complete class definition and sample usage. This is the first of several modules that deal with the OOP aspects of C++. The mechanics of defining classes and using objects is relatively simple. Taking full advantage of them is not. The problem from a presentation point of view is all of the OOP constructs in C++ are very interrelated. It is difficult to talk about one area without touching on others. For example, methods and constructors are used in the sample program, but have not been discussed yet. They are necessary for a complete class example. These and other OOP constructs are discussed in separate modules. Refer to *Object Oriented Programming Using Turbo C++*, also published by Wordware Publishing, Inc., for a more in depth look at OOP.

8. Continue the learning sequence with Module 21.

Module 15
COMPILE MENU

DESCRIPTION

After debugging a program, you will want to compile it to an executable file (.EXE) so it can be run as a stand-alone program without Borland C++. The Compile menu provides the means to compile a program into either an object file (.OBJ) or executable file. The object file can be linked with other object files to build a large program from several small modules.

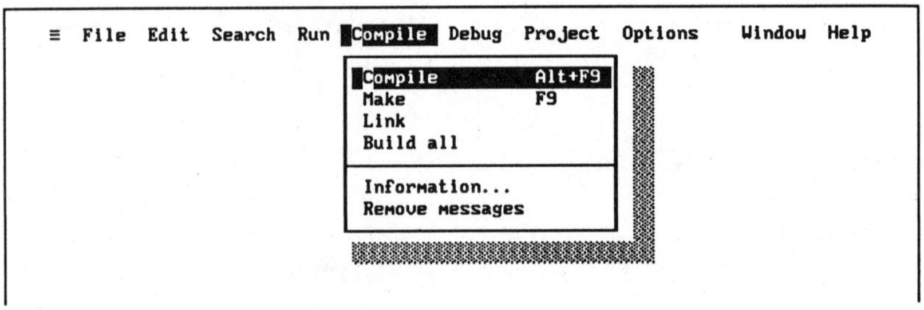

Compile	Compiles the source in edit window into object format. Separate object files can be linked into an executable program. This selection uses the filename of the file in the edit window and adds the .OBJ extension.
Make	Compiles any file that has changed since the last time the program was compiled. The DOS time and date are used to determine which files need compiling. A dependency structure is specified in a Make File. The executable filename is built by taking the filename in the edit window and changing the extension to .EXE.
Link	Links one or more object files into an executable .EXE file.
Build all	All of the files associated with the file in the edit window are recompiled.
Information...	Pops up a summary of the current compile statistics, including the file information.
Remove messages	Clears compile/link error messages from the message window.

APPLICATIONS

Compiling a program translates source code into machine executable instructions. Borland C++ offers several ways of compiling programs. (The Run menu compiles the program into memory when required for debugging.) The program can be compiled into either object (.OBJ) or executable (.EXE) program files. Individual modules can be compiled individually into object files, then linked to build the executable program. The executable program is run by typing its name at the DOS prompt.

Borland C++ can determine the modules to compile if a make file is set up for the program. (Make files are discussed in Module 30.) Make the file creation time and date to determine which modules to compile. Make compiles any module whose source code has been changed since the last executable file was created. Be sure to set the PC clock to the correct time and date at power up. Otherwise, modules may be compiled even when there is no change to the source file.

HANDS-ON ACTIVITY

This sample session demonstrates creating an executable program and how to run the program from the DOS prompt.

1. Type **BC** and press **Enter** to load and run Borland C++.
2. Press **Alt-F** to activate the File menu, select the Open... option, and press **Enter**.
3. Type **MOD2.CPP** at the filename prompt then press **Enter** to load the source code for MOD2.CPP into the edit window.
4. Press **Alt-C** to pull down the Compile menu.

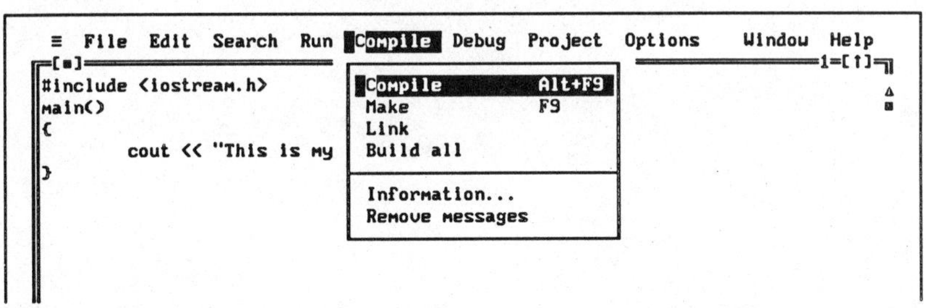

5. Move the selection bar to Build all and press **Enter** to begin compilation.

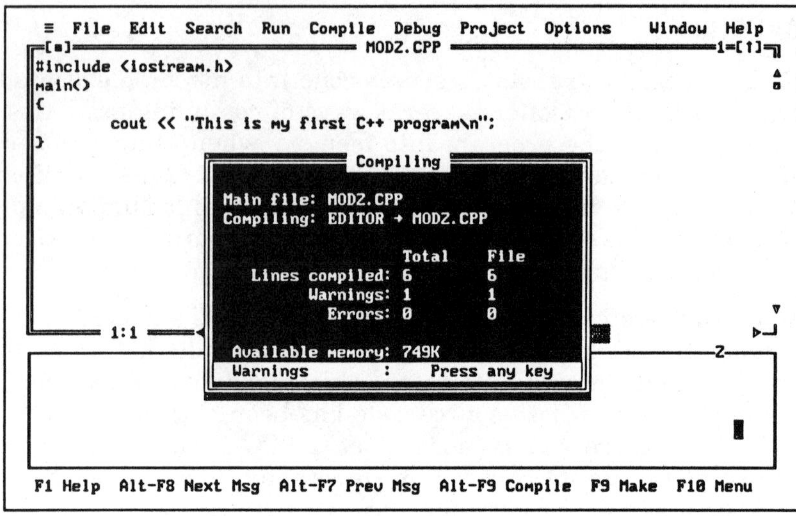

The compile window shows the progress of the compilation and link process. The executable filename is displayed in the window. Thus, MOD2.EXE is the resulting executable file.

6. Press **Enter** when the compile completes.
7. Press **Alt-X** to exit Borland C++ and return to the DOS prompt.
8. At the DOS prompt, type **DIR *.EXE** followed by **Enter** to display the executable programs in the current directory. Verify that MOD2.EXE is present.
9. Type **MOD2** and press **Enter** to execute the program.
10. Continue the learning sequence with Module 24.

Module 16

COMPILER DIRECTIVES

DESCRIPTION

Borland C++ includes two compilers, BC and BCC. The IDE is integrated with the BC to provide an interactive development environment. The operation of BC is described extensively in this book.

The second C++ compiler, BCC, is run from the DOS command line. It represents a more traditional approach to program development where the edit, compile, and link are separate and distinct steps. Running BCC instead of BC provides the programmer the option of using different programming tools, for example a different text editor.

The differences in the actual compilers are small. Code that compiles with BC will compile with BCC. The most visible difference is that BCC generates slightly smaller .EXE files because debugging information is not included by default.

APPLICATIONS

Borland C++ includes a number of options for compiling C++ programs from the command line. The general form is:

```
C:> BC [options] file[.cpp] file2[.cpp] ...
```

Where:

options is one or more items from the following list of BCC compiler options. Each option begins with a '-' or a '/.' The options are case sensitive, so be sure to use the specified alphabetic case when specifying options. -B and -b are two different options.

NOTE [ ] denote optional entries in the command.

The following lists each BCC option and a short description.

-1	80186/80286 Instructions. This option causes the compiler to generate instructions for the 80186/80286 processor. BCC generates 8086 instructions by default.
-1-	8086 Instructions. This is the default.
-2	80286 Protected Mode Instructions. BCC will generate code for an 80286 processor running in protected mode. DOS normally does not run in protected mode.
-A	ANSI keywords only.
-A-	Borland C++ keywords only. This is the default.
-AT	Borland C++ keywords only.
-AK	Accept K&R keywords only.
-AU	Accept only Unix keywords.
-B	Compile via assembly.
-C	Allow nested comments. Nested /* ... */ comment lines are not normally allowed in C. Specify this option to allow comment nesting.
-C-	Do not allow nested comments. This is the default.
-Dxxx	Define symbol. This option defines the symbol, named xxx, to the compiler. Setting symbol values is useful on the command line to specify compile time options to control conditional compilation. This is an alternative to editing the source code.
-Exxx	Use xxx as the alternate assembler name for this compile.
-Fc	Create COMDEFs.
-Ff	Automatically create far variables.
-Ff=size	Automatically creates far variables and sets the threshold to *size*.
-Fm	Set -Fc, -Ff, and -Fs options with one command.
-Fs	Assume DS=SS regardless of the memory model used.
-G	Generate code for speed.
-G-	Generate code for size. This is the default.
-H	Use and generate precompiled headers.
-H-	Do not use precompiled headers.
-Hu	Use, but do not generate precompiled headers.
-H=name	Specify filename of precompiled headers.
-Iname	Set include files directory.
-Jg	Generate and merge template instances.
-Jgd	Do not allow duplicate template instances errors.

-Jgx	Generate external references for template instances.
-K	Generate unsigned char.
-K-	Generate signed characters. This is the default.
-Lxxx	Set libraries directory.
-M	Generate link map.
-N	Check stack overflow.
-O1	Optimize for smallest possible code.
-O2	Optimize for fastest possible code.
-Od	Disable optimization.
-P	Force C++ compile.
-Pext	Do C++ compile and set default extension to *ext.*
-P-	Compile C or C++ depending on file extension. This is the default setting.
-P-ext	Compile C or C++ dependent on file extension and set default extension to *ext.*
-Qe	Compiler uses all available EMS memory. This is the default.
-Qe-	Compiler does not use any EMS memory.
-Qx	Compiler uses extended memory.
-R	Compiler generates ObjectBrowser information.
-S	Produce assembly language output.
-Txxx	Set assembler option.
-T-	Clear previous assembler options.
-Uxxx	Undefine macro named *xxx.*
-Vx	Virtual table control options.
-W	Generate .OBJ file for Windows with exportable functions.
-WD	Generate Windows .OBJ file to be linked with DLL exportable functions.
-WDE	Generate Windows .OBJ file to be linked as a DDL with explicit export functions.
-WE	Generate Windows .OBJ file using explicit export functions.
-WS	Generate Windows .OBJ file using smart callbacks.
-X	Suppress autodependency output.
-Yx	Enable overlay control.
-Z	Optimize register usage.
-a	Generate word alignment.
-a-	Generate byte alignment. This is the default setting.
-b	Treat enums as integers.

-b-	Treat enums as bytes where possible.
-c	Compile only. This generates .OBJ files.
-d	Merge duplicate strings on.
-d-	Set merge duplicate strings off. This is the default setting.
-exxx	Link step only. xxx is the executable filename to generate.
-f	Use Floating Point. This is the default.
-f-	Do not use Floating Point.
-ff	Generate fast Floating Point option.
-ff-	Generate ANSI Floating Point code.
-f87	Generate code for 8087 Floating Point processor instruction set.
-f287	Generate code for the 80287 Floating Point processor instruction set.
-gN	Stop after N warnings.
-h	Generate fast huge pointer arithmetic.
-iN	Set max identifier length to N.
-jN	Stop after N errors.
-k	Standard stack frame.
-lx	Set Linker option.
-l-x	Supress Linker option.
-mx	Set Memory Model.
-nxxx	Output file directory.
-oxxx	Set object filename.
-p	Compile with Pascal calling conventions.
-pr	Compile with fastcall conventions with parameters in registers when possible.
-p-	Compile with C calling conventions. This is the default setting.
-r	Use register variables.
-r-	Do not use register variables.
-rd	Use only declared register variables in registers.
-tDe	Create DOS .EXE file.
-tDc	Create DOS .COM file.
-tW	Create Windows file. This is the same as the -W option.
-u	Underscores on externs. This is the default.
-u-	Disables underscore on extern names.
-v	Source level debugging on.
-v-	Source level debugging on.

-vi	Set inline function handling.
-w	Set warning display on.
-y	Produce line number information.
-zxxx	Set segment names.

This module concludes the learning sequence.

Module 17

CONDITIONALS

DESCRIPTION

C++ conditionals are a central part of all the if related statements. Conditional statements determine which portions of an if statement to execute.

```
if(conditional_statements){
     true_statements;
}else{
     false_statements;
}
```

The conditional operators in C++ are:

Operator	*Name*
<	Less Than
>	Greater Than
==	Equals
!=	Not Equal
<=	Less Than or Equal
>=	Greater Than or Equal

Conditional operators can be used in any order. Each conditional operator is either relational or logical. Relational operators test two expressions.

```
if(x==y){
     cout << "x is equal to y";
}
```

Compound conditionals are allowed. Compound conditions are evaluated left to right starting from the innermost parenthesis pair. The evaluation order may be explicitly ordered via additional ( ) pairs. Compound conditions are connected with logical statements (&& and | |):

```
if((x > y) && (y < z)){
     a = 0;
}
```

This if statement reads "If x is greater than y and y is less than z."

APPLICATIONS

Use conditionals as the condition expression portion of if statements. Conditionals are evaluated to true or false. The control statement (if) then acts upon the true or false. Conditionals are evaluated left to right unless the order is explicitly changed with parentheses.

Enclosing compound conditionals in parentheses is good coding practice. The compile generates the same code with or without the parentheses in most cases. Always using parentheses to explicitly show each conditional expression is for the benefit of the code reader. The following example does not use parentheses:

```
if(dollars < 0 && cents > 0){
      statements;
}
```

Contrast the same if statement using parentheses:

```
if((dollars < 0) && (cents > 0)){
      statements;
}
```

These two examples are identical from the compiler's point of view. The second version does not require as much effort to determine exactly what the code does. The parenthesis pairs must match.

HANDS-ON ACTIVITY

The sample session illustrates both a simple and a compound conditional statement.

1. Type **BC** and press **Enter** to start up the compiler.
2. Press **Alt-FN** to pull down the File menu and create a new file.
3. Type the following code into the NONAME00.CPP edit window:

```
#include <iostream.h>

void main()
{
      long i;

      cout << "Module 17\n\n";
      cout << "Type a number followed by Enter: ";
      cin  >> i;
      if(i == 0){
            cout << "The number is ZERO.\n";
      }
```

```
        if((i != 0) && (i < 0)){
             cout << "The number is negative.\n";
        }
        if((i >= 1) || (i == 99)){
             cout << "The number is positive.\n";
        }
}
```

4. Press **Alt-RR** to compile and run the sample program.

```
 ≡ File  Edit  Search  Run  Compile  Debug  Project  Options    Window  Help
[■]═══════════════════════ NONAME00.CPP ══════════════════════1=[↑]═
#include <iostream.h>

void main()
{
        long i;

        cout << "Module 17\n\n";
        cout << "Enter a number followed by Enter: ";
        cin  >> i;
        if(!(i == 0)){
                cout << "The number is not ZERO.\n";
        }
        if((i != 0) && !(i > 0)){
                cout << "The number is negative.\n";
═*═══ 13:76 ═══
────────────────────────── Message ──────────────────────────2─



 F1 Help  F2 Save  F3 Open  Alt-F9 Compile  F9 Make  F10 Menu
```

5. Type **99** then press **Enter.**

```
C:\NORM\TEST>bc
Module 17

Type a number followed by Enter: 99
_
```

6. The sample program completes execution then returns to Borland C++. Press **Alt-F5** to view the user screen.

```
C:\NORM\TEST>noname01
Module 17

Enter a number followed by Enter: 99
The number is not ZERO.
The number is positive.

C:\NORM\TEST>
```

7. Continue the learning sequence with Module 59.

Module 18

CONSOLE I/O

DESCRIPTION

C automatically opens several I/O file descriptors attached to the console. The console is the computer screen and keyboard. The file descriptors are:

Descriptor	*Meaning*
stdin	Standard Input
stdout	Standard Output
stderr	Standard Error

stdin and stdout may be redirected to/from files on the command line by using < for stdin and > for stdout. stderr may not be redirected. For example:

```
C:> ANY_PROG <INPUT.FIL >OUTPUT.FIL
```

This statement runs ANY_PROG and uses INPUT.FIL for stdin and OUTPUT.FIL as stdout.

There are several library functions that specifically deal with the *std* file descriptors. The standard I/O function include:

Function	*Description*
getchar	Get the next character from stdin
gets	Get the next string from stdin
perror	Print string to stderr
putchar	Put character to stdout
puts	Put string to stdout
printf	Print a formatted string to stdout
scanf	Read formatted input from stdin

stdin, stdout, and stderr may be used like any other file descriptor in file-related functions such as fgets( ).

Each of these functions is discussed individually in its own separate module. The function prototypes for both the functions and file descriptors are in <stdio.h>.

Continue the learning sequence with Module 49.

Module 19
CONST

DESCRIPTION

In C++, const defines a variable whose value cannot be changed. The value for a constant is specified at compile time. const is the preferred way to define a constant in C++. const can also be used as a type modifier in a function prototype calling sequence to specify an argument that cannot be changed.

APPLICATIONS

Use const to define program constants.

The general form for defining a constant is:

```
const type NAME = value;
```

Where 'const' is the type modifier, 'type' is one of the C++ basic data types, 'NAME' is the constant name, and value is the value to set the constant to. The valid data types are:

- int
- short
- long
- float
- double
- char

Type int is assumed when no type is specified. A valid constant definition is:

```
const ZERO = 0;
```

This example defines a constant integer with a value of 0.

> ***NOTE*** Constant names are usually all uppercase to distinguish them from variables. This is a common C/C++ convention that has been followed since the beginnings of the language.

A constant character array is often useful:

```
const char HI[] = "Hello there";
```

HI is a character constant string that contains *Hello there.*

const can also be used as an argument modifier in a function call to specify that the contents of an argument cannot be changed. (C++ functions are described in Module 47.) For example:

```
test_const(const int X);
```

Specifying this prototype for the C++ function test_const( ) prevents changing of the value of X by test_const.

Turbo C++ contains many built-in system constants which are specified in .h files. For example, math.h defines M_PI as 3.14159265358979323846.

HANDS-ON ACTIVITY

This sample session uses const to begin a program that illustrates ways of defining constants.

1. Type **BC** and press **Enter** at the DOS prompt to execute Borland C++.
2. Press **Alt-F** to activate the File menu. Select New by typing **N**.
3. Type the following source code:

```
#include <iostream.h>
#include <math.h>
const int ZERO = 0;                // global constant
int test_const(const int x);       // Function prototype

main()
{
      int y = 3;                   // variable initialized to 3
      int a;

      cout << "Module 19\n";
      a = test_const(y);           // call the test function
      cout << "a: " << a << ", y: " << y << "\n";
}
int test_const(const int x)
{
      int a;
      cout << "Testing test_const\n";
      x = M_PI * x;                // this will be an error
      return a;
}
```

4. Press **Alt-F** to drop down the File menu. Select **Save as...** and use CONSTANT.CPP as the filename.
5. Press **Alt-F9** to compile the program. Assigning a value to x in test_const generates a compile error.

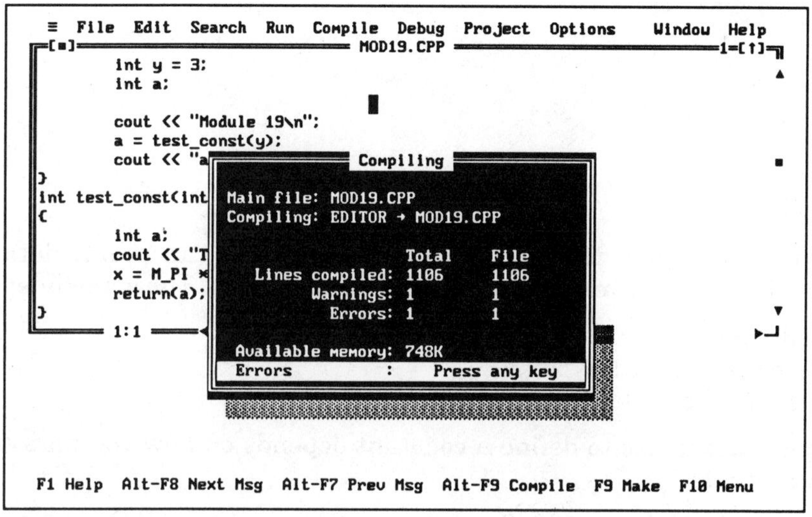

6. Press **Enter** to return to the edit window.
7. Change the line

```
x = M_PI * x;
```

to

```
a = M_PI * x;
```

8. Press **F2** to save the program, then **Alt-F9** to compile and run CONSTANT.CPP.
9. Press **Alt-F5** to view the output of CONSTANT.CPP in the user window.

```
Module 19
Testing test_const
a: 9, y: 3
```

10. Press **Alt-X** to exit Turbo C++ and return to the DOS prompt.
11. Continue the learning sequence with Module 36.

Module 20
CONSTANTS

DESCRIPTION

Constants are values that do not change. Constants can be any data type in C++. There are several ways of defining constants. These include:

- #define - Preprocessor
- const - Any data type
- enum - Compiler assigned value

The construct to use to define a constant depends on how you plan to use it in a program.

A constant defined using #define is handled by the Borland C++ preprocessor. The literal is substituted directly into the source code before the compiler sees it. This is the traditional way to define a constant in C. #define is covered in detail in Module 26.

const creates a variable whose value cannot be changed after initialization. The const keyword was introduced with the ASNI C standard. The operation of const in ANSI C and C++ is not identical. const is covered in detail in Module 19.

enum is a relatively new way of defining constants in C. Each constant defined using enum is assigned a unique value. enum is discussed in detail in Module 36.

Each of the ways to define a C++ constant is covered in separate modules.

Continue the learning sequence with Module 19.

Module 21

CONSTRUCTORS

DESCRIPTION

A constructor is a special C++ function which allocates memory for an object. Constructors are declared in the class definition. A constructor is called automatically each time an object is declared. A default constructor that simply allocates memory for the object is called if one is not specified. Multiple constructors are allowed providing each has a unique calling sequence.

The constructor name is the name of the class. There are two ways of implementing a constructor, 1) in the class definition and 2) as a separate function. Defining the constructor inline with the class definition may be done when the initialization code is short. Simply put the entire function definition in the class definition as in the example discussed in the applications section.

The longer the constructor code, the better candidate it is for implementation as a separate function. Constructors with external code must still be declared in the class definition. External constructors have the form:

```
Class_name::Class_name()
{
     initialization_code;
}
```

Constructors have many benefits:

- They provide a very convenient place for special initialization code.
- They provide a convenient place to put debug code.
- They can be used as constructors from the base class in a derived class.
- Default function call values may be used.
- Constructors can be overloaded.

APPLICATIONS

Use constructors when initialization of an object requires more code than simply allocating memory. Define constructors within the class definition if the code is only a few lines of code. For longer constructors, use an external function definition.

An example class definition with both internal and external constructors is:

```
class stuff{
      int int_stuff;
      char *char_ptr_stuff:
public:
      stuff(){                          // constructor
            char_ptr_stuff = new char [100];
      };
      stuff(int);                       // constructor
};
stuff::stuff(int size)
{
      char_ptr_stuff = new char [size];
}
```

Two constructors are defined for stuff; the one after the *public*: statement simply allocates 100 bytes of memory and saves the pointer to it, and the other accepts the number of bytes to allocate as a parameter. The constructor stuff(int) still must be declared in the class statement, even though the function is external.

Constructors are functions with special names that are executed as part of the process of creating a class instance.

HANDS-ON ACTIVITY

This sample program defines and manipulates a simple class.

1. Start the compiler from the DOS prompt.
2. Press **Alt-FN** to pull down the File menu and create a new file.
3. Type the following code. (You can save some time by not typing the comments.)

```
#include <iostream.h>
#include <stdio.h>
#include <string.h>
#include <conio.h>

class SomeClass{
          int int_SomeClass;
```

```
            char *char_SomeClass;
      public:
            SomeClass(){                        // constructor
                  char_SomeClass = new char [100];
                  strcpy(char_SomeClass,"ABCDEFG");
                  int_SomeClass = 0;
            };
            SomeClass(char*,int);               // constructor
            void dump();
};
SomeClass::SomeClass(char *string, int size)
{
      char_SomeClass = new char [size];
      strcpy(char_SomeClass,string);
      int_SomeClass = 47;
}
void SomeClass::dump()
{
      cout << "int_SomeClass : " << int_SomeClass << "\n";
      cout << "char_SomeClass : " << char_SomeClass << "\n";
      cout << "\n";
}
void main()
{
      int   integer;
      char  string1[80];

      clrscr();
      cout << "Module 21\n";
      cout << "This module illustrates constructors\n\n";
      cout << "Enter a number: ";
      cin  >> integer;
      cout << "Type a string: ";
      gets(string1);
      cout << "Creating object1\n";
      SomeClass object1;
      cout << "Creating object2\n";
      SomeClass object2(string1,27);
      cout << "\nDumping object1...\n";
      object1.dump();
      cout << "\nDumping object2...\n";
      object2.dump();

      cout << "\nPress any key to exit\n";
      do {;} while(!kbhit());
}
```

4. Press **Alt-RR** to compile and run the sample program.

```
Module 21
This module illustrates constructors

Enter a number:
```

5. Type **47** and press **Enter**. The following is displayed:

```
Module 21
This module illustrates constructors

Enter a number: 47
Type a string:
```

6. Type **Never complain and never explain.**, then press **Enter**. The following is displayed:

```
Module 21
This module illustrates constructors

Enter a number: 47
Type a string: Never complain and never explain.
Creating object1
Creating object2

Dumping object1...
int_SomeClass : 0
char_SomeClass : ABCDEFG

Dumping object2...
int_SomeClass : 47
char_SomeClass : Never complain and never explain.

Press any key to exit
```

7. Press any key to exit the sample program and return to Borland C++.
8. Press **Alt-X** to exit Borland C++ and return to DOS.

The sample program creates two objects, object1 and object2. Each uses a different constructor. The method, dump( ), displays the contents of an object. The program invokes dump( ) for each object to show that the constructors work.

9. Continue the learning sequence with Module 64.

Module 22

CONTINUE

DESCRIPTION

The *continue* statement is a "branch to the beginning of a loop" command. The general usage of continue is:

```
if(expression){ continue; }
```

continue takes the place of goto for this situation. The continue construct may be used with do, for, or while loops.

APPLICATIONS

Use continue in a for loop to skip some statements, but continue with the loop. The continue statement can be used to perform statements the first time through the for loop:

```
condition = 0;
for(i=0;i<42;i++){
      statements;
      if(condition){ continue; }
      condition = 1;
      first_time_only();
}
```

The function call to *first_time_only( )* will execute only when condition is zero, the first time through the loop.

continue can be used with the while loop also:

```
i = 0;
while(i<10){
      i++;
      if(i == 1){ continue; }
      cut << "First time through.";
}
```

The do loop is similar:

```
i = 0;
do{
      ch = string[i++];
      if(ch == 'X'){ continue; }
      cut << "The character not X\n";
}while(ch);
```

The continue statement is not used frequently. But there are times when it is very convenient.

HANDS-ON ACTIVITY

The sample program illustrates the continue statement. It outputs a string the first time through a loop, then prints a '.' each time after the first.

1. Type **BC** and press **Enter** to start up the compiler.
2. Type **Alt-FN** to pull down the File menu and create a new file.
3. Type the following code into the NONAME00.CPP edit window:

```
#include <iostream.h>
#include <stdio.h>
#include <string.h>
#include <conio.h>

void main()
{
      int  i;
      int  len;
      int  truth;
      char value;
      char string[80];

      clrscr();
      cout << "Module 22\n\n";
      cout << "The continue statement\n";

      cout << "Enter a string: ";
      gets(string);
      len   = strlen(string);
      truth = 0;
      for(i=0;i<len;i++){
            putchar('.');
            if(truth){ continue; }
            truth = 1;
            cout << "First time through";
      }
      cout << "\n\nPress any key to exit";
```

```
        do {;} while(!kbhit());
    }
```

4. Press **Alt-RR** to compile and run the sample program.

```
Module 22
The continue statement

Enter a string: 1234567890
```

5. Type **Test the continue statement** and press **Enter**. The following is displayed:

```
Module 22
The continue statement

Enter a string: 1234567890
.First time through.........

Press any key to exit
```

6. Press any key to exit the sample program and return to Borland C++.
7. Continue the learning sequence with Module 99.

Module 23
COUT, <<

DESCRIPTION

Using Stream I/O is different from using the file-based I/O functions because streams are defined as classes that use overloaded operators instead of function calls. The operator <<, when used with a stream descriptor in front and a variable after it, performs the "put to" operation rather than the left shift operation that << normally performs.

cout may be redirected on the command line to read from a file instead of the keyboard. The usage syntax is:

```
#include <iostream.hgg
cout << variable;
```

Typical usage is:

```
#include <iostream.hgg
    ...
char string[80];
    ...
cin << string;
```

<< writes a value to the cout standard output stream. Multiple "put to" operators may be used together to write multiple variables to the output device. The computer screen is the default output device associated with cout.

```
cout << variable_1 << variable_2;
```

The << operator is overloaded for all standard C++ data types. The output will be converted to ASCII string form according to the data type of the variables used in the statement. If *variable_1* is a character array and *variable_2* is an integer, the correct data conversion is done automatically in both cases.

APPLICATIONS

Use << to write a field to the standard output (cout) stream. An advantage of using << is convenience. The compiler automatically opens stdout and creates cout. The programmer does not have to explicitly open or close the stream nor specify the error handling code normally associated with opening a stream.

Command line I/O redirection works for <<. Files specified on the command line with a leading **gg** are written to rather than the screen. For example:

```
C:\gg ANY_PROG ggFILE.OUT
```

This command runs ANY_PROG and redirects stdout to FILE.OUT. << writes to FILE.OUT rather than the screen.

HANDS-ON ACTIVITY

This program uses << to write variables to the screen.

1. Start Borland C++ and open a new file window.
2. Type the following code in the file window:

```
#include <iostream.hgg
#include <stdio.hgg
#include <string.hgg
#include <conio.hgg

void main()
{
      int  integer   = 27;
      float big_num  = 12.34E7;
      char ch        = 'A';
      char string[]  = "Time is the great physician.";

      clrscr();
      cout << "Module 23\n";
      cout << "This module exercises <<\n\n";
      cout << "Output a string: " << string  << "\n";;
      cout << "Output an int  : " << integer << "\n";
      cout << "Output a float : " << big_num << "\n";
      cout << "Output a char  : " << ch      << "\n";
      cout << "\nPress any key to exit";
      do {;} while(!kbhit());
}
```

3. Press **Ctrl-F9** to run the program.

```
Module 23
This module exercises <<

Output a string: Time is the great physician.
Output an int  : 27
Output a float : 1.234e+08
Output a char  : A

Press any key to exit
```

4. Press any key to exit the sample program and return to Borland C++.
5. Press **Alt-X** to exit Borland C++ and return to DOS.
6. Continue the learning sequence with Module 14.

Module 24

DEBUG MENU

DESCRIPTION

The Debug menu provides a level of detail and interaction past what is available in the Run menu. The Run menu provides tracing capabilities on a line by line basis. The Debug menu lets the programmer examine individual pieces of the program such as variables, the call stack, and watch points. The capabilities provided in the Debug menu are very powerful and can save tremendous amounts of time debugging a program.

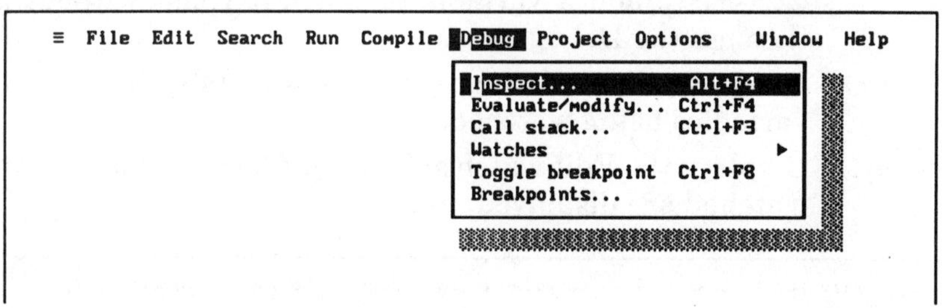

Inspect... The contents data structures such as variables can be examined by selecting this item. Alt-F4 invokes Inspect... directly. A submenu is used for specifying the item to dump.

Evaluate/ modify... This menu selection pops up a submenu for entering a C++ expression to evaluate. The value of a variable can be changed using Evaluate/modify. Use Ctrl-F4 to invoke the Evaluate/modify submenu directly from an edit window.

Call stack... Selecting this menu item shows the contents of the call stack. Each time a Borland C++ function is called, its return address is placed on the call stack. Displaying the call stack shows the hierarchy of calls to get to this point in the program. Ctrl-F3 is the shortcut key for this item.

Watches... A watch is a variable in the program that the debugger "watches." Each time the variable changes, the new value is displayed. Selecting Watches pops up a submenu to specify watch points. The options available on the Watches submenu is discussed below.

Toggle breakpoint	This selection causes the current line to be toggled on/off as a breakpoint for debugging. The shortcut key is Ctrl-F8.
Breakpoints...	The Breakpoints selection displays a submenu to manipulate breakpoints.
Watches submenu	The Watches submenu controls Borland C++'s watch facility. This submenu is used to change the variables that the debugger watches.

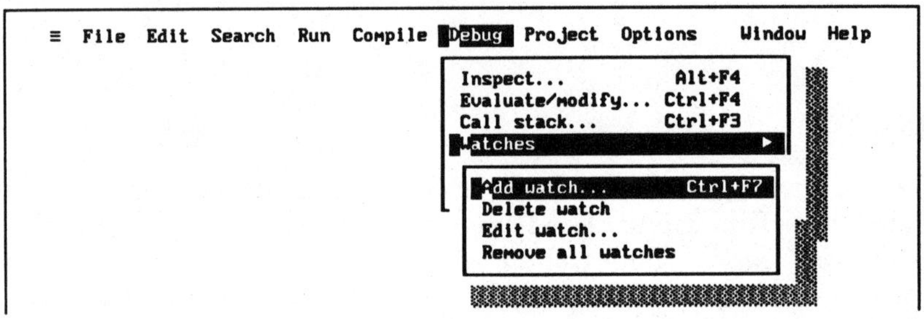

Add watch...	Select this item to add variables to the watch list. Use Ctrl-F7 to add a variable to the watch list without going through the Debug menu.
Delete watch	Use this submenu item to remove a variable from the list of variables being watched.
Edit watch...	Displays the Edit watch submenu. All of the variables being watched are displayed.

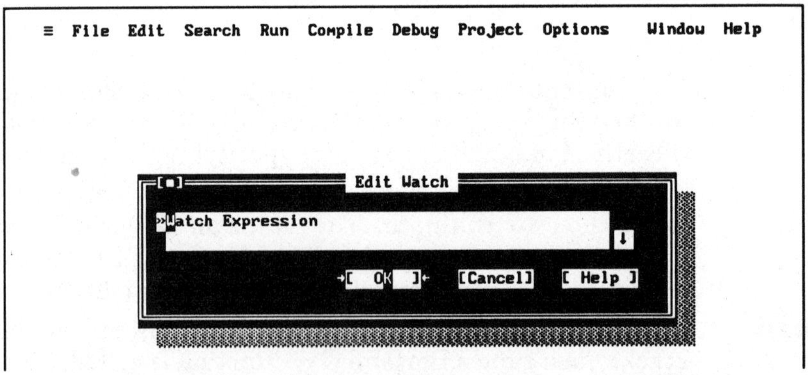

Remove all watches	All watch variables are cleared. Their values are unchanged, but the debugger no longer reports value changes.

APPLICATIONS

The Debug menu provides a way to get very detailed information about the state of your program during development. Watching the value of a variable change during execution frequently makes finding program problems much easier.

Be sure that source files are saved before using the Debug menu to alter variable values. It is possible to corrupt the Programmer's Platform by changing pointers to invalid memory locations. The PC may lock up completely when this happens, requiring you to boot it again.

HANDS-ON ACTIVITY

This session illustrates debugging with the aid of watches and breakpoints.

1. Start Borland C++.
2. Press **Alt-F** to activate the File menu.
3. Select New and press **Enter** to open an edit window for a new file.
4. Type the following code into the edit window:

```
#include <iostream.h>
#include <stdio.h>
#include <string.h>
#include <conio.h>

void main()
{
     int  i;
     char ch;

     clrscr();
     cout << "Module 24\n\n";
     cout << "Simple program for debugging \n\n";

     i  = 0;
     ch = 'a';
     i  = ch;

     cout << "\n\nPress any key to exit";
     do {;} while(!kbhit());
}
```

5. Press **Alt-C** to activate the Compile menu then type **M** to compile the program.
6. Press **Alt-RT** to trace into the program. The *main()* line is highlighted. This is the next line to execute.

7. Move the cursor to the line with *i = 0;* and press **Alt-D** to pull down the debug menu.
8. Type **T** to toggle a breakpoint on. The line will change color to red indicating that program execution will stop when the line is reached.
9. Press **Ctrl-F9** to begin program execution. Program execution will stop at the line with the breakpoint set.
10. Press **F7** to execute the current line.
11. Press **Alt-D** then type **I** to pop up the Inspect dialog box.
12. Type **i** then press **Enter**. The current value of the variable i is displayed.
13. Press **F7** twice to move execution past the line *i = ch;*. The value of *i* changes from zero to 97.
14. Press **Ctrl-F9** to execute the remainder of the program.
15. Press any key to exit the screen display and return to the compiler.
16. Press **Alt-X** to exit Borland C++ and return to DOS.
17. Continue the learning sequence with Module 73.

Module 25
DEFAULT

DESCRIPTION

The *default* statement is the catch-all label in a switch statement. The syntax for default is:

```
default:
        statements;
```

The default statement is the last label in a switch construct. If the switch expression evaluates to a value not covered by a specific case, program flow branches to the default.

Refer to the module about SWITCH for complete examples of using default within a switch statement.

Continue the learning sequence with Module 44.

Module 26
#DEFINE, #UNDEF

DESCRIPTION

#define is a preprocessor command that defines a preprocessor symbol, constant, or macro. #undef undefines a previously defined symbol, constant, or macro. #define has the following syntax:

```
#define symbol
#define constant 99
#define macro(p1)      (p1 * 2)
```

symbol can be tested for existence by the #ifdef statement. The preprocessor substitutes 99 for every occurrence of *constant* in the source code. *macro* defines a macro with one parameter, p1. The parameter value is substituted in the macro body, then the body is substituted for the macro call in the code. For example:

```
value = macro(4);
```

will be translated into:

```
value = (4 * 2);
```

by the preprocessor before the compiler sees the code.

#undef undefines a previously defined item. The syntax is:

```
#undef symbol
```

Constants and macros can also be undefined, but that is rarely done in practice.

APPLICATIONS

Use #define to define a symbol, constant, or macro for the preprocessor. Use #undef to undefine a previously defined item. #define is not used as much in C++ as in C. C++ has the *const* modifier that should be used instead of #define for constants.

A prime use of preprocessor symbols is selecting code to build a specific version of a program.

```
#define ANSI
# define BCC                  // This a comment

#ifdef ANSI
#include <stdio.h>
#include <stdlib.h>
#endif

#ifdef BCC
#include <stdio.h>
#endif
```

Define either ANSI, for an ANSI C compiler, or BCC, for Borland C++. The BCC symbol is commented out in this example. The code tests for the existence of the symbol ANSI. When ANSI exists, the code up to the #endif is compiled. The test for the BCC symbol fails so the code up to the #endif is ignored. This technique is referred to as conditional compilation.

A define macro can be used as shorthand for longer code sequences that are used often. The C++ inline functions can be used for many instead of a preprocessor macro.

```
#define debug(str)     (cout << str)
     ...
debug("This outputs a Debug message.\n");
     ...
```

The debug macro outputs a debug message. This can be useful during program development. Once development is complete, change the definition of debug( ) to:

```
#define debug(str)     ()
```

and recompile the program. The debug messages remain in the code for later use if necessary but are ignored when the new version is compiled.

HANDS-ON ACTIVITY

The example program in this module defines a preprocessor symbol, constant, and macro. The session starts from the DOS prompt.

1. Type **BC** and press **Enter** to run Borland C++.
2. Press **Alt-FN** to pull down the File menu and begin a new file.
3. Type the following program code:

```
#define BCC
#define TESTING
#define BLANK          ' '

#ifdef TESTING
#define DEBUG(STR)     (cout << STR)
#else
#define DEBUG(STR)
#endif

#ifdef BCC
#include <iostream.h>
#include <stdio.h>
#include <string.h>
#include <conio.h>
#elif
#include <stdio.h>
#include <string.h>
#endif

void main()
{
     char string[80];

     clrscr();
     cout << "Module 26\n";
     cout << "#define and #undef\n\n";
     cout << "Type a string: ";
     gets(string);
     if(string[0] == BLANK){
          DEBUG("Leading Blank\n");
     }
     DEBUG(string);

     cout << "\n\nPress any key to exit";
     do {;} while(!kbhit());
}
```

4. Press **Alt-R** and **Enter** to compile and run the program.

```
Module 26
#define and #undef

Type a string:
```

5. Type **Life is a joke that's just begun.** and press **Enter.**

```
Module 26
#define and #undef

Type a string: Life is a joke that's just begun.
Life is a joke that's just begun.

Press any key to exit
```

If the string is entered with a leading blank, the "Leading blank" message will also be displayed.

6. Press **Alt-X** to exit Borland C++ and return to DOS.
7. Continue the learning sequence with Module 54.

Module 27
DELETE

DESCRIPTION

After memory is allocated by the new operator, it is deallocated with *delete*. delete is often used in class destructors. The format of a delete statement is:

```
delete name;
```

Where name is the name of the pointer value returned from a previous new operation. Sample usage is:

```
char *string;
     ...
string = new char[80];
     ...
delete string;
```

This statement allocates memory for an 80 byte character array and returns a pointer to it. The delete operator deallocates memory allocated by new.

APPLICATIONS

Use the delete operator to deallocate memory allocated by new. It is frequently used in destructors to deallocate memory for an object that is being destroyed. delete is analogous to free in C.

HANDS-ON ACTIVITY

This sample program allocates memory using new then removes it via delete.

1. Run Borland C++ from the DOS prompt.
2. Pull down the File menu and create a new file.

3. Type the following code into the edit window:

```
#include <iostream.h>
#include <stdio.h>
#include <string.h>
#include <conio.h>
#include <alloc.h>

void main()
{
      unsigned long memory;
      char  *string;

      clrscr();
      cout << "Module 27\n";
      cout << "This module exercises delete\n\n";
      memory = coreleft();
      cout << "Memory remaining: " << memory << "\n";
      cout << "Reserve 10000 bytes for a string...\n\n";
      string = new char [10000];
      if(!string){
            cout << "Could not allocate memory.\n";
      }
      memory = coreleft();
      cout << "Memory remaining: " << memory << "\n";
      cout << "Type a string: ";
      gets(string);
      cout << "string now contains: " << string << "\n";
      cout << "Now give the memory back.\n\n";
      delete(string);
      memory = coreleft();
      cout << "Memory remaining: " << memory << "\n";
      cout << "\nPress any key to exit\n";
      do {;} while(!kbhit());
}
```

4. Press **Alt-RR** to compile and run the sample program.

```
Module 27
This module exercises delete

Memory remaining: 59536
Reserve 10000 bytes for a string...

Memory remaining: 49520
Type a string:
```

5. Type **Justice is truth in action.** and press **Enter**. The following is displayed:

```
Module 27
This module exercises delete

Memory remaining: 59536
Reserve 10000 bytes for a string...

Memory remaining: 49520
Type a string: Justice is truth in action.
string now contains: Justice is truth in action.
Now give the memory back.

Memory remaining: 59536

Press any key to exit
```

6. Press any key to exit the sample program and return to Borland C++.
7. Press **Alt-X** to exit Borland C++ and return to DOS.

The sample program allocates 10,000 bytes of memory using new, reads a string into that memory, then deallocates it with delete. The amount of free memory is displayed before and after allocation operations to show the results of the allocation. The amount of memory shown may vary depending on the number of device drivers and TSRs resident in your computer.

8. Continue the learning sequence with Module 62.

Module 28

DERIVED CLASSES AND INHERITANCE

DESCRIPTION

Derived classes and inheritance go hand-in-hand. A derived class inherits data structures and methods from an existing or base class. The derived class adds new data or methods to create an extension of the original class.

A derived class that inherits from a single base class has the characteristic of single inheritance. When multiple base classes are combined in a derived class, then the derived class has multiple inheritance. C++ supports both single and multiple inheritance.

The format for defining a derived class is:

```
class derivedclass : public|private|protected baseclass{
      class_definition;
};
```

Where *derivedclass* is the new class being defined and baseclass is an existing class. The derived class now has access to items from the base class.

The progression of deriving classes can continue as far as necessary to fit a particular application. The ability to derive classes makes classes into building blocks for constructing an application.

Borland C++ provides an extensive library of classes. Most generic data structures, from lists to stacks to queues, already exist and are waiting for you to use. The class libraries take advantage of the concept of derived classes.

APPLICATIONS

Use a derived class to add new data and procedures to an existing class. Assuming that the base class exists, is fully tested, and works, the advantages of deriving new classes include:

- Reduced development time
- Reduced testing time
- Hidden complexity
- Reduced program maintenance

The primary reason is that classes are self-contained. Once a class has been written and tested, it will work correctly where ever used.

Define a base class:

```
class BaseClass{
protected:
     int  status;
     char string[80];
public:
     show();
};
```

BaseClass is very simple, with two variables, *status* and *string*, and a single method, *show( )*. The data items in BaseClass cannot be accessed by derived classes unless the protection is specified as protected. This example uses protected, but real applications should leave the data private and provide methods to manipulate the data instead of allowing direct access to the data. The point here is the protection of the data within a class should be a conscious decision by the programmer.

The next step is a class that inherits BaseClass:

```
class DerivedClass : public BaseClass{
     char name[80];
public:
     void load_name(char*,char*)
};
```

DerivedClass inherits the data from BaseClass and can use the data and methods as if they were defined locally. Notice that protection for the base class is specified. The protection can be public or protected or private just as with data and methods.

The method *load_name( )* uses data from both classes.

```
void DerivedClass::load_name(char *stuff,char *thing)
{
     strcpy(name,stuff);
     strcpy(string,thing);
}
```

string is defined in BaseClass but used as if it is part of DerivedClass. Likewise, show( ) can be used with DerivedClass objects.

HANDS-ON ACTIVITY

This sample program defines and manipulates a simple class.

1. Type **BC** and press **Enter** to start up the compiler from the DOS prompt.

2. Press **Alt-FN** to pull down the File menu and create a new file.
3. Type the following code into the NONAME00.CPP edit window:

```
#include <iostream.h>
#include <stdio.h>
#include <string.h>
#include <conio.h>

class BaseClass{
protected:
      int  status;
      char string[80];
public:
      void show(void);
};
class DerivedClass : public BaseClass{
      char name[80];
public:
      void load_name(char*,char*);
};

void BaseClass::show(void)
{
      cout << "BaseClass string: " << string << "\n";
};
void DerivedClass::load_name(char *stuff,char *thing)
{
      strcpy(name,stuff);
      strcpy(string,thing);
}

void main()
{
      char  variable_1[80];
      char  variable_2[80];

      clrscr();
      cout << "Module 28\n";
      cout << "This module illustrates derived classes\n\n";
      cout << "Creating Derived Object\n";
      DerivedClass DObject;
      cout << "Now collect data to load...\n";
      cout << "Type a string: ";
      gets(variable_1);
      cout << "Type a string: ";
      gets(variable_2);
      cout << "Call a method for the derived object...\n";
      DObject.load_name(variable_1,variable_2);
```

```
        cout << "Call a method from the base class...\n";
        DObject.show();

        cout << "\nPress any key to exit\n";
        do {;} while(!kbhit());
    }
```

4. Press **Alt-RR** to compile and run the sample program.

```
Module 28
This module illustrates derived classes

Creating Derived Object
Now collect data to load...
Type a string:
```

5. Type **This goes to the DerivedClass** and press **Enter**. The following is displayed:

```
Module 28
This module illustrates derived classes

Creating Derived Object
Now collect data to load...
Type a string: This goes to the DerivedClass
Type a string:
```

6. Type **This string is headed for BaseClass**, then press **Enter**. The following is displayed:

```
Module 28
This module illustrates derived classes

Creating Derived Object
Now collect data to load...
Type a string: This goes to the DerivedClass
Type a string: This string is headed for BaseClass
Call a method for the derived object...
Call a method from the base class...
BaseClass string: This string is headed for BaseClass

Press any key to exit
```

7. Press any key to exit the sample program and return to Borland C++.
8. Press **Alt-X** to exit Borland C++ and return to DOS.

The sample program shows an object created for a derived class that accesses data and uses both data and methods from the base class.

9. Continue the learning sequence with Module 75.

Module 29
DESTRUCTORS

DESCRIPTION

Destructors are the inverse of constructors. A destructor removes an object from memory. C++ provides an implicit or default destructor. The programmer may also provide a destructor in place of the default one.

The destructor name is formed by prepending a "~" to the class name. For example, the destructor for class AnyClass is ~AnyClass.

```
AnyClass::~AnyClass()
{
     destructor_code;
}
```

A destructor may be written as an external function, such as ~AnyClass above, or it may be defined internally to the class declaration:

```
class AnyClass{
     int number;
public:
     ~AnyClass(){ statements; }
}
```

The primary restrictions associated with destructors include:

- Automatically called when object goes out of scope
- No parameters allowed
- Must use delete to deallocate memory allocated by new in the object's constructor

APPLICATIONS

Use destructors to remove an object from memory. Destructors provide a convenient place to put debug and error checking code. The destructor is automatically called when an object goes out of scope.

A destructor may be declared as part of the class definition or as a separate method. The following definition of AnyClass defines the destructor as part of the class definition:

```
class AnyClass{
      int offset;
      char *one_string;
public:
      AnyClass(){ one_string = new char [80];};
      ~One_class(){ delete one_string;};
};
```

An alternative way of defining ~AnyClass is:

```
class AnyClass{
      int offset;
      char *one_string;
public:
      AnyClass(){ one_string = new char [80];};
      ~One_class();
};

AnyClass::~AnyClass()
{
      delete one_string;
      cout << "AnyClass destructor executed...\n";
}
```

Complex destructors should be broken out of the class definition as the second example shows.

Destructors cannot take arguments and cannot be overloaded. Since the destructor is executed automatically by C++ when an object goes out of scope, there is no place to supply parameters. In practice, these restrictions are quite reasonable.

A destructor provides a place to insert code to:

- Deallocate memory
- Debug
- Other processing

C++ has no way of knowing what memory is allocated for a particular object or if the memory is still in use. The destructor must deallocate any memory allocated using *new* by the constructor.

Destructors are functions with special names that execute as part of the process of removing an object.

HANDS-ON ACTIVITY

This sample program defines a class with destructors.

1. Type **BC** and press **Enter** to start up the compiler from the DOS prompt.
2. Press **Alt-FN** to pull down the File menu and create a new file.
3. Type the following code into the NONAME00.CPP edit window:

```
#include <iostream.h>
#include <stdio.h>
#include <string.h>
#include <conio.h>

class AnyClass{
        int  number;
        char *character;
    public:
        AnyClass(char*,int);            // constructor
        ~AnyClass();                    // destructor
};
AnyClass::AnyClass(char *string, int size)
{
    number    = size;
    character = new char [size];
    strcpy(character,string);
    cout << "In Constructor\n";
}
AnyClass::~AnyClass()
{
    delete character;
    cout << "In Destructor\n";
}
void do_object2(char *string,int value)
{
    AnyClass object2(string,value);
}
void main()
{
    int  integer;
    char string1[80];

    clrscr();
    cout << "Module 29\n";
    cout << "This module examines destructors\n\n";
    cout << "Enter a number: ";
    cin  >> integer;
    cout << "Type a string: ";
    gets(string1);
```

```
        cout << "Creating object1\n";
        AnyClass object1(string1,integer);
        cout << "Creating object2 in a function...\n";
        do_object2(string1,27);
        cout << "Back in main(). \n";
        cout << "Destructor for object1 is not called until program exit.";

        cout << "\nPress any key to exit\n";
        do {;} while(!kbhit());
}
```

4. Press **Ctrl-F9** to compile and run the program.

```
Module 29
This module examines destructors

Enter a number:
```

5. Type **27** and press **Enter**. The following is displayed:

```
Module 29
This module examines destructors

Enter a number: 27
Type a string:
```

6. Type **Never take anything for granted.**, then press **Enter**. The following is displayed:

```
Module 29
This module examines destructors

Enter a number: 27
Type a string: Never take anything for granted.
Creating object1
In constructor
Creating object2 in a function...
In constructor
In destructor
Back in main().
Destructor for object1 is not called until program exit.

Press any key to exit
```

7. Press any key to exit the sample program and return to Borland C++.
8. Press **Alt-F5** to view the final message.

```
Module 29
This module examines destructors
```

```
Enter a number: 27
Type a string: Never take anything for granted.
Creating object1
In constructor
Creating object2 in a function...
In constructor
In destructor
Back in main().
Destructor for object1 is not called until program exit.

Press any key to exit
In destructor
```

9. Press **Alt-X** to exit Borland C++ and return to DOS.

The sample program creates two objects, object1 and object2. One is created in main( ) and the other in a function. object1 stays in scope from the time of its creation until main( ) terminates. The object2 is created in do_object2( ). object2 is in scope for the life of the function. The destructor is called automatically when the do_object2( ) exits.

10. Continue the learning sequence with Module 27.

Module 30

DEVELOPING LARGE PROGRAMS

DESCRIPTION

Borland C++ is an excellent development environment for developing very large programs. Large programs are best implemented as multiple modules. Development is much faster using the modular approach. Compile time is generally less because only those modules with changes have to be compiled each time a change is made rather than the entire program. Small modules are usually easier to debug as well.

Two features of the Borland compiler system that contribute to the ease of developing large programs are the *Project File* and the *make* utility. The project files are associated with the IDE compiler and make works with the command line compiler. Each provides the capability of specifying build dependencies.

MAKE is designed to be used with the command line compiler BCC. It is derived from the Unix make utility. Make is primarily used with the compiler to build programs with multiple source and object file dependencies. It is not limited to the compile process; make can be used to automate any process that involves selecting files to manipulate based on file creation dates.

Make uses the creation date of a file to determine if it has changed since the previous make operation. The program uses this information to determine which other file in the dependency list must be recreated. There is a "rule" associated with each dependency list that will be executed if the file is out of date. For example, the .EXE file depends on the .OBJ files, which in turn depend on the .CPP files. So when a .CPP file changes, the corresponding .OBJ file is out of date and must be recreated. The .EXE file is out of date because an .OBJ file has been updated. The rule for recreating the .OBJ file is to compile the .CPP file that changed and the rule for the .EXE file is linking the object files. This all sounds much more confusing than it is in practice.

The dependencies and rules are automatically read from a file named MAKEFILE. The make command allows any filename to be specified. The general syntax for a make rule is:

```
target_file : dependent_files
          command
```

The target_file must start in column 1 and command must have a leading tab character. There must be a blank before and after the ":" in the target line.

PROJECT FILE is accessed via the Project menu in the integrated compiler, BC. A project file serves the same purpose as the make except it can only be used to compile programs. In other words, the dependency rules are fixed. The Project menu follows:

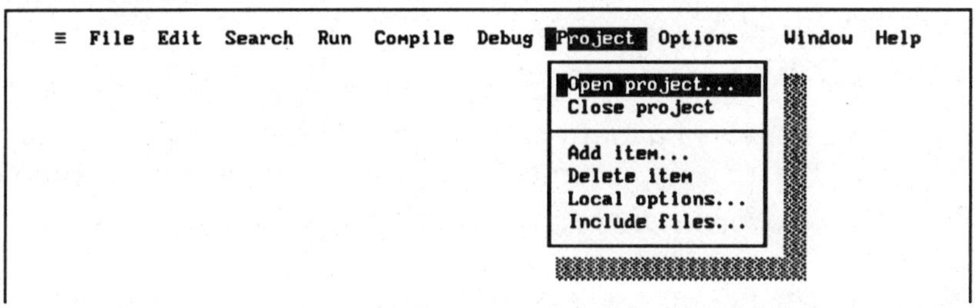

Refer to Module 73 for a detailed discussion of the Project menu and how to create and manipulate a project file.

APPLICATIONS

Use make with the BCC command line compiler to build multiple module programs. Use project files with BC to identify modules that make up a multiple module program.

Assume the following dependency tree for a program:

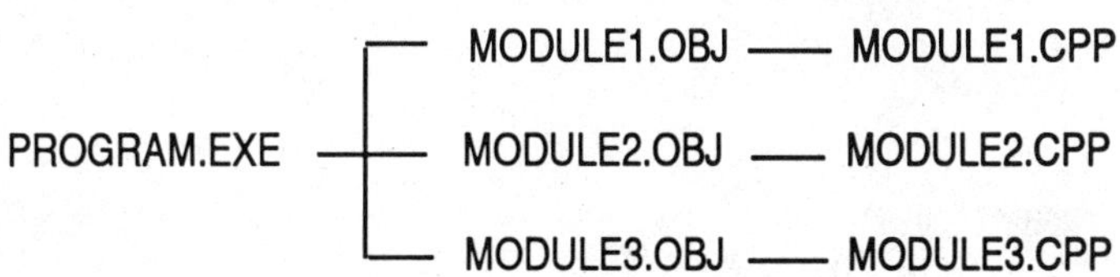

PROGRAM.EXE depends on MODULE1.OBJ, MODULE2.OBJ, and MODULE3.OBJ. MODULE1.OBJ depends on MODULE1.CPP. MODULE2.OBJ depends on MODULE2.CPP and MODULE3.CPP depends on MODULE3.CPP. The .OBJ files could also depend on header (.H) files as well.

The simplest MAKEFILE. to compile PROGRAM.EXE is:

```
PROGRAM.EXE : MODULE1.OBJ MODULE2.OBJ MODULE3.OBJ
	BCC MODULE1.OBJ MODULE2.OBJ MODULE3.OBJ

MODULE1.OBJ : MODULE1.CPP
	BCC -c MODULE1.CPP
	...
```

Don't forget that the *target,* PROGRAM.EXE in the first rule and MODULE1.OBJ in rule two, must start in column one and the BCC command is preceded by a tab.

The make utility is not used very often in Borland C++ because of the wonderful development provided by the IDE compiler. make is a necessity in many other C and C++ compilers.

HANDS-ON ACTIVITY

This program consists of a main program and three modules. Make builds the program. This activity assumes BCC is installed and operational.

1. Type **BC** and press **Enter** to start up the compiler from the DOS prompt.
2. Press **Alt-FN** to pull down the File menu and create a new file.
3. Type the following code into the NONAME00.CPP edit window:

```
#include <iostream.h>
#include <stdio.h>
#include <string.h>
#include <conio.h>

void funct1(void);
void funct2(void);
void funct3(void);

void main()
{

     clrscr();
     cout << "Module 30\n";
     cout << "Illustrate make\n\n";

     funct1();
     funct2();
     funct3();
```

```
    cout << "\nPress any key to exit\n";
    do {;} while(!kbhit());
}
```

4. Press **Alt-F** and select **Save as...** from the menu. Type **mod30.cpp** for the filename.
5. Press **Alt-FN** to start a new file and type the following code:

```
#include <stdio.h>
void funct1()
{
    printf("Function 1\n");
}
```

6. Save this file as **funct1.cpp**.
7. Open a new file, enter the following code, then save as **funct2.cpp**.

```
#include <stdio.h>
void funct2()
{
    printf("Function 2\n");
}
```

8. Open a new file, enter the following code, then save as **funct3.cpp**.

```
#include <stdio.h>
void funct3()
{
    printf("Function 3\n");
}
```

9. Press **Alt-FN** to open an edit window for the makefile and type the following code:

```
mod30.exe : mod30.obj funct1.obj funct2.obj funct3.obj
    bcc funct1.obj funct2.obj funct3.obj

mod30.obj : mod30.cpp
    bcc -c mod30.cpp

funct1.obj : funct1.cpp
    bcc -c funct1.cpp

funct2.obj : funct2.cpp
    bcc -c funct2.cpp

funct3.obj : funct3.cpp
    bcc -c funct3.cpp
```

10. Save this code as MAKEFILE.
11. Press **Alt-X** to exit BC.
12. At the DOS prompt, type **make** then press **Enter**. The whole program is compiled the first time make executes. Thereafter, only those source files that have changed will be recompiled.
13. Type **mod30** to execute the program.

```
Module 30
Illustrate make

Function 1
Function 2
Function 3

Press any key to exit
```

14. Press any key to exit the sample program and return to DOS.
15. Continue the learning sequence with Module 70.

Module 31

DO

DESCRIPTION

The do loop is a structured looping construct. The exit condition is checked at the end of the loop. The do syntax is:

```
do{
      statements;
}while(expression);
```

The expression is a variable, a comparison, or result of a function call that evaluates to True or False. The while branches back to do when expression is True. Control falls through to the next portion of code if expression evaluates to False.

APPLICATIONS

Use a do loop in the following situations:

- The number of times to loop is not known at the beginning of the loop.
- The test for exit must be at the bottom of the loop.

The do loop code always executes at least one time. This contrasts with the while loop whose code may not be processed at all. A typical do loop is:

```
do{
      status = some_function();
      x      = status + 27;
}while(!status);
```

This loop continues to execute as long as status is zero. Presumably, a status value of zero means success in this case.

Both continue and break may be used with the do loop.

HANDS-ON ACTIVITY

The sample program illustrates a do loop.

1. Start the compiler.
2. Press **Alt-FN** to pull down the File menu and create a new file.
3. Type the following code into the NONAME00.CPP edit window:

```
#include <iostream.h>
#include <stdio.h>
#include <string.h>
#include <conio.h>

void main()
{
      int  i;
      int  len;
      char ch;
      char string[80];

      clrscr();
      cout << "Module 31\n\n";
      cout << "The do loop \n\n";

      cout << "Enter a string: ";
      gets(string);
      cout << "The string is: " << string << "\n";
      cout << "Its length is: ";
      i = 0;
      do{
            ch = string[i++];
            cout << ".";
      }while(ch);

      cout << (i-1) << "\n";
      cout << "Compare that with the result of strlen\n";
      len   = strlen(string);
      cout << "strlen is    : " << len;

      cout << "\n\nPress any key to exit";
      do {;} while(!kbhit());
}
```

4. Press **Alt-RR** to compile and run the sample program.

```
Module 31

The do loop

Enter a string:
```

5. Type **ABCDE** and press **Enter**. The following is displayed:

```
Module 31

The do loop

Enter a string: ABCDE
The string is: ABCDE
Its length is: ......5
Compare that with the result of strlen
strlen is    : 5

Press any key to exit
```

6. Press any key to exit the sample program and return to Borland C++.

Notice that the program prints six dots. The loop executes six times, but the length is five. The trailing null character is the sixth character. One is subtracted from i before being displayed to take the extra time through the loop into consideration.

7. Continue the learning sequence with Module 18.

Module 32

EDIT MENU

DESCRIPTION

The Edit menu provides the means to perform common editing operations that manipulate groups of lines. Editing functions such as cutting and pasting lines are accessed from this menu. Individual editing keystrokes are covered in detail in Module 33, Edit Window.

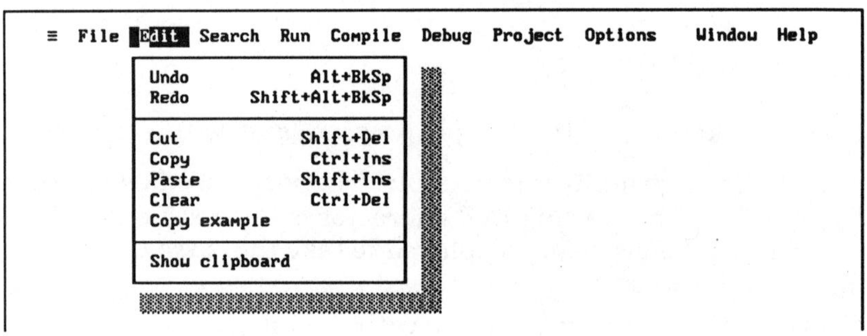

APPLICATIONS

The options available via the Edit menu are:

Undo	Select this menu item to put the edit buffer back to its state before the last edit or cursor movement. Continued execution of the Undo command will eventually place the edit buffer in its original state.
Redo	Redo undoes the most recent Undo command.
Cut	Delete marked text. The deleted text is moved to the Programmer's Platform Clipboard. The shortcut command for this selection is Shift-Del.
Copy	Copy the marked text to the Clipboard. The shortcut command for this selection is Ctrl-Ins.
Paste	Copy the text in the Clipboard to the current cursor position. The shortcut command for this selection is Shift-Ins.

Clear	Clear the text from the current editing window and begin a new editing session. The shortcut command is Ctrl-Del.
Copy example	Copies example code from the help window to the Clipboard so it can be pasted into an edit window.
Show clipboard	This selection opens a window that shows the current contents of the clipboard. Text on the clipboard can be modified while the window is active.

MARKING TEXT Several of the Edit menu commands require text be marked prior to the edit operation. Marking text can be done two ways. The first is move the cursor to the beginning of the block and press Ctrl-KB. Move the cursor to the end of the block and press Ctrl-KK. The marked text is displayed in reverse video.

Positioning the editor cursor is a matter of moving the mouse cursor to the desired location and clicking the left mouse button once. The editor cursor jumps to the mouse cursor position.

Marking a block of text is similar to positioning the cursor.

1. Move the mouse cursor to the start of text block,
2. Hold the left mouse button down,
3. Move the mouse cursor to the end of the text block, and
4. Release the mouse button.

The text between the start of the block and the position of the mouse cursor is highlighted to show the text that has been marked.

HANDS-ON ACTIVITY

This session demonstrates cutting and pasting of text using the Programmer's Platform Edit menu. Other Edit menu options that require marking the text are not covered as separate examples because their operation follows the same basic steps as the cut and paste procedure. The steps assume that the current directory contains the example C++ source file from Module 2.

1. Start Borland C++ by typing **BC** and pressing **Enter**.
2. Press **Alt-F** to activate the File menu.
3. Press **F3** to call up the Open submenu and select MOD2.CPP.

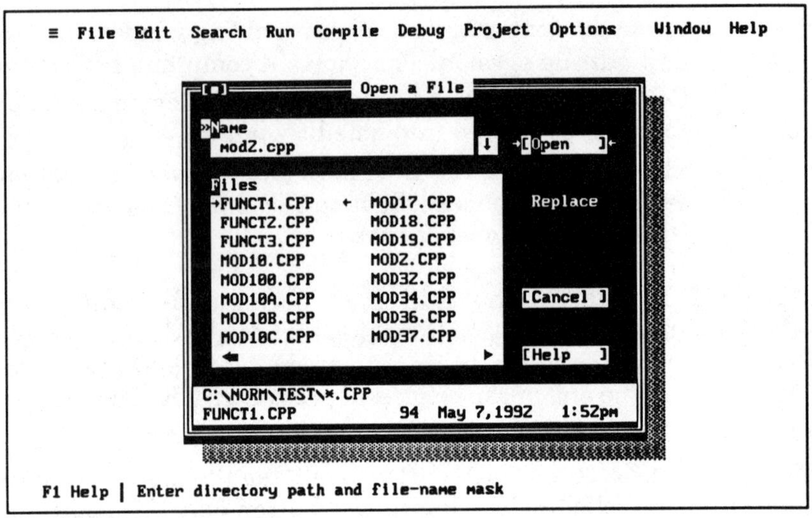

4. Move the cursor to the '{' in line 3 and press **Ctrl-KB** to mark the beginning of the block.
5. Move the cursor to the '}' in the last line of the code and press **Ctrl-KK.** The text between the '{' and '}' is highlighted.

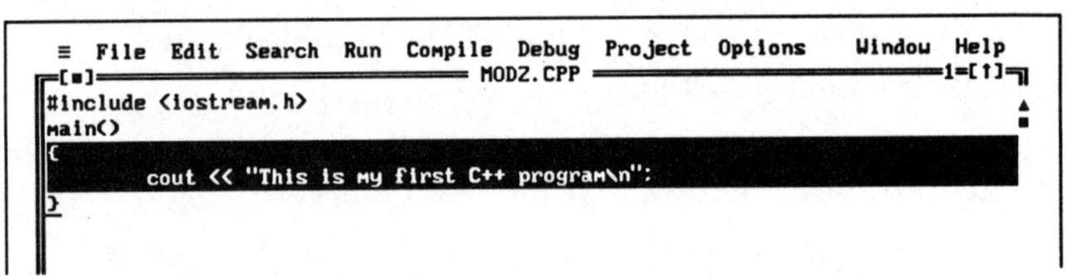

6. Press **Alt-E** to pull down the Edit menu.
7. Select Cut by typing **t**. The highlighted text is removed from the edit window.

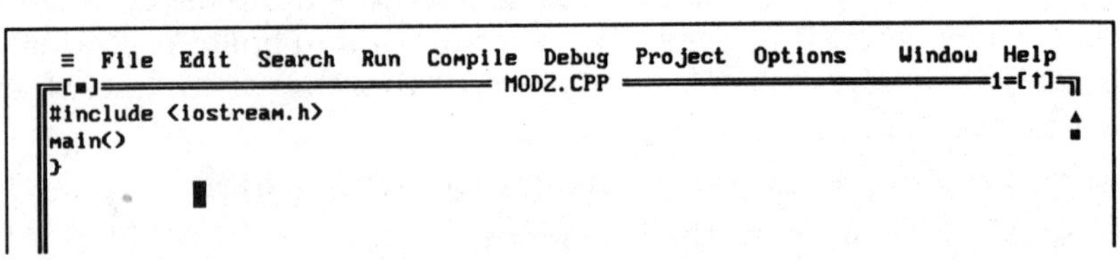

8. Activate the Edit menu again by pressing **Alt-E** and select the Paste option. The deleted text is placed at the cursor. Text on the Clipboard can be pasted multiple times.
9. Press **Alt-X**. Notice the following.

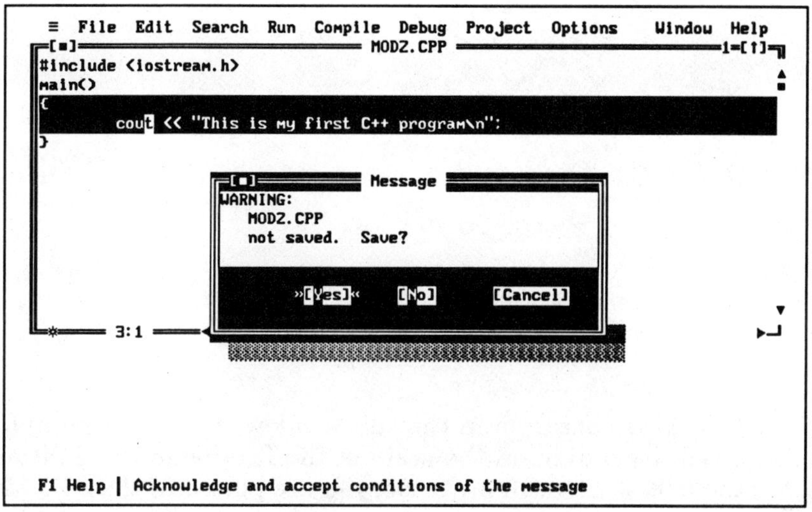

10. A message box is generated because MOD2.CPP was modified and not saved. Type **N** to exit back to DOS without saving the file or **Y** to save it.
11. Continue the learning sequence with Module 81.

Module 33
EDIT WINDOW

DESCRIPTION

Borland C++ begins operation in the edit window. A file may be automatically displayed depending on the state of the Programmer's Platform at the end of the last session. In any case, you are placed in the edit window when there is a source file open. The built-in text editor responds to a combination of pull-down menus and command key sequences. This module covers the commands available in the Borland C++ text editor.

The command structure of the Borland C++ editor is based on WordStar. If you are already comfortable editing with WordStar or another editor that also uses the WordStar commands, you will be comfortable editing in Borland C++ from the start. Those familiar with WordStar should review the section later in this module describing the differences between the two editors.

COMMAND STRUCTURE The Borland C++ text editor has a command structure. The command structure can be divided into categories:

- Basic cursor control commands
- Quick cursor control commands
- Block commands
- Print control commands
- Other

Basic cursor control is performed with dedicated keys such as Down Arrow or control keys that operate on a single character. Quick editing commands move the cursor 'quickly' by groups of characters. Block commands work with marked blocks of text. Print commands insert nonprinting commands into the source file. The final grouping is any command that does not fit into the above command groupings. The Borland C++ editing commands are not mnemonic, but do follow a logical structure that is well suited to the touch typist.

BASIC CURSOR CONTROL Editing commands that fall into this category move the cursor around the file in small, usually one-character, increments. They are all single character commands that use either a dedicated key or control character sequence.

PC keyboards include several dedicated editing keys. Borland C++ takes advantage of these keys for user convenience. The editing keys and their definition are discussed below.

Up Arrow	Move the cursor to the previous line.
Down Arrow	Move the cursor to the next line.
Left Arrow	Move the cursor one character to the left. The cursor stops when the beginning of the current line is reached.
Right Arrow	Move the cursor one character to the right. The cursor stops when the end of line is reached.
Home	Move to the first character on the first line of the screen.
End	Move to the last character of the last line of the screen.
PgUp	Scroll the cursor up 20 lines to the previous screen.
PgDn	Scroll the cursor down 20 lines to the next screen.

Borland C++ also utilizes control keys for cursor control. These are arranged in a diamond shape. Keys on the top row (with the E character) cause motion in the up direction. Keys on the row with X cause down motion. Keys from the D right cause cursor motion in the right or forward direction. Keys from the S left cause motion in the left or backward direction. The basic editing diamond is:

```
       ↑
       E
   ←S     D→
       X
       ↓
```

All keys in the editing diamond are Ctrl keys. This means hold the Ctrl key down while pressing the letter on the keyboard. For example, Ctrl-D causes the cursor to move one character to the right.

Ctrl-E	Move the cursor to the previous line. This key has the same effect as pressing the Up Arrow key.
Ctrl-X	Move the cursor to the next line. Ctrl-X is equivalent to the Down Arrow key.
Ctrl-D	Move the cursor forward one character. Ctrl-D and the Right Arrow key perform the same action.
Ctrl-S	Move the cursor backward one character. Pressing Ctrl-S has the same action as pressing the Left Arrow key.

Add R and C to the basic editing diamond. The editing diamond now looks like this:

```
     ↑
     E   R
  ←S   D→
     X   C
     ↓
```

These commands move the cursor a screen at a time.

Ctrl-R — Move to the previous screen. The cursor is moved up 20 lines. Ctrl-R performs the same action as the PgUp key.

Ctrl-C — Jump to the next screen. The cursor is moved down 20 lines. This key is equivalent to the PgDn key.

There are more basic editing commands. These scroll the whole screen up or down a line rather than moving the cursor.

```
       ↑
  W    E    R
  ←S     D→
  Z    X    C
       ↓
```

Ctrl-W — Scroll the screen to the previous line. The cursor remains in position. Ctrl-PgUp also performs this action.

Ctrl-Z — Scroll the screen to the next line in the text. The cursor remains in position, while the whole screen moves one line. Ctrl-PgDn also scrolls the screen.

The final set of basic editing commands jump forward or backward a word at a time.

```
           ↑
     W     E     R
  ← A  S      D  F →
     Z     X     C
           ↓
```

Ctrl-A — Move the cursor to the previous word. Ctrl-A is the same as Ctrl-Left Arrow.

Ctrl-F — Move the cursor to the next word. This key does the same action as Ctrl-Right Arrow.

This set of editing commands is enough to move around a text file easily and perform basic editing.

QUICK COMMANDS These editing commands move 'quickly' around the source file. Quick commands are prefixed with Ctrl-Q. Various search type capabilities along with inserting and deleting lines are also included. The command diamond is extended intact with the quick commands. For example, Ctrl-QD jumps to the end of the line and Ctrl-QS jumps to the beginning of the line. Many of the commands in this category can also be accessed via the Search menu.

Ctrl-QS	Move the cursor to the beginning of the current line.
Ctrl-QD	Move the cursor to the end of the current line.
Ctrl-QE	Move the cursor to the top of the screen. Pressing Ctrl-QE performs the same action as pressing the Home key.
Ctrl-QX	Move the cursor to the end of the screen. Performs the same action as End.
Ctrl-QR	Jump to the beginning of the text window. Ctrl-PgUp also performs this action.
Ctrl-QC	Jump to the end of the text window. Pressing Ctrl-PgDn has the same effect.
Ctrl-Qn	Jump to place marker n; where n is 0 thru 9. A place marker is set with Ctrl-Kn.
Ctrl-QF	Search for a text string. This action can also be performed by pulling down the Search menu and selecting Find...
Ctrl-QA	Search for a text string and replace it with a new text string. Selecting Replace... from the Search menu also does this.
Ctrl-QL	Restore deleted characters within the line. This command does not restore a whole line deleted with Ctrl-Y. Also performed via Restore in the Edit menu.
Ctrl-QY	Delete from the current cursor position to the end of the line.

BLOCK COMMANDS These commands deal with manipulating blocks of text. The text block must be marked before it can be used. Ctrl-KB marks the start of a block and Ctrl-KK marks the end. The marked text is highlighted. Any of the other block commands can be used on the block at that point. Ctrl-KH hides the marked text when you are done with it.

Ctrl-KB	Mark the beginning of a text block.
Ctrl-KK	Mark the end of a text block.
Ctrl-KT	Mark the current word.
Ctrl-KC	Copy marked text to the current cursor position. This function can be performed via the Copy selection in the Edit menu.

Ctrl-KV	Move the marked text block to the current cursor position. The same as a Cut then a Paste in the Edit menu.
Ctrl-KY	Delete the marked text block.
Ctrl-KR	Read file and insert text at current cursor position.
Ctrl-KW	Write the marked text to disk. A window pops up for specifying the filename.
Ctrl-KH	Hide the current text block. This command restores marked text to normal video.
Ctrl-KP	Print the marked text block.
Ctrl-KI	Indent the marked text block.
Ctrl-KU	Unindent the marked text block.
Ctrl-Kn	Set place marker 'n'; where 'n' is 0 thru 9. Ctrl-Qn jumps to place marker 'n.'
Ctrl-KS	Save the contents of the edit window to disk and continue editing. The Save selection in the File menu also performs this action.

The mouse can be used to mark and hide blocks of text as an alternative to the Ctrl-KB Ctrl-KK command sequence.

OTHER EDITING COMMANDS Several other commands are available that do not fall clearly into the other categories. These commands are described here.

Ctrl-Pc	Control character prefix; where 'c' is a control character. For example, Ctrl-PG inserts a Ctrl-G character in the text.
Ctrl-V	Toggle insert/overtype mode.
Ctrl-Y	Delete the current line.
Ctrl-G	Delete the character under the cursor. The Del key also performs this action.
Ctrl-T	Delete the current word.
Ctrl-H	Delete the previous character. The Backspace key also performs this action.
Ctrl-N	Insert a blank line at the cursor.
Ctrl-I	Insert a tab character or eight spaces depending on the setting of tab mode.
Ctrl-OT	Toggle tab mode on/off.
Ctrl-OI	Toggle auto-indent mode on/off.
Ctrl-L	Repeat the last search operation.
Ctrl-Right Arrow	Jump to the beginning of the next word. Pressing Ctrl-F has the same effect.

Ctrl-Left Arrow	Jump to the beginning of the previous word. The same as Ctrl-A.
Ctrl-Home	Move the cursor to the beginning of the text window. This key performs the same action as Ctrl-QR.
Ctrl-End	Move the cursor to the end of the text window. Pressing Ctrl-QC also performs this function.

APPLICATIONS

The editing commands identified in this module provide complete editing control over your editing session. The Borland C++ editor can be used to edit any ASCII file, in addition to source code. Having a complete text editor built into the Programmer's Platform saves a great deal of time during program development compared to the conventional approach of separating the editor from the compiler.

DIFFERENCES WITH WORDSTAR Most of the Borland C++ commands follow WordStar command conventions. Several differences should be pointed out for those that are already comfortable with WordStar.

Command	*Borland C++ Action*	*WordStar Action*
Ctrl-QL	Restores line	Runs spelling checker
Ctrl-P	Inserts control character	Inserts print command
Ctrl-KD	Activates menu bar	Saves file and exits
Ctrl-KQ	Activates menu bar	Quits editing current file
Ctrl-S	Stops at start of line	Continues to previous line
Ctrl-D	Stops at end of line	Continues to next line

Continue the learning sequence with Module 20.

Module 34
ELSE

DESCRIPTION

The else operator is used in conjunction with *if*. It provides an alternate execution path. The statements after else are executed when the condition is false. The format of an if statement with an else clause is:

```
if(condition)
     true_statement;
else
     false_statement;
```

or

```
if(condition){
     true_statements;
}else{
     false_statements;
}
```

The same rules apply to the { } as with a simple if statement; the { } are optional for single statements and required for multiple statements. The condition expression also operates the same way. For example:

```
if(a != 0){
     cout << "a is not equal to zero.";
}else{
     cout << "a is equal to zero.";
}
```

APPLICATIONS

Use *else* when an explicit program action is required for the false condition.

The equals error produces code that will never be executed with the else statement. The condition portion of the if has "=" instead of "==". The condition is always true when that happens. For example:

```
if(i = 1){
     cout << "True";
}else{
     cout << "This will never execute!";
}
```

The true statements always execute. What is meant in this case is:

```
if(i == 1){
     cout << "True";
}else{
     cout << "This executes when i is not 1.";
}
```

Good coding practice dictates always using the '{' and '}' for clarity to explicitly mark the statements associated with the if. The potential problem is maintenance. Refer to the *IF* module for a discussion of the maintenance problem.

HANDS-ON ACTIVITY

The sample session shows how to use else in an if construct to produce alternate action.

1. Type **BC** and press **Enter** to start up the compiler.
2. Press **Alt-FN** to pull down the File menu and create a new file.
3. Type the following code into the NONAME00.CPP edit window:

```
#include <iostream.h>

void main()
{
     long i;
     char string[80];

     cout << "Module 34\n\n";
     cout << "Enter a number followed by Enter: ";
     cin  >> i;
     if(i == 0){
          cout << "The number is ZERO.\n";
     }
     if(i < 0){
          cout << "The number is negative.\n";
     }else{
          cout << "The number is positive.\n";
     }
     if(i = 1){
          cout << "i=1 is always true!\n";
     }else{
```

```
            cout << "This never executes!\n";
        }
}
```

4. Press **Alt-R** and type **R** to compile and run the sample program.

```
Module 34
Enter a number followed by Enter: _
```

5. Type **99**. The program compares the number to zero and prints the response based on the if statement.

```
Module 34
Enter a number followed by Enter: 99
The number is positive.
```

The final line illustrates the equal error where "=" is used instead of "==" in a comparison.

```
Module 34
Enter a number followed by Enter: 99
The number is positive.
i=1 is always true!
```

6. Press **Alt-F5** to view the user screen.
7. Press **Alt-X** to exit the program and return to the DOS prompt.
8. Continue the learning sequence with Module 35.

Module 35
ELSE IF

DESCRIPTION

The *else if* statement is a nested if that executes as part of a false condition for the next outer if statement. An if statement with one or more nested if statements is a compound statement. The else if statement executes when its condition is true. The branch is taken when the condition evaluates to false. The format of an else if statement is:

```
if(condition)
     one_statement;
else if(condition_2)
     another_statement;
```

or

```
if(condition){
     statements;
}else if(condition_2){
          nested_statements;
      }
}
```

The *if(condition_2)* is considered a single statement by the compiler.

The { } are optional and must balance for single statements and are required when multiple statements are executed. The condition is an expression that evaluates to true or false. *condition_2* is tested only when *condition* is false. False is zero and true is any nonzero value.

The condition_2 expression may be any of the expressions for a simple if statement:

- Conditional operator
- Function that returns a value
- Variable
- Compound conditions

Refer to Module 53 for discussions on valid if expressions.

APPLICATIONS

Use the *else if* statement when a condition only applies to the false portion of a previous if or another else if.

Always use the '{' and '}' for clarity to explicitly mark which statement's associated with the else if. The else if statement is an extension to the simple if operator.

C++ provides the *switch* as an alternative to deeply nested else if statements. Compound if statements that nest more than one or two levels are prone to error and are frequently difficult to debug. Consider using switch or refactor code that nests multiple levels.

HANDS-ON ACTIVITY

The sample session illustrates nested if statements. Three integer values are tested to determine the largest value.

1. Type **BC** and press **Enter** to start up the compiler.
2. Press **Alt-FN** to pull down the File menu and create a new file.
3. Type the following code into the NONAME00.CPP edit window:

```
#include <iostream.h>

void largest(long,long,long);      // prototype

void main()
{
      long a = 0;
      long b = 88;
      long c = 99;

      cout << "Module 35\n\n";
      cout << "Testing the default values: \n";
      cout << " A: " << a;
      cout << " B: " << b;
      cout << " C: " << c << "\n";
      largest(a,b,c);

      cout << "Now, you test the else if code...\n";
      cout << "Enter A: ";
      cin  >> a;
      cout << "\nEnter B: ";
      cin  >> b;
      cout << "\nEnter C: ";
      cin  >> c;
      largest(a,b,c);
}
```

```
void largest(long a, long b, long c)
{
     if(a > b){
          if(a > c){
               cout << "A is the largest.\n";
          }
     }else if(b > c){
               cout << "B is the largest.\n";
          }else{
               cout << "C is the largest.\n";
          }
}
```

4. Press **Alt-RR** to compile then run the sample program.

```
C:\NORM\TEST>bc
Module 35

Testing the default values:
 A: 0 B: 88 C: 99
C is the largest.
Now, you test the else if code...
Enter A:
```

5. Type a number for A, B, then C. The program compares the numbers and prints the response based on the nested if/else if statements.

```
Testing the default values:
 A: 0 B: 88 C: 99
C is the largest.
Now, you test the else if code...
Enter A: 27
Enter B: 0
Enter C: 12
```

6. Press **Alt-F5** to show the user screen with output.

```
Testing the default values:
 A: 0 B: 88 C: 99
C is the largest.
Now, you test the else if code...
Enter A: 27
Enter B: 0
Enter C: 12
A is the largest.
```

7. Press **Alt-X** to exit the sample program and return to DOS.
8. Continue the learning sequence with Module 17.

Module 36
ENUM

DESCRIPTION

enum is one C++ data type. Other data types include struct, union, typedef, and class. Each of these is discussed separately. Defining a variable as an enumerated data type allows the programmer to define sets of related variables, set acceptable values for a variable, and assign a name to a number.

The general form of an enumerated data type is:

```
enum set_name{member1,member2,...membern}var1,var2,...varn
```

where enum is the data type, set_name is the name of the set, and member1...membern are the names of the variables belonging to the set.

The first member in an enum data type is given a value of 0 and each additional member is given a value of one greater than the previous member. This can be overridden by declaring a different value for the individual member.

APPLICATIONS

Use enum to let the compiler assign values to associated constants. Consider the following two C++ statements.

```
enum numbers{zero,one,two,three}widget;
enum more_numbers{zero,one,five=5,six}sproket;
```

In the first statement the set numbers contain the four members zero, one, two, and three. As stated previously, the first member is assigned a value of zero and each additional member's value is incremented by one. This means zero equals 0, one equals 1, two equals 2, and three equals 3.

Now look at the second statement. The set more_numbers contains the members zero, one, five, and six. As in the first statement, the first member zero is assigned the value of 0 and the second member is assigned the value of 1. But the third member five has been given a value of 5 in the statement. This overrides the C++ default of assigning a value of 1 greater than the previous. Since the value of five is 5, the value assigned the next member, six, is one greater than the previous or 6.

One important thing to remember about enumerated data types is that member names cannot be used as names of other variables.

HANDS-ON ACTIVITY

1. Start Borland C++.
2. Press **Alt-F** to activate the File menu. Select New by typing **N**.
3. Type the following source code:

```
#include <iostream.h>
#include <stdio.h>
#include <string.h>
#include <conio.h>

enum numbers{zero,one,two,three}value;

main()
{
      clrscr();
      cout << "Module 36\n";
      cout << "This module uses enum\n\n";

      cout << "Assign a number to value...\n";
      value = zero;
      cout << "value is: " << value << "\n";

      cout << "Assign a constant to value...\n";
      value = 99;
      cout << "value is: " << value << "\n";

      cout << "\nPress any key to exit";
      do {;} while(!kbhit());
}
```

4. Press **Ctrl-F9** to compile and run the program.

```
Module 36
This module uses enum

Assign a number to value...
value is: 0
Assign a constant to value...
value is: 99

Press any key to exit
```

Notice that the assignment of 99 to value caused a compiler warning message. The message is caused by assigning a constant to an enumerated value.

5. Continue the learning sequence with Module 56.

Module 37
ERROR HANDLING

DESCRIPTION

Error handling is an area often overlooked by even the best intentioned programmer. Ignoring error testing and recovery can lead to programs with unpredictable behavior at best and programs that crash frequently.

C and C++ provide features that aid error processing. These are varied and include:

Feature	*Usage*
stderr	Error file descriptor
errno	System variable with last error number
perror	Function that prints system error message
eof	Function that checks for end of file
clearerr	Function to clear error status on files
strerror	Function to return pointer to errno message

In addition, many system functions return a success/fail value that can be tested. This is true for the I/O functions. Writing an error class to test for and report specific program errors is also relatively easy.

The important thing is to take advantage of status return values and handle errors as soon as they happen. Failing to trap an error can cascade and cause errors in unrelated areas of the program. These types of program bugs are often hard to track down.

APPLICATIONS

Use the error detection and handling features of the language to construct robust programs. An obvious question is "How do I process errors?" This section shows one approach.

Assume the following code segment:

```
        ...
descriptor = fopen(file_name,"r");
        ...
fputs(string,descriptor);
        ...
```

There are several things wrong with this code. First of all, the file is opened in mode "r" for read. The first operation performed on that file is to write to it. The biggest problem is not testing the status returns. The fputs( ) call does not capture its status information. The errors that can be tested for include:

- File open failure
- Unsuccessful write

Several steps that can be added to this code are:

- Test for successful file open.
- Use perror( ) or errno to generate an error message.
- Write an error message to stderr.
- Set errno to a unique value to mark where error occurs.

The revised code segment is:

```
        ...
descriptor = fopen(file_name,"r");
if(!descriptor){
        perror();              // print system error message
        fprintf(stderr,"The filename is: %s\n",file_name);
        exit(errno);
}
        ...
status = fputs(string,descriptor);
if(status == EOF){             // Write not successful
        abort(999);            // Mark error location
}
        ...
void abort(int location)
{
        perror();
        fputs("Error writing to output file\n",stderr);
                ...
}
```

The changes in the code consists of an if statement to test for and handle an error each place a status indicator is returned. The first test is for a valid file open. Most of the built-in system functions set a global variable named errno. perror( ) uses the value of errno to print an error message to stderr. The fprintf( ) function also prints the filename to stderr. These two actions give a clear indication of the problem when the file cannot be opened. exit( ) is a system function that terminates the program. The batch command language in many operating systems can use the value returned via exit( ) to control processing further.

The code for testing the success or failure of the fputs( ) call is handled differently. When the test for failure is true, a dedicated error handling function, abort( ), is called to perform the error processing. A separate error processing function does two things: it provides a standard way of handing errors and can save a few lines of code in the rest of the program.

Adding five or six lines of code every place a status value is returned may seem painful, but it is more than worth the effort during program maintenance.

HANDS-ON ACTIVITY

This program illustrates one approach to error handling.

1. Type **BC** and press **Enter** to start up the compiler.
2. Press **Alt-FN** to pull down the File menu and create a new file.
3. Type the following code into the edit window:

```
#include <iostream.h>
#include <stdio.h>
#include <stdlib.h>
#include <string.h>
#include <conio.h>

void abort(int);

void main()
{
      int  status;
      FILE *descriptor;
      char filename[80];
      char string[80];

      clrscr();
      cout << "Module 37\n";
      cout << "This module demonstrates error handling\n\n";
      cout << "Enter filename: ";
      gets(filename);
```

```
        descriptor = fopen(filename,"r");
        if(!descriptor){
            perror("Input File:");
            fprintf(stderr,"The filename is: %s\n",filename);
            exit(errno);
        }
        printf("Enter a string: ");
        gets(string);
        status = fputs(string,descriptor);
        if(status == EOF){              // Write not successful
            abort(999);                 // Mark error location
        }
        cout << "\n\nPress any key to exit";
        do {;} while(!kbhit());
    }
    void abort(int location)
    {
        perror("Abort");
        fputs("\n",stderr);
        fputs("Error writing to output file\n",stderr);
        fprintf(stderr,"Location code is: %d\n",location);
        exit(errno);
    }
```

4. Save the program by selecting **Save as** from the File pull-down menu and typing **MOD37.CPP**, then pressing **Enter**.
5. Press **Alt-RR** to compile and run the program.

```
Module 37
This module demonstrates error handling

Enter filename:
```

6. Type **ZZZ.ZZZ**, then press **Enter**. Any nonexistent filename will work for testing the error handling associated with the fopen( ) call.

```
Module 37
This module demonstrates error handling

Enter filename: ZZZ.ZZZ

Input File: No such file or directory
The filename is: ZZZ.ZZZ
```

perror( ) requires a string argument. The text after the colon is generated based on the value of errno. The call to exit( ) causes immediate program termination; you must press **Alt-F5** to view the screen.

7. Press **Ctrl-F9** to run the sample program again.

```
Module 37
This module demonstrates error handling

Enter filename:
```

8. Type **MOD37.CPP** then press **Enter**. This is a valid filename.

```
Module 37
This module demonstrates error handling

Enter filename: MOD37.CPP
Enter a string: There is moderation even in excess.

Abort: Error 0
Error writing to output file
Location code is: 999

Press any key to exit
```

This run has a valid filename, so it gets past the fopen( ) error test. This error is generated by the attempt to write to a file opened for read only access. The fputs( ) call returns the error status. perror( ) generates the "Error 0" message because fputs did not set errno.

9. Press any key to exit MOD37.CPP and return to Borland C++.
10. Press **Alt-X** to exit Borland C++ and return to DOS.
11. Continue the learning sequence with Module 87.

Module 38
EXIT( )

DESCRIPTION

The function exit( ) is called to terminate a program at some point other than the end of main( ). exit( ) automatically closes all open files and sets an error status for DOS. The calling syntax is:

```
#include <stdlib.h>
void exit(int);
```

The integer parameter is the exit status. An exit status of zero is considered "normal" termination. Other values indicate an error.

APPLICATIONS

Use exit( ) to end program execution and return to the operating system. The most common situations to use exit( ) in are:

- To terminate a program when an error is detected
- When the user selects a quit program option

Many operating systems can act upon the exit value of a program.

The following code segment detects a file open failure then terminates the program via exit( ):

```
descriptor = fopen("bad_file","r");
if(!descriptor){
     cout << "Could not open file\n";
     exit(errno);
}
```

If the input file, bad_file, cannot be opened, there is no point in continuing. errno is the global error number variable that is set by most system routines to indicate what error was detected.

```
switch (ch){
     ...
case 'q':
     ...
```

```
        exit(0);
        ...
    }
```

This code segment is typical of the user selecting quit from a menu. Exit is called to terminate execution, but the status flag is zero to indicate normal program termination.

HANDS-ON ACTIVITY

This program uses exit( ) to terminate program execution.

1. Start Borland C++.
2. Open a new File window by pressing **Alt-FN**.
3. Type the following code in the NONAME00.CPP window:

```
#include <iostream.h>
#include <stdio.h>
#include <string.h>
#include <conio.h>
#include <stdlib.h>

void main()
{
    char ch;

    clrscr();
    cout << "Module 38\n";
    cout << "This module uses exit\n\n";
    cout << "Type a string (q exits): ";
    do{
        ch = getchar();
        switch (ch){
        case 'q':
            cout << "Quit was selected\n";
            exit(0);
        default:
            ;
        }
    }while(ch);

    cout << "\nPress any key to exit";
    do {;} while(!kbhit());
}
```

4. Press **Ctrl-F9** to run the program.

```
Module 38
This module uses exit

Type a string (q exits):
```

5. Type **AbCdEfGqHiJkLm**, then press **Enter**. The following is displayed:

```
Module 38
This module uses exit

Type a string (q exits): AbCdEfGqHiJkLm
Quit was selected
```

6. The program automatically returns to Borland C++. Press **Alt-F5** to view the screen.
7. Press **Alt-X** to exit Borland C++ and return to DOS.
8. Continue the learning sequence with Module 51.

Module 39

FCLOSE( )

DESCRIPTION

fclose( ) closes a file opened by a previous call to fopen( ). The file buffers are flushed automatically as part of the file close process. The syntax for fclose( ) is:

```
#include <stdio.h>
int = fclose(FILE*);
```

The return value is zero on success.

The process of program shutdown will automatically close all open files. However, this provides no opportunity to trap error conditions. Always explicitly close files so proper error handling can be included.

APPLICATIONS

Use fclose( ) to close a file previously opened by fopen( ). fclose( ) does not distinguish between input and output files. A typical sequence that uses fclose( ) is:

```
#include <stdio.h>
   ...
int  status;
FILE *descriptor;
char string[80];
   ...
descriptor = fopen("MOD39.CPP","r");
   ...
status = fgets(string,MAXLINE,descriptor);
   ...
status = fclose(descriptor);
```

The code segment opens the file MOD39.CPP, reads the first line into string, then closes the file. A real program also would include testing the return values for the I/O function calls for error returns.

HANDS-ON ACTIVITY

The sample program illustrates the fclose.

1. Start the compiler, select New File from the pull-down menu bar, then type the following code:

```
#include <iostream.h>
#include <stdio.h>
#include <string.h>
#include <conio.h>

#define MAXLINE 80

void main()
{
      int  status;
      char string[128];
      char file_name[80];
      char *buffer;
      FILE *descriptor;

      clrscr();
      cout << "Module 39\n\n";
      cout << "The fclose statement\n";

      cout << "Enter a filename: ";
      cin  >> file_name;
      cout << "Opening the file...\n";
      descriptor = fopen(file_name,"r");
      if(!descriptor){         // zero means open error
            cout << "Could not open " << file_name << "\n";
      }
      cout << "Read the first line...\n";
      buffer = fgets(string,MAXLINE,descriptor);
      if(!status){
            cout << "Error reading input file.\n";
      }
      cout << "The first line is: " << string;
      status = fclose(descriptor);
      if(status){              // zero means success
            cout << "Could not close file.\n";
      }
      cout << "\nPress any key to exit";
      do {;} while(!kbhit());
}
```

2. Press **Alt-F**, then select **Save as...** from the File menu.
3. Type **MOD39.CPP** then press **Enter** to save the source code.
4. Press **Alt-RR** to compile and run the sample program.

```
Module 39

The fclose statement
Enter a filename:
```

5. Type the name of a file in your current directory, then press **Enter**. Type **MOD39.CPP** if you did step 4. The following is displayed:

```
Module 39

The fclose statement
Enter a filename: MOD39.CPP
Opening the file...
Read the first line...
The first line is: #include <iostream.h>

Press any key to exit
```

6. Press any key to exit the sample program and return to Borland C++.
7. Continue the learning sequence with Module 43.

Module 40
FGETS( )

DESCRIPTION

fgets( ) reads the next line from a file. The line of text is treated as a string. fgets( ) uses a file descriptor obtained from a call to fopen( ). The syntax is:

```
#include <stdio.h>
char* fgets(char*,int, FILE*);
```

fgets( ) returns the address of the character string on success, or zero on failure. The first argument is the address of a character array to read the next line into. The integer is one plus the maximum number of bytes to read. The FILE* is the file descriptor. A typical call is:

```
#include <stdio.h>
#define MAXLINE   80
      ...
FILE *descriptor;
char *status;
char string[80];
      ...
status = fgets(string,MAXLINE,descriptor);
```

fgets( ) includes the newline character in the line placed in the input buffer.

APPLICATIONS

Use fgets( ) to read a string from a file stream. A string in this case corresponds to a line in a text file. The file must be opened using fopen( ) with a mode of "r" prior to being accessed by fgets( ).

stdin may be used as the file descriptor to read a line from the keyboard. This may be done when a program reads from the keyboard sometimes and from a file other times. No modifications are necessary for the same code to handle both input sources in this situation.

Code must explicitly be added to applications that do not need the newline that fgets( ) leaves on the end of the string to remove it before processing.

HANDS-ON ACTIVITY

This program uses fgets( ) to read a file and display 10 lines at a time on the screen. The sample program is a simple version of more. The number of lines per screen may be easily changed by modifying the value of MAXLINE in the code. The output display screens in the following sample session assumes that the source code has been saved as MOD66.CPP after typing it in.

1. Start Borland C++ and open a new file window.
2. Type the following code in the file window:

```
#include <iostream.h>
#include <process.h>
#include <stdio.h>
#include <string.h>
#include <conio.h>
#define MAXLINE  80
#define PAGE     10
#define FOREVER  for(;;)

void main()
{
      FILE *descriptor;
      int  lines;
      char ch;
      char *status;
      char buffer[128];
      char file_name[80];

      clrscr();
      cout << "Module 40\n";
      cout << "This module uses fgets\n\n";
      cout << "Enter filename: ";
      gets(file_name);
      descriptor = fopen(file_name,"r");
      if(!descriptor){
            cout << "Cannot open " << file_name << ".\n";
            exit(0);
      }
      lines = 0;
      clrscr();
      FOREVER{
            status = fgets(buffer,MAXLINE,descriptor);
            if(!status){            // Got EOF
                  break;
            }
            cout << buffer;
            lines++;
```

```
            if(!(lines%PAGE)){     // "Page Break"
                cout << "\n\n Press Q to exit; any key to continue";
                do {;} while(!kbhit()); // Wait for key
                ch = getch();
                if(ch == 'Q' || ch == 'q'){ break; }
                clrscr();
            }
        }
        fclose(descriptor);

        cout << "\nPress any key to exit";
        do {;} while(!kbhit());
    }
```

3. Press **Ctrl-F9** to run the program.

```
Module 40
This module uses fgets

Enter filename:
```

4. Type **MOD40.CPP**, then press **Enter**. The following is displayed:

```
Module 40
This module uses fgets

Enter filename: MOD40.CPP
```

5. The screen clears and the first ten lines of the file are displayed:

```
#include <iostream.h>
#include <stdio.h>
#include <string.h>
#include <conio.h>
#define MAXLINE  80
#define PAGE     10
#define FOREVER  for(;;)

void main()
{

Press Q to exit; any key to continue
```

6. Press **Enter** to display the next screen of the file.

```
    FILE *descriptor;
    int  lines;
    char ch;
    char *status;
    char buffer[128];
    char file_name[80];

    clrscr();
    cout << "Module 40\n";

Press Q to exit; any key to continue
```

7. Press **q** to quit at this point. The final prompt is displayed:

```
Press any key to exit
```

8. Press any key to exit the sample program and return to Borland C++.
9. Press **Alt-X** to exit Borland C++ and return to DOS.
10. Continue the learning sequence with Module 45.

Module 41

FILE I/O

DESCRIPTION

C and C++ have a rich set of I/O functions. The file I/O functions operate in conjunction with file descriptors that are assigned by opening the file. The I/O functions discussed in this book are:

Function	*Description*
fopen	Associate a file descriptor with a filename
fclose	Close a file
fgetc	Get the next character from a file
ungetc	Put character back into input stream
fgets	Get the next string from a file
fputs	Put string to a file
fprintf	Print a formatted string to a file
fscanf	Read formatted input from a file

Each of these functions is discussed individually in its own module. The function prototypes for both the functions and file descriptors are in <stdio.h>.

Advanced file I/O functions are not discussed in detail in this book. The I/O functions listed above provide a great deal of power. C++ also includes a set of file I/O stream classes for manipulating files. These are discussed in the STREAM I/O module.

Continue the learning sequence with Module 39.

Module 42
FILE MENU

DESCRIPTION

This module describes the Programmer's Platform File menu. The File menu is Borland C++'s interface to MS-DOS source files. File operations such as load, save, and print are performed from this menu.

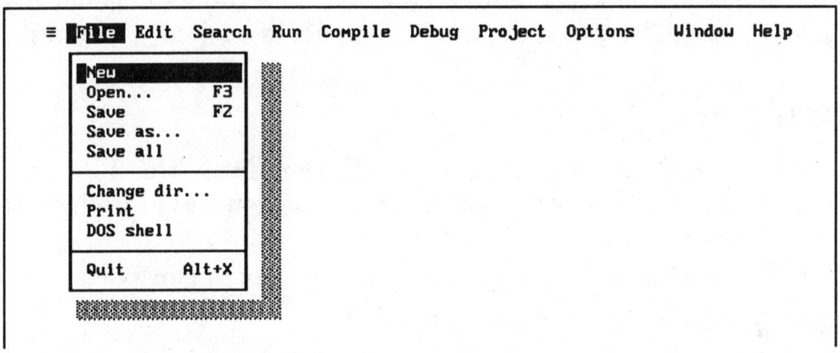

APPLICATIONS

The File menu is accessed by pressing Alt-F. The entries in this menu are:

New — Selecting New opens a new editing window with a default filename of NONAME00.C. After completing the editing session, set the new filename via the Save as... File menu.

Open... — Select OPEN... to open a new source file and load it into the editor. The filename is selected from a submenu that allows the filename to be typed in directly or selection of a file from the current directory. Use the F3 key as a shortcut to the OPEN... submenu.

Save — This menu item saves the current file in the editing window. The filename is unchanged. The F2 key is the shortcut keystroke that invokes Save.

Save as... — Use this item to save the file being edited in the current edit window and change its name. A submenu provides the place to enter the filename.

Save all — Select *Save all* to save all files modified during this session.

Change dir... — Allows you to change both the current directory and disk drive. A submenu is used to specify the new directory.

Print — Print provides a means to print the entire file or a portion of the file in the current edit window.

DOS Shell — This selection spawns a new version of COMMAND.COM. This allows you to run other programs without completely exiting from Borland C++. Type EXIT to restart the Programmer's Platform.

Quit — Quit exits Borland C++ and returns to the DOS prompt. The current directory is left pointing to the directory the Programmer's Platform used for source code. The Alt-X key also exits Turbo C++.

NOTE menu items that end in '...' indicate that a submenu will pop up when the item is selected. The submenu generally provides a place to enter information such as a filename.

HANDS-ON ACTIVITY

This session uses the Open... menu selection from the File menu to illustrate submenus for selecting files. The same general procedure applies to other menus.

1. Type **BC** at the DOS prompt and press **Enter** to run Borland C++.
2. Select the File menu by pressing **Alt-F**.
3. Press **Enter** to activate the Open... submenu.

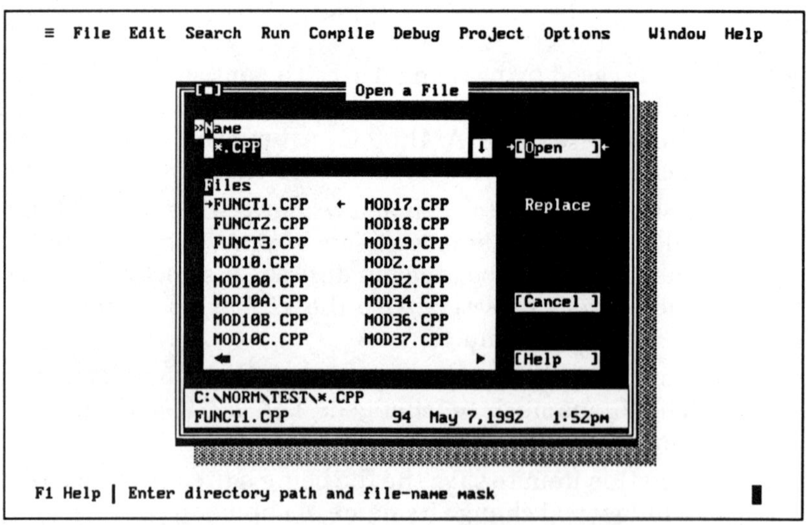

The cursor is left on the Name Field. This field is a template for which filenames to include in the list of files. The default is *.CPP. That means that all files in the current directory ending with the extension '.CPP' are listed. The file types can be changed to C files by typing *.C. A single file not in the Files List can be selected by typing its name.

4. Press **Tab** to highlight the first file in the Files Field.
5. Move the menu bar to the desired file and press **Enter** to load the file into the editor.
6. Press **Alt-X** to exit Borland C++ and return to DOS.
7. Continue the learning sequence with Module 32.

Module 43

FOPEN( )

DESCRIPTION

fopen( ) opens a file. The I/O functions identified in the FILE I/O module may access a file after a successful call to fopen( ). The file access mode is specified as part of the calling sequence along with the filename. The syntax for fopen( ) is:

```
#include <stdio.h>
FILE* = fopen(const char* name,const char * mode);
```

The return value is the file descriptor used for other file I/O functions. The file descriptor is zero when an error occurs in the fopen( ) call. The valid mode values are:

Value	*Mode*
r	Read from an existing file
w	Write to a new or existing file
a	Append to the end of an existing file
r+	Read/write an existing file
w+	Update
a+	Append for update
b	Binary file type modifier
t	Text file type modifier

The mode is a string, and so must be enclosed in double quotes. Using the update, '+,' modes are advanced usages that are used in conjunction with functions not covered in this text. Update mode I/O requires a file positioning function, such as fseek( ), be used between file writes and reads. Otherwise, the read may not read the correct file location.

APPLICATIONS

Use fopen( ) to make a file accessible to a program. fopen( ) distinguishes between input and output files. A typical sequence that uses fopen( ) is:

```
#include <stdio.h>
   ...
FILE *descriptor;
char filename[80];
char string[80];
   ...
descriptor = fopen(filename,"r");
if(!descriptor){
     cout << "Could not open file.\n";
}
```

Checking the return value is very important with fopen( ) because all references to the file are tied to the file descriptor. Failing to test for the zero file descriptor can cause problems in other parts of the program. The contents of the file may be read after calling fopen( ).

HANDS-ON ACTIVITY

The sample program illustrates the fopen( ). Start Borland C++ from the DOS prompt then perform the following steps.

1. Press **Alt-FN** to pull down the File menu and create a new file.
2. Type the following code:

```
#include <iostream.h>
#include <stdio.h>
#include <string.h>
#include <conio.h>

void main()
{
     char file_name[80];
     FILE *descriptor;

     clrscr();
     cout << "Module 43\n\n";
     cout << "The fopen statement\n";

     cout << "Enter a filename: ";
     cin  >> file_name;
     cout << "Opening the file...\n";
     descriptor = fopen(file_name,"r");
     if(!descriptor){        // zero means open error
          cout << "Could not open " << file_name << "\n";
     }
     cout << "\nPress any key to exit";
     do {;} while(!kbhit());
}
```

3. Press **Alt-RR** to compile and run the sample program.

```
Module 43

The fopen statement
Enter a filename:
```

4. Type **XXX.XXX**, then press **Enter**. The following is displayed:

```
Module 43

The fopen statement
Enter a filename: XXX.XXX
Opening the file...
Could not open XXX.XXX

Press any key to exit
```

5. Press any key to exit the sample program and return to Borland C++.

This program shows fopen( ) with a nonexistent file. The result of the call is tested and an error message printed. If you saved the source file, run the program again with a valid filename. The program exits properly, even though the file was not closed.

6. Continue the learning sequence with Module 48.

Module 44
FOR

DESCRIPTION

The *for* statement is a C++ looping construct. The for statement executes the statements within the loop a specified number of times. The general usage of the for statement is:

```
for(initialization;exit_expression;end_of_loop){
      statements;
      if(skip_the_rest){ continue; }
      if(time_to_exit){ break; }
}
```

where *initialization* represents one or more statements done before the loop starts execution. Initializing variables is done in *initialization.* The *exit_expression* tests for *end of loop.* Finally, the statement(s) that make up end_of_loop, such as incrementing the counter, are performed at the bottom of the loop.

The brace pair, { }, is optional if a single statement is executed within the loop. Braces are required for multiple statements. The rules about using braces are the same as for the *if* statement. The break operator may be used to exit the for loop before the normal end of loop is reached. The continue operator causes control to branch directly to the start of the loop, in effect skipping a portion of the loop.

A typical for loop is:

```
for(i=0,j=1;i<10;i++,j++){
      cout << i;
}
```

This loop is performed 10 times. Both the initialization and end_of_loop portions of the for may contain zero, one, or more statements. Separate multiple statements with a comma.

APPLICATIONS

Use the for loop when the number of times to execute the loop is known at the start of the loop. Manipulating strings is frequently done with for because the string length can be calculated and used in the exit_expression.

Any of the C++ looping constructs may be used in a given situation. A do or while loop can be coded to perform the exact operation of a for loop. Choosing a looping construct is often a matter of personal preference.

Loops may be nested. Nested loops past two levels are not very readable, just as nested if statements are not readable. Anytime a program has loops nested more than two levels deep, the code should be refactored. Frequently, moving the nested loop into a function helps readability a great deal. It also makes tracking bugs easier. An example nested for loop is:

```
for(i=0;i<length;i++){
        statements;
        for(j=0;j<27;j++){
                more_statements;
        }
}
```

Nested for loops are sometimes used when processing multiple dimensioned arrays.

A variation on the for loop is FOREVER:

```
#define FOREVER  for(;;)
        ...
FOREVER{
        statements;
        if(exit_condition){ break; }
}
```

This is an endless for loop. There is no exit condition in the for statement. There must be an explicit test and break executed for control to branch out of the loop. FOREVER is not included in most C/C++ text books. It is sometimes convenient and the name, FOREVER, makes its purpose obvious.

HANDS-ON ACTIVITY

The sample program illustrates the for loop. It types a character string, one character at a time.

1. Type **BC** and press **Enter** to start up the compiler.
2. Press **Alt-FN** to pull down the File menu and create a new file.

3. Type the following code into the NONAME00.CPP edit window:

```
#include <iostream.h>
#include <stdio.h>
#include <string.h>
#include <conio.h>

#define FOREVER  for(;;)

void main()
{
      int  i;
      int  len;
      char value;
      char string[80];

      clrscr();
      cout << "Module 44\n\n";
      cout << "The for loop\n";

      cout << "Enter a string: ";
      gets(string);
      cout << "\nOutput the string, one char at a time\n\n";
      len = strlen(string);
      for(i=0;i<len;i++){
            value = string[i];
            putchar(value);
      }
      cout << "\nNow, do the same thing with FOREVER...\n\n";
      i = 0;
      FOREVER{
            value = string[i++];
            if(value == '\0'){ break; }
            putchar(value);
      }
      cout << "\n\nPress any key to exit";
      do {;} while(!kbhit());
}
```

4. Press **Alt-RR** to compile and run the sample program.

```
Module 44

The for loop
Enter a string:
```

5. Type **abcdefgABCDEFG** and press **Enter**. The following is displayed:

```
Module 44

The for loop
Enter a string: abcdefgABCDEFG

Output the string, one char at a time

abcdefgABCDEFG

Now, do the same thing with FOREVER...

abcdefgABCDEFG

Press any key to exit
```

6. Press any key to exit the sample program and return to Borland C++.
7. Continue the learning sequence with Module 22.

Module 45

FPUTS( )

DESCRIPTION

fputs( ) writes a character string to a file. The file must be opened prior to calling fputs( ) via fopen( ). The syntax is:

```
#include <stdio.h>
int fputs(const char*,FILE*);
```

fputs( ) returns EOF on failure, otherwise the return value is an undetermined nonnegative value. Each call to fputs( ) appends a newline character to the end of the string. stdout may be used as the file descriptor for fputs( ). A typical call is:

```
#include <stdio.h>
      ...
FILE *descriptor;
int  status;
char string[80];
      ...
descriptor = fopen(file_name,"w");
      ...
status = puts(string,descriptor);
```

APPLICATIONS

Use fputs( ) to write a string to an output stream. A newline character is automatically appended to the string by fputs( ). Thus, each string written using fputs( ) is a line in the output file.

stdout and stderr may be used as the descriptors. Using fputs( ) for all output is a technique for programs that write messages to the screen or to a file depending on some variable value. The code may be simplified using this approach as opposed to having similar code write to the screen sometimes and a file sometimes.

HANDS-ON ACTIVITY

This program uses fputs( ) to copy a file. The sample program is another version of MOD76.CPP that uses fputs( ) in place of fputc( ) calls. Be sure to save the source code as MOD45.CPP before compiling the sample program.

1. Start Borland C++.
2. Open a new file window by pressing **Alt-FN**.
3. Type the following code:

```
#include <iostream.h>
#include <stdio.h>
#include <string.h>
#include <conio.h>

#define MAXLINE 100

void main()
{
     long  i = 0;
     int   success;
     FILE  *fd_in;
     FILE  *fd_out;
     char  file_in[80];
     char  file_out[80];
     char  buffer[128];
     char  *status;

     clrscr();
     cout << "Module 45\n";
     cout << "This module uses fputs to copy a file\n\n";
          /*
          | Read filenames
          */
     cout << "Enter input filename:  ";
     gets(file_in);
     cout << "Enter output filename: ";
     gets(file_out);
          /*
          | Open files
          */
     fd_in = fopen(file_in,"r");
     if(!fd_in){
          cout << "Could not open file: " << file_in <<"\n";
     }
     fd_out = fopen(file_out,"w");
     if(!fd_out){
          cout << "Could not open file: " <<file_out<<"\n";
     }
```

```
        /*
        | Copy file_in to file_out using fgets and fputs
        */
    do{
        status     = fgets(buffer,MAXLINE,fd_in);
        if(!status){
            break;
        }
        success     = fputs(buffer,fd_out);
        if(success == EOF){
            fputs("Error writing output file\n",stderr);
        }
        i++;
        if(!(i%10)){ putchar('.'); }
    }while(1);
    cout << "\nCopied " << i << " lines.\n\n";

    fputs("Press any key to exit",stdout);
    do {;} while(!kbhit());
}
```

4. Press **Ctrl-F9** to run the program.

```
Module 45
This module uses fputs to copy a file

Enter input filename:  MOD45.CPP
```

5. Type the input filename **MOD45.CPP**, then press **Enter**. The following is displayed:

```
Module 45
This module uses fputs to copy a file

Enter input filename:  MOD45.CPP
Enter output filename:
```

6. Next, type the output filename **TRASH.DAT**, and press **Enter**. The copy begins. A '.' is displayed for each 10 lines copied.

```
Module 45
This module uses fputs to copy a file

Enter input filename:  MOD45.CPP
Enter output filename: TRASH.DAT
.....
Copied 59 lines

Press any key to exit
```

7. Press any key to exit the sample program and return to Borland C++.
8. Press **Alt-X** to exit Borland C++ and return to DOS.

fputs( ) can be used in place of cout when writing strings to the screen. cout has the advantage of automatically writing any built-in C data type. fputs( ) only handles strings.

9. Continue the learning sequence with Module 37.

Module 46
FRIEND FUNCTIONS

DESCRIPTION

A friend method or function is a function that is granted access to private data items within a class. This feature provides flexibility for application implementation. The syntax for declaring a friend function is:

```
class ClassName{
      data_structures;
public:
      friend void any_function();
};
```

A method in another class may be declared a friend:

```
class ClassName{
      data_structures;
public:
      friend void AnyClass::any_method();
};
```

Finally, a class may be a friend:

```
class ClassName{
      data_structures;
public:
      friend class AnyClass;
};
```

Any method in a friend class may access private data items in the class.

APPLICATIONS

Use friend functions, methods, or classes when access must be granted to data items that are normally private. Selective access is afforded this way. The protection is more restricted than protected or public, but less than private.

The necessity for declaring a friend usually comes about because access to otherwise private data is needed by an entity not part of the class. Be cautious of classes with numerous friends. It is a sign that the class structure is not quite correct and needs to be redesigned.

HANDS-ON ACTIVITY

This program defines a stack class. A function is declared a friend to allow access to the stack pointer.

1. Type **BC** and press **Enter** to start up the compiler from the DOS prompt.
2. Press **Alt-FN** to pull down the File menu and create a new file.
3. Type the following code into the NONAME00.CPP edit window:

```
#include <iostream.h>
#include <stdio.h>
#include <string.h>
#include <conio.h>

class BaseClass{
      char B_string[80];
public:
      BaseClass(char *tmp){ strcpy(B_string,tmp); }
      friend void show(BaseClass);
};
void show(BaseClass BC)
{
      cout << BC.B_string << "\n";
}

void main()
{
      char  string1[80] = "";

      clrscr();
      cout << "Module 46\n";
      cout << "Public Protection Demonstration\n\n";
      cout << "Type a string: ";
      gets(string1);
      BaseClass one_object(string1);
      cout << "Now access from a friend function\n";
      show(one_object);

      cout << "\nPress any key to exit\n";
      do {;} while(!kbhit());
}
```

4. Press **Ctrl-F9** to compile and run the sample program.

```
Module 46
Friend Function

Type a string:
```

5. Type **Youth is a blunder; Manhood a struggle; Old Age a regret.** and press **Enter**. The following is displayed:

```
Module 46
Friend Function

Type a string: Youth is a blunder; Manhood a struggle; Old Age a regret.
Now access from a friend function
Youth is a blunder; Manhood a struggle; Old Age a regret.

Press any key to exit
```

6. Press any key to exit the sample program and return to Borland C++.
7. Press **Alt-X** to exit Borland C++ and return to DOS.
8. Continue the learning sequence with Module 57.

Module 47
FUNCTIONS

DESCRIPTION

Functions are the smallest addressable unit of code in C++. Every C++ program consists of one or more functions. Functions provide a way to partition a program into smaller, more manageable pieces of code.

The rules for functions are:

- Every program must have a function named main( ).
- Every function should have a function prototype.
- A function can return only one value.
- Every function should perform a single action.
- Follow the naming rules in Module 63.

Failure to follow the first two rules cause error messages during compilation. The fourth rule is not checked by the compiler. It is enforced by the programmer who wants to write programs that are easier to write and maintain.

A function declaration has several portions:

- Type declaration
- Function identifier
- Parameter list

The body of a function is enclosed in '{' and '}'. For example:

```
void My_Character(char ch)
{
     cout << "My Character is: " << ch << "\n";
}
```

The function name is *My_Character*; it returns no value (void) and expects a single character argument (ch). The function name may, optionally, be enclosed in parentheses.

A function prototype is the function declaration terminated with a ';'. The prototype for My_Character( ) is:

```
void My_Character(char);
```

The argument name is not necessary in the prototype. The function prototype must occur before the function. Function prototypes are frequently defined in header (.H) files. See the module *#include* for the discussion of header files.

APPLICATIONS

A large program divided into multiple small functions that each perform a single action is easier to understand and maintain than a large monolithic main( ) function. Programs are also much easier to debug and test when broken down into simple functions.

Function prototypes allow the compiler to check that all calling sequences are correct at compile time. This extra level of compiler checking prevents obscure bugs that are hard to track down because an argument was passed as character when the called function expects an integer argument.

HANDS-ON ACTIVITY

The following session illustrates the use of functions in C++. The traditional first program when learning C or C++ is "Hello World". This is used as the basis for this session.

1. Start Borland C++.
2. Press **Alt-FN** edit a new file.
3. Type the following code into the edit window:

```
#include <iostream.h>

      // Function Prototypes
int  Hello_World();
int  two_times(int);

void main()                           // Function declaration for main
{
      int count;

      cout << "Module 47\n";
      count = Hello_World();          // Call a function
      cout << "count is " << count << "\n";

      count = two_times(count);       // A function with
                                      //  parameter and return
```

```
                                        // value
        cout << "count is now " << count << "\n";
}

int Hello_World()
{
        const VALUE = 99;

        cout << "Hello World\n";
        return(VALUE);
}

int two_times(int value)
{
        int temp;

        temp = value * 2;               // multiply param by 2
        return(temp);
}
```

4. Press **Alt-R** to pull down the Run menu, then type **R** to compile and run the sample program.

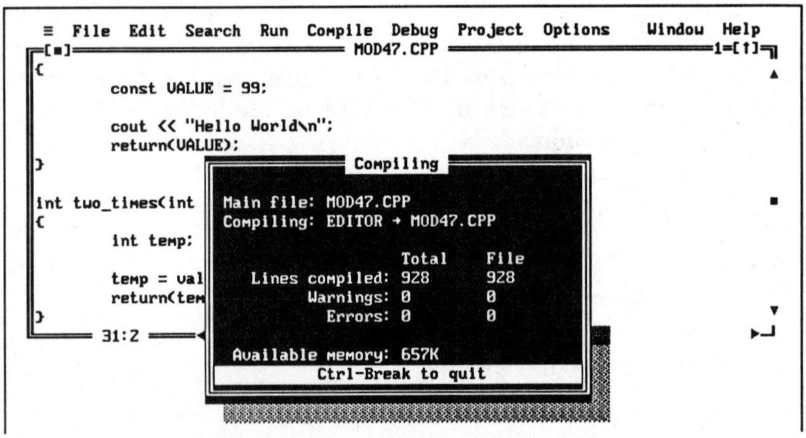

5. Press **Alt-F5** to see the results of program execution.

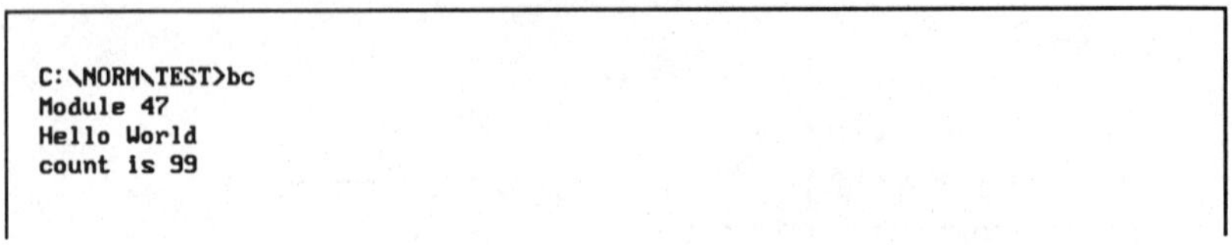

6. Press **Alt-X** to exit Borland C++ and return to DOS.
7. Continue the learning sequence with Module 96.

Module 48

GETC( ), FGETC( )

DESCRIPTION

The functions getc( ) and fgetc( ) read the next character from the file referenced by a valid file descriptor. The syntax is:

```
#include <stdio.h>
int getc(FILE*);
int fgetc(FILE*);
```

EOF is returned on error. Typical calls are:

```
#include <stdio.h>
     ...
char ch;
FILE *descriptor;
     ...
ch = getc(descriptor);
     ...
ch = fgetc(descriptor);
```

Many C compilers implement getc( ) as a preprocessor macro that is compiled as a fgetc( ) call.

APPLICATIONS

Use fgetc( ) when character input is desired from a file. The file must be opened prior to its file descriptor being referenced. Use fopen( ) to open a file for reading. The file should be closed via fclose( ) prior to exiting back to DOS.

HANDS-ON ACTIVITY

This program uses fgetc( ) to type the contents of a file.

1. Start Borland C++ and open a new file window.
2. Type the following code:

```
#include <iostream.h>
#include <stdio.h>
#include <string.h>
#include <conio.h>

void main()
{
     char  ch;
     FILE *descriptor;

     cout << "Module 48\n";
     cout << "This module uses getc\n\n";
     cout << "Opening MOD48.CPP...\n";
     descriptor = fopen("MOD48.CPP","r");
     if(!descriptor){
          cout << "File not found.\n";
     }
     cout << "Type the file.\n\n";
     cout << "--------------------------------\n";
     do{
          ch = fgetc(descriptor);
          if(ch == EOF){
               cout << "\nGot EOF from fgetc()\n";
          }else{
               cout << ch;
          }
     }while(ch != EOF);

     cout << "\nPress any key to exit";
     do {;} while(!kbhit());
}
```

3. Press **Alt-F**, then select **Save as...** to save the program. Use the filename MOD48.CPP.

4. Press **Alt-RR** to compile and run the program.

```
Module 48
This module uses fgetc

Opening MOD48.CPP...
Type the file.

--------------------------------------------
#include <iostream.h>
#include <stdio.h>
#include <string.h>
#include <conio.h>

void main()
{
      char  ch;
      FILE *descriptor;

      cout << "Module 48\n";
      cout << "This module uses getc\n\n";
      cout << "Opening MOD48.CPP...\n";
      descriptor = fopen("MOD48.CPP","r");
      if(!descriptor){
            cout << "File not found.\n";
      }
      cout << "Type the file.\n\n";
      cout << "--------------------------------\n";
      do{
            ch = fgetc(descriptor);
            if(ch == EOF){
                  cout << "\nGot EOF from fgetc()\n";
            }else{
                  cout << ch;
            }
      }while(ch != EOF);

      cout << "\nPress any key to exit";
      do {;} while(!kbhit());
}


Got EOF from fgetc()

Press any key to exit
```

5. Press any key to exit the sample program and return to Borland C++.
6. Press **Alt-X** to exit Borland C++ and return to DOS.

Notice that fgetc( ) reads the '\n' that ends every line in the file. A simple extension to the sample program is modifying it to query the user for a filename. The new program becomes a simple TYPE program with that single change.

7. Continue the learning sequence with Module 94.

Module 49

GETCHAR( )

DESCRIPTION

The I/O function *getchar( )* reads the next character from stdin. stdin is the keyboard by default. It may be redirected to take input from a file on the command line. The usage syntax is:

```
#include <stdio.h>
int getchar(void);
```

getchar uses stdin as the input file descriptor. A typical call is:

```
#include <stdio.h>
    ...
char ch;
    ...
ch = getchar();
```

The getchar( ) call above is equivalent to:

```
ch = getc(stdin);
```

Many C compilers implement getchar( ) as a preprocessor macro that is compiled as the getc(stdin) call.

One characteristic of getchar( ) should be mentioned here. The compiler echoes characters automatically as they are typed at the keyboard. getchar( ) does not actually see the characters until the Enter key is pressed. The whole input line is buffered by the system. The sample program illustrates the behavior described here. The action of getchar( ) in Borland C++ is compatible with C compilers on other types of computers.

APPLICATIONS

Use getchar( ) when character input is desired from the standard input stream. One of the main advantages of using getchar( ) is convenience. stdin is automatically opened by the compiler. That means the programmer does not have to explicitly open the file and specify the error handling code associated with opening a file. Likewise, stdin is automatically closed upon program exit.

Additional code may be saved by taking advantage of command line I/O redirection. Files may be specified on the command line and getchar( ) reads the file rather than the keyboard. Input redirection is specified using the < character in front of a filename on the command line. For example:

```
C:\> APROGRAM <FILE.INP
```

This command runs APROGRAM and redirects stdin. getchar( ) reads from FILE.INP rather than the keyboard.

HANDS-ON ACTIVITY

This program uses getchar( ) and getc( ) to read from the keyboard and from a file.

1. Start Borland C++ and open a new file window.
2. Type the following code:

```
#include <iostream.h>
#include <stdio.h>
#include <string.h>
#include <conio.h>

void main()
{
     char  ch;

     cout << "Module 49a\n";
     cout << "This module uses getchar\n\n";
     cout << "Type some string (Q to quit): ";
     do{
          ch = getchar();
          if(ch == EOF){
               cout << "Got EOF from getchar()\n";
               break;
          }
          cout << ch;
     }while(ch != 'Q');
     cout << "\nGot Q uit character from stdin.\n";

     cout << "\nPress any key to exit";
     do {;} while(!kbhit());
}
```

3. Press **Alt-F**, then select **Save as...** to save the program. Use the filename MOD49A.CPP.

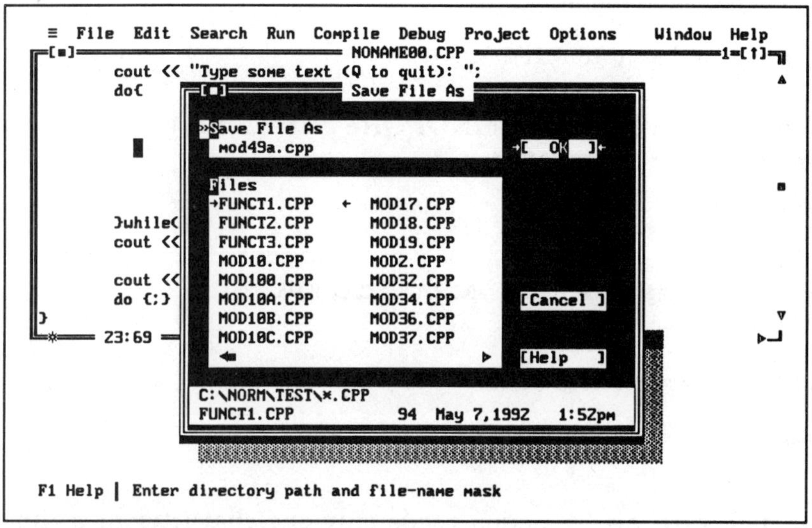

4. Press **Alt-CM** to compile MOD49A.CPP.

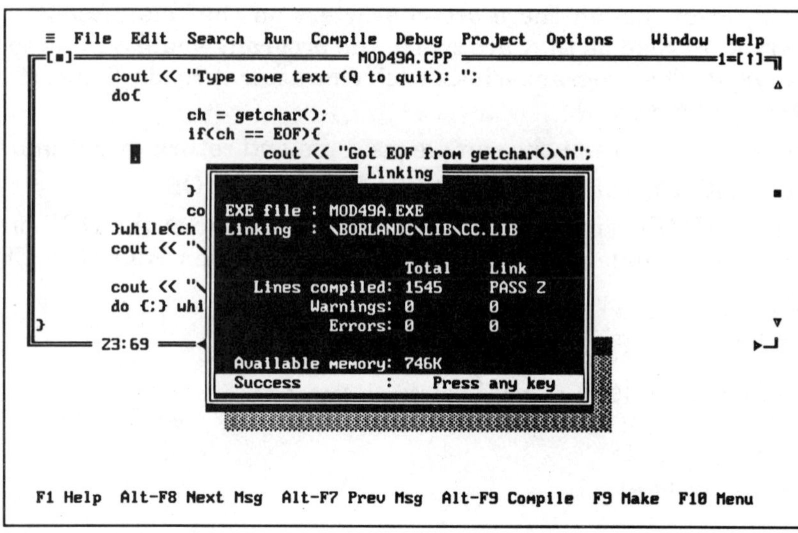

5. Press **Alt-RR** to run the program.

```
Module 49a
This module uses getchar

Type some string (Q to quit):
```

6. Type **ABCDEFGHIJKLMNOPQRSTUVWXYZ** and press **Enter**. The following is displayed:

```
Module 49a
This module uses getchar

Type some string (Q to quit): ABCDEFGHIJKLMNOPQRSTUVWXYZ
ABCDEFGHIJKLMNOPQ

Got Q uit character from stdin.

Press any key to exit
```

Even though getchar( ) function reads only one character at a time, the characters are not available until the Enter key is pressed. The program illustrates this quite well. The program stops reading when the character 'Q' is read, even though there are characters on the line after it. If the characters were read as they are typed, the program would quit as soon as the Q is typed. The program echoes each character it reads. Thus, the last character displayed is Q.

7. Press any key to exit the sample program and return to Borland C++.
8. Press **Alt-X** to exit Borland C++ and return to DOS.
9. Type **MOD49A <mod49a.cpp**, then press **Enter** at the DOS prompt to run the sample program with input coming from MOD49A.CPP.

```
Module 49a
This module uses getchar

Type some string (Q to quit): #include <iostream.h>
#include <stdio.h>
#include <string.h>
#include <conio.h>

void main()
{
     char  ch;

     cout << "Module 49a\n";
     cout << "This module uses getchar\n\n";
     cout << "Type some string (Q to quit): ";
```

```
        do{
              ch = getchar();
              if(ch == EOF){
                    cout << "Got EOF from getchar()\n";
                    break;
              }
              cout << ch;
        }while(ch != 'Q');
        cout << "\nGot Q
  Got Q uit character from stdin.

  Press any key to exit
```

The < causes getchar( ) to read characters from MOD49A.CPP rather than the keyboard. The first Q encountered in the file causes the program to quit.

10. Press any key to exit the program and return to the DOS prompt.

A useful experiment is substituting the following line

```
ch = getc(stdin);
```

for the getchar( ) call in MOD49A.CPP. Repeat steps three through ten, except use MOD49B in place of MOD49A in the instructions. The results will be identical.

This code illustrates using getchar( ) to read from the keyboard and from a file. There are several related I/O function. See modules GETS( ), PUTCHAR( ), and PUTS( ) for further discussions of using Console I/O functions.

11. Continue the learning sequence with Module 50.

Module 50
GETS( )

DESCRIPTION

The I/O function *gets( )* reads the next character string from stdin. A line of text is the string in this case. stdin is the keyboard. It may be redirected on the command line to read from a file instead of the keyboard. The usage syntax is:

```
#include <stdio.h>
char* gets(char*);
```

gets( ) returns the address of the character string on success, or zero on failure. stdin is the input file descriptor for gets( ). A typical call is:

```
#include <stdio.h>
     ...
char *status;
char string[80];
     ...
status = gets(string);
```

The gets( ) call reads a string from standard input into the character array named string. The return value, status, will be the address of string on success or zero on failure. The above call to gets( ) is equivalent to:

```
status = fgets(stdin,MAXLINE,string);
```

Some C compilers implement gets( ) as a preprocessor macro that calls fgets( ) with stdin as the file descriptor.

APPLICATIONS

Use gets( ) to read a string from the standard input (stdin) stream. An advantage of using gets( ) is convenience. The compiler automatically opens stdin. The programmer does not have to explicitly open or close the file and specify the error handling code associated with opening a file.

Command line I/O redirection also works for gets( ). Files specified on the command line with a leading **<** are read rather than reading the keyboard. For example:

```
C:\> APROGRAM <FILE.INP
```

This command runs APROGRAM and redirects stdin. gets( ) reads from FILE.INP rather than the keyboard.

HANDS-ON ACTIVITY

This program uses gets( ) to read strings from the keyboard.

1. Start Borland C++ and open a new file window.
2. Type the following code in the file window:

```
#include <iostream.h>
#include <stdio.h>
#include <string.h>
#include <conio.h>

void main()
{
        char *status;
        char string[80];

        cout << "Module 50\n";
        cout << "This module uses gets\n\n";
        cout << "Type a string: ";
        status = gets(string);
        if(!status){
                cout << "Error Reading stdin.\n";
        }
        cout << "\nThe string is: " << string << "\n";

        cout << "\nPress any key to exit";
        do {;} while(!kbhit());
}
```

3. Press **Ctrl-F9** to run the program.

```
Module 50
This module uses gets

Type a string:
```

4. Type **Never take anything for granted.**, then press **Enter**. The following is displayed:

```
Module 50
This module uses gets

Type a string: Never take anything for granted.

The string is: Never take anything for granted.

Press any key to exit
```

The characters typed on the keyboard are buffered and automatically echoed to the screen. The characters are not available to gets( ) until the Enter key is pressed.

5. Press any key to exit the sample program and return to Borland C++.
6. Press **Alt-X** to exit Borland C++ and return to DOS.
7. Continue the learning sequence with Module 77.

Module 51

GOTO

DESCRIPTION

Both C and C++ support the *goto* statement even though they are structured languages. goto should be used sparingly. The other, structured looping constructs such as for, do, and while are sufficient for 99% of looping situations. The goto syntax is:

```
    goto label;
         ...
label:
```

goto is an unconditional branch to the label.

APPLICATIONS

Use the goto statement to branch to a specific place in the program. Occasionally, it is necessary to branch to a common location from different places in the program. Branching to the end of main( ) to perform shutdown activities is one such example.

Too many gotos is bad coding practice. Code that uses many goto statements is hard to maintain, tends to have many bugs, and generally should be restructured to eliminate as many goto statements as possible. Code with many gotos is unstructured and often referred to as spaghetti code.

HANDS-ON ACTIVITY

The sample program illustrates the goto statement.

1. Type **BC** and press **Enter** to start up the compiler.
2. Pull down the File menu and select **NEW** to create a new file.
3. Type the following code:

```
#include <iostream.h>
#include <stdio.h>
#include <conio.h>

void main()
```

```
{
	int  i;
	int  len;
	char ch;
	char string[80] = "String";

	clrscr();
	cout << "Module 51\n";
	cout << "The goto statement\n\n";

	cout << "goto Skip_string\n";
	goto Skip_string;
	cout << "Enter a string: ";
	gets(string);
Skip_string:
	cout << "The string is: " << string << "\n";
	i = 0;
	do{
		ch = string[i++];
		cout << ".";
		cout << "goto XXX\n";
		goto XXX;
	}while(ch);
XXX:
	if(i){
		cout << "goto Exit_program\n";
		goto Exit_program;
	}
	goto Skip_string;
Exit_program:
	cout << "\nPress any key to exit\n";
	do {;} while(!kbhit());
}
```

4. Press **Alt-RR** to compile and run the sample program.

```
Module 51
The goto statement

goto Skip_string
The string is: String
.goto XXX
goto Exit program

Press any key to exit
```

5. Press any key to exit the sample program and return to Borland C++.
6. Continue the learning sequence with Module 93.

Module 52

HELP MENU

DESCRIPTION

Borland C++ has a context sensitive help system built into the Programmer's Platform. This module describes accessing the help system.

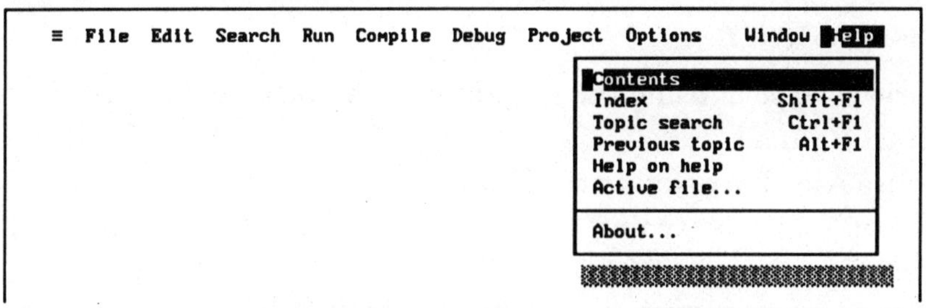

Contents Selecting Contents pops up a window that contains the table of contents for the entire help system. The table of contents is arranged by topic.

Index This item opens a window with individual help entries arranged alphabetically. Shift-F1 can be used to activate the index.

Topic search Choose this selection to open a help window with broad topics such as Main menu or Editor. This menu provides a good starting point for general browsing of the help system when you don't know the exact command to ask for help with. Use the right mouse button or Ctrl-F1 to access this menu entry directly.

Previous topic The help system keeps a stack of the help requests made in a session up to the current point. The Previous topic selection uses this information to backtrack to the previous help topic. The help window is closed when the top level is reached. The Alt-F1 key activates this function.

Help on help The Programmer's Platform help system also provides help on help. This can be accessed directly by pressing F1 twice.

Active file... This option allows you to choose which help file is active, IDE and C++, ObjectWindows API, or Turbo Vision API.

About... Pop up a dialog box with copyright and version number.

APPLICATIONS

The Programmer's Platform help system can save a great deal of time during development by providing the capability of looking up information from language syntax to library calling sequences.

A very powerful feature of the help system is that many entries include examples that can be copied into an editor window. The ability to experiment with working library functions saves time typing the source code from the help window because typing mistakes are eliminated.

HANDS-ON ACTIVITY

The various ways of using the Help menu are illustrated in this session.

1. Start Borland C++.
2. Press **Alt-H** to activate the Help menu.
3. Select Topics by typing **T**. You can also press **Ctrl-F1** to access the Topics dialog box directly.

```
≡  File  Edit  Search  Run  Compile  Debug  Project  Options   Window  Help

              ╔═[■]═══════════ Help ═══════════1═[↑]═╗
              ║Turbo Help Index                      ▲
              ║                                      ■
              ║!
              ║!=
              ║#
              ║#define
              ║#elif
              ║#else
              ║#endif
              ║#error
              ║#if
              ║#ifdef
              ║#ifndef                               ▼
              ║#include
              ╚◄                                    ►┘

F1 Help on help  Alt-F1 Previous topic  Shift-F1 Help index  Esc Close help
```

4. Move the cursor to #define using either the mouse or the arrow keys and press **Enter** to pop up the #define entry.

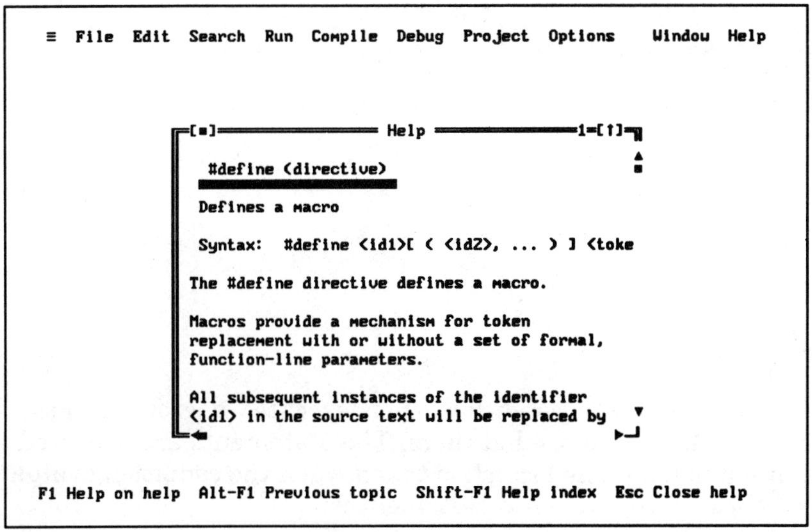

5. Press **Esc** to close the Help menu.
6. Press **Alt-X** to return to the DOS prompt.
7. Continue the learning sequence with Module 33.

Module 53

IF

DESCRIPTION

The *if* operator tests a condition, then executes a group of associated statements or branches around them. The statements are executed when the condition is true. The branch is taken when the condition evaluates to false. The basic format of an if statement is:

```
if(condition)                              if(condition){
     one_statement;          or                 statements;
                                           }
```

The { } are optional for single statements but required for multiple statements. The condition is an expression that evaluates to true or false. False is zero and true is any nonzero value.

The condition expression may be any of the following:

- Conditional operator
- Function that returns a value
- Variable
- Compound conditions

Conditional operators include ==, <, >, etc. For example:

```
if(x==y){
     cout << "x is equal to y";
}
```

Conditional operators are discussed in a separate module.

A function call can be used as the conditional. C expressions are executed from the inside out. Thus, a function call inside the parentheses will be called before the condition is evaluated:

```
if(strlen(x) > 5){
     cout << "x is a long string."
}
```

strlen is called before the if condition is evaluated. The result of the call is tested for greater than five and the string output if the condition is true. An alternate usage is:

```
if((len = strlen(x)) > 5){
      cout << "x is a long string."
}
```

The difference between the two if statements is the length is assigned to len, which allows len to be used later.

Variables are valid conditions.

```
len = strlen(x);
if(len){
      cout << "len is greater than zero.";
}
```

Compound conditions are allowed. Compound conditions are evaluated left to right starting from the innermost parenthesis pair. The evaluation order may be explicitly ordered via additional ( ) pairs. Compound conditions are connected with logical operators:

```
if((x > y) && (y < z)){
      a = 0;
}
```

The if statement reads "If x is greater than y and y is less than z."

```
if((ch == 'A') || (ch == 'a')){
      cout << "ch is an A.";
}
```

The '| |' means *or.* A condition can be tested for false even though the default test is true. A false condition is flagged using a '!'.

```
if(a != 0){
      cout << "a is not equal to zero.";
}
```

APPLICATIONS

Use the *if* statement to act upon the results of a condition test to control the program flow. if is the most basic of control structures in C++.

There are some facts about the if statement to keep in mind when writing code to prevent obscure program bugs:

- The result of an '=' is always true.
- You should always use braces.

A very common error is forgetting the second equal sign in a comparison. The condition becomes = instead of ==. The condition is always true when that happens. For example:

```
if(i = 1){
     cout << "True";
}
```

The true statements always execute. What is meant in this case is:

```
if(i == 1){
     cout << "True";
}
```

Good coding practice dictates always using the '{' and '}' for clarity to explicitly mark the statements associated with the if. The potential problem is maintenance. Suppose you code an if statement like:

```
if(dollars < 0)
     cout << "In the red";
```

Later another statement needs to execute when dollars is less than zero.

```
if(dollars < 0)
     cout << "In the red";
     black = get_more_money(dollars);
```

Forgetting to add the { }, as in the example, is a surprisingly common mistake that is frequently hard to find. This is how the example should have been written:

```
if(dollars < 0){
     cout << "In the red";
     black = get_more_money(dollars);
}
```

Always using { } will prevent this error from occurring.

HANDS-ON ACTIVITY

The sample session illustrates if usage. The user enters a number. The program uses several if statements to determine if the number is negative, zero, or positive.

1. Type **BC** and press **Enter** to start up the compiler.
2. Press **Alt-FN** to pull down the File menu and create a new file.
3. Type the following code into the NONAME00.CPP edit window:

```
#include <iostream.h>
#include <string.h>
```

```
void main()
{
      long i;
      char string[80];

      cout << "Module 53\n\n";
      cout << "Enter a number followed by Enter: ";
      cin  >> i;
      if(i == 0){
            cout << "The number is ZERO.\n";
      }
      if(i < 0){
            cout << "The number is negative.\n";
      }
      if(i > 0)
            cout << "The number is positive.\n";
      cout << "\nType a word: ";
      cin  >> string;
      i  = strlen(string);
      if(i){
            cout << "The string length is: " << i << "\n";
      }
      if(i = 1){
            cout << "i=1 is always true!\n";
      }
}
```

4. Press **Alt-C** and type **M** to compile the sample program.

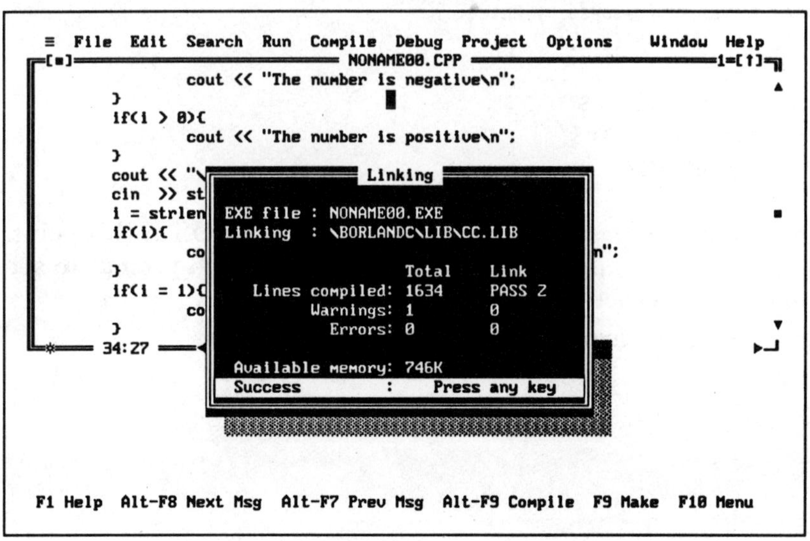

5. Press **Alt-X** to exit Borland C++ and return to the DOS prompt.
6. Type **NONAME00** and press **Enter** to execute the sample program. The following screen is displayed:

```
Module 53
Enter a number followed by Enter: _
```

7. Type a number between –9 and +9. The program compares the number to zero and prints the response based on the if statement.

```
Module 53
Enter a number followed by Enter: 9
The number is positive.

Type a word: _
```

8. Type **STRING** and press **Enter** at the prompt.

```
Module 53
Enter a number followed by Enter: 9
The number is positive.

Type a short string: STRING
The string length is: 6
```

The final line illustrates the equal error where "=" is used instead of "==" in a comparison.

```
Module 53
Enter a number followed by Enter: 9
The number is positive.

Type a short string: STRING
The string length is: 6
i=1 is always true!
```

9. The sample program automatically returns to DOS at this point. Run NONAME00 again using different values at each prompt to see how the program reacts.
10. Continue the learning sequence with Module 34.

Module 54

#IF, #ELSE, #ELIF, #ENDIF

DESCRIPTION

The preprocessor supports testing of symbol and constant values. These tests and actions are compile time events. The preprocessor *#if* construct supports the following statements:

Statement	*Description*
#if	Test a preprocessor condition
#else	False statements follow
#elif	Else if
#endif	End a #if construct

The syntax for each part of the #if statement is:

#if constant-expression
preprocessor statements or code for true evaluation
#elif constant-expression2
preprocessor statements or code for true evaluation
#else
preprocessor statements or code for false evaluation
#endif

The constant expression must evaluate to true or false. Preprocessor statements must start in column one so they cannot be indented to delimit the true and false portions of the construct.

APPLICATIONS

Use the #if construct to evaluate conditions to choose alternate lines to include in a program at compile time. The following operators may be used in the constant expression:

Operator	*Description*
<	Less than
>	Greater than
==	Equal
<=	Less than or equal

>=	Greater than or equal
!=	Not equal

The tests can involve only constants, including preprocessor defined constants.

```
#if ERROR == FATAL
     cout << "Fatal Error\n";
     exit(errno);
#else
     cout << "Non-fatal Error\n";
#endif
```

This code segment assumes two constants, ERROR and FATAL, are already defined. The programmer controls which code is compiled by setting the value of ERROR to FATAL. When ERROR equals FATAL, the "Fatal Error" message is output and the program exits. When ERROR is not equal FATAL, the "Non-fatal Error" prints and program execution continues. Remember these are compile time tests to determine which source code to pass on to the compiler.

HANDS-ON ACTIVITY

The example program shows a typical preprocessor #if construct. This session assumes BC has already been started.

1. Press **Alt-FN** to begin a new file.
2. Type the following program code:

```
#include <iostream.h>
#include <stdio.h>
#include <string.h>
#include <conio.h>

#define DEBUG        54

void main()
{
     char string[80];

     clrscr();
     cout << "Module 54\n";
     cout << "Preprocessor #if construct\n\n";
     cout << "Type a string: ";
     gets(string);
#if DEBUG == 54
     cout << "DEBUG was selected at compile time\n";
     cout << "The string is: " << string << "\n";
```

```
#else
     cout << "Not debugging...\n";
#endif

     cout << "\nPress any key to exit";
     do {;} while(!kbhit());
}
```

3. Press **Alt-R** and **Enter** to compile and run the program.

```
Module 54
Preprocessor #if construct

Type a string:
```

4. Type **History is philosophy from examples.** and press **Enter**.

```
Module 54
Preprocessor #if construct

Type a string: History is philosophy from examples.
DEBUG was selected at compile time
The string is: History is philosophy from examples.

Press any key to exit
```

5. Press **Alt-X** to exit Borland C++ and return to DOS.
6. Continue the learning sequence with Module 55.

Module 55

#IFDEF, #IFNDEF

DESCRIPTION

The preprocessor supports testing a symbol to determine if it currently exists or not. The *#ifdef* tests a symbol and evaluates to true when the symbol has been previously defined. *#ifndef* takes the true path if the symbol does not exist. The other preprocessor conditional statements, #else, #elif, and #endif, also work with #ifdef and #ifndef. The syntax for these statements are:

```
#ifdef symbol
preprocessor or source true statements
#else
preprocessor or source false statements
#endif

#ifndef symbol
preprocessor or source true statements
#else
preprocessor or source false statements
#endif
```

These statements evaluate the existence or nonexistence of the symbol to determine whether or not to include a group of lines in the compile.

APPLICATIONS

Use the #ifdef and #ifndef statements to include or exclude sections of code in a compile. These preprocessor statements are frequently used to create compile option selection for a program. Assume the following code segment is in a word processing program:

```
#define BIG_BUFF
#define INSERT_MODE
#define AUTO_BACKUP
      ...
```

These options cause the program to be compiled with big buffers, start in insert mode, and do automatic backup. The symbols are used in the following way:

```
     ...
#ifdef BIG_BUFF
     alloc_buff(BIG);
#else
     alloc_buff(SMALL);
#endif

     ...
#ifndef INSERT_MODE
     edit_mode = OVERSTRIKE;
#endif
     ...
#ifdef AUTO_BACKUP
     if(that_time()){
          write_backup();
     }
#endif
```

Picking the symbols to define at the start of a large program can tailor the program to whatever degree allowed by the options designed in the program. This preprocessor usage remains a very valid and valuable feature for C++ programs as it was for C programs.

HANDS-ON ACTIVITY

This sample program illustrates #ifdef and #ifndef.

1. Type **BC** and press **Enter** to run Borland C++.
2. Press **Alt-FN** to pull down the File menu and begin a new file.
3. Type the following program code:

```
#include <iostream.h>
#include <stdio.h>
#include <string.h>
#include <conio.h>

#define WRITE
#define LINE1
#define LINE2

void main()
{
     char string[80];
     clrscr();
     cout << "Module 55\n";
```

```
        cout << "Preprocessor #ifdef construct\n\n";
#ifdef WRITE
#ifdef LINE1
        cout << "Type a string: ";
        gets(string);
        cout << "Line 1 was: " << string << "\n\n";
#endif
#ifdef LINE2
        cout << "Type a string: ";
        gets(string);
        cout << "Line 2 was: " << string << "\n\n";
#endif
#endif
        cout << "\nPress any key to exit";
        do {;} while(!kbhit());
}
```

4. Compile and run the sample program.

```
Module 55
Preprocessor #ifdef construct

Type a string:
```

5. Type **A University should be a place of light,** and press **Enter**.

```
Module 55
Preprocessor #ifdef construct

Type a string: A University should be a place of light,
Line 1 was: A University should be a place of light,
Type a string:
```

6. Respond by typing **of liberty, and of learning.** then press **Enter**.

```
Module 55
Preprocessor #ifdef construct

Type a string: A University should be a place of light,
Line 1 was: A University should be a place of light,
Type a string: of liberty, and of learning.
Line 2 was: of liberty, and of learning.

Press any key to exit
```

7. Press any key to exit the program and return to Borland C++.
8. Press **Alt-X** to exit Borland C++ and return to DOS.
9. Continue the learning sequence with Module 16.

Module 56

#INCLUDE

DESCRIPTION

Borland C++ defines a large number of system header files that define data structures, function prototypes, and constants. The general form is:

```
#include <system.h>
```

to include a system level file header. The '<' and '>' tell the compiler to search the C++ system directories for system.h. A local header file has a slightly different form:

```
#include "local.h"
```

Only the current directory is searched for local.h in this case.

When the compiler encounters a #include statement, the contents of the specified file are compiled as if the code is contained in the current source file.

A large number of system file headers are included with Borland C++. Some header files apply only to the C++ compiler and others apply only to the C compiler.

APPLICATIONS

Large programs are best broken into multiple modules. Frequently, data structures must be shared between the modules. Global data structures are usually defined in header files. The #include directive allows multiple modules to reference common header files. The traditional file extension for header files is ".h."

Use #include to reference system files. You will find that almost every C program includes <stdio.h> and almost every C++ program will include <iostream.h>.

Local header files should define global information. Structure declarations for records are typically defined in a ".h" file for example. Variables used locally by a function are better defined in the function.

HANDS-ON ACTIVITY

The example program in this module references both system and local header files. The session starts from the DOS prompt.

1. Start Borland C++.
2. Press **Alt-FN** to pull down the File menu and begin a new file.
3. Type the following program code:

```
// local.h
char header_name[]="local.h";
int  global;
```

4. Press **Alt-FA** to pop up the Save File As menu. Type **local.h** as the filename and press **Enter**.

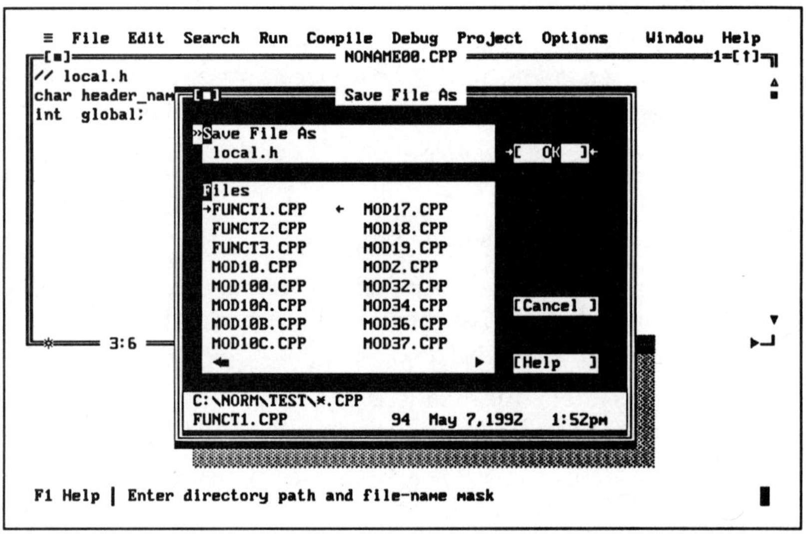

5. Press **Alt-FN** to access the File menu and start another new file.
6. Type the following code:

```
#include <iostream.h>
#include "local.h"

main()
{
      char ch;

      cout << "Module 56\n";
      global = 99;
      cout << "The header_name in local.h is ";
      cout << header_name << "\n";
```

```
        cout << "The value of global is: ";
        cout << global << "\n";
}
```

7. Press **Alt-FA** to pop up the Save File As menu. Type **mod56.cpp** as the filename.
8. Press **Alt-R** and **Enter** to compile and run mod56.cpp.
9. Press **Alt-F5** to view the user window with the results of run.

```
C:\NORM\TEST>bc
Module 56

The header_name in local.h is Local.h
The value of global is 99
```

10. Press **Alt-X** to exit Borland C++ and return to DOS.

This sample program shows that items defined in a .h file are accessable to a program when that file is referenced by the #include statement.

11. Continue the learning sequence with Module 8.

Module 57
INLINE

DESCRIPTION

One of the down sides to Object Oriented Programming (OOP) is programs tend to contain many very small functions. This can hurt program execution speed because function calls are relatively slow. C++ uses the *inline* statement to tell the compiler to compile the function code directly into the program rather than as a function call. Declaring an inline function tends to speed up execution if the function is called often. It also generates a larger executable file. A function call is generally only six or eight bytes. Rarely is the inline function code that small. The syntax for declaring an inline function is:

```
inline void any_function(void);
```

APPLICATIONS

Use inline functions when execution speed is critical in an application. Inline functions take more memory than normal functions but usually execute faster.

Functions called only a few times in a session should not be declared inline. Guard against the temptation to use inline for too many functions! Generally, one or two small functions that execute often cause the most dramatic speed improvement in a program.

A good candidate for inlining might be the function that moves the cursor in a word processing program. It is usually small and executed often.

HANDS-ON ACTIVITY

This sample program defines two functions and a main. The two functions are identical except one is a normal function and one is declared inline. The elapsed number of computer clock ticks is computed and displayed after executing each 10,000 times. The times shown in the example may be different depending on your computer and the version of Borland C++ you use.

1. Type **BC** and press **Enter** to start up the compiler from the DOS prompt.
2. Press **Alt-FN** to pull down the File menu and create a new file.
3. Type the following code:

```
#include <iostream.h>
#include <stdio.h>
#include <string.h>
#include <conio.h>
#include <time.h>

inline int faster(float x,int a,int b,int c)
{
      int y;
      y = x;
      x = x + 1;
      return(x);
}
int fast(float x,int a,int b,int c)
{
      int y;
      y = x;
      x = x + 1;
      return(x);
}

void main()
{
      int  i;
      int  value;
      clock_t start;
      clock_t stop;

      clrscr();
      cout << "Module 57\n";
      cout << "This module has an inline function\n\n";
      cout << "Execute fast 10,000 times\n";
      start = clock();
      for(i= 0; i<10000;i++){
            value = fast(1,2,3,4);
      }
      stop = clock();
      cout << "Elapsed: " << (stop - start) << "\n";

      cout << "Execute faster 10,000 times\n";
      start = clock();
      for(i= 0; i<10000;i++){
            value = faster(1,2,3,4);
```

```
        }
        stop = clock();
        cout << "Elapsed: " << (stop - start) << "\n";


        cout << "\nPress any key to exit\n";
        do {;} while(!kbhit());
}
```

4. Press **Alt-RR** to compile and run the sample program.

```
Module 57
This module has an inline function

Execute fast 10,000 times
Elapsed: 135
Execute faster 10,000 times
Elapsed: 91

Press any key to exit
```

5. Press any key to exit the sample program and return to Borland C++.
6. Press **Alt-X** to exit Borland C++ and return to DOS.
7. Continue the learning sequence with Module 67.

Module 58

INT

DESCRIPTION

The *int* operator sets aside 16 bits of storage for a variable to be used as an integer number. The two-byte size limits the value range that an int variable can represent. The range for a signed int is –32,768 to +32,767. An unsigned int can represent 0 to +65,535.

The following example lists several ways to define an int variable:

```
auto int two_bytes;
static int integer sixteen_bits;
int stuff;
static unsigned int integer trash;
unsigned int zero_to_65535;
```

The modifier short is a synonym for int. See Module 82 for a discussion of short.

APPLICATIONS

Use int variables when the values to be represented can fit into a two-byte representation. Counters and indexes most frequently fall into this category. Other uses of int variables include structures and files to minimize memory requirements compared to using long variables.

HANDS-ON ACTIVITY

The sample session illustrates the use of int integers. The program defines an int variable, stuff. stuff is incremented in a pair of loops until it overflows to negative.

1. Type **BC** and press **Enter** to start up the compiler.
2. Press **Alt-FN** to pull down the File menu and create a new file.

3. Type the following code into the NONAME00.CPP edit window:

```
#include <iostream.h>

void main()
{
	int   i;
	int stuff;
	unsigned int trash;

	cout << "\nCount up to 32,000 by 1000.\n";
	stuff = 0;
	for(i=0;i<32;i++){
		cout << stuff;
		stuff += 1000;          // Add 1000 to stuff
	}
	cout << "\nKeep on counting to see what happens...\n";
	for(i=0;i<32;i++){
		cout << stuff;
		stuff = stuff + 1000;
	}
}
```

4. Press **Alt-RR** to compile the program, then run it.
5. Press **Alt-F5** to view the user screen.

```
C:\NORM\TEST>bc
Module 58

count up to 32,000 by 1000.
0 1000 2000 3000 4000 5000 6000 7000 8000 9000 10000 11000 12000 13000 14000 150
00 16000 17000 18000 19000 20000 21000 22000 23000 24000 25000 26000 27000 28000
 29000 30000 31000
Keep on counting to see what happens...
32000 -32536 -31536 -30536 -29536 -28536 -27536 -26536 -25536 -24536 -23536 -225
36 -21536 -20536 -19536 -18536 -17536 -16536 -15536 -14536 -13536 -12536 -11536
-10536 -9536 -8536 -7536 -6536 -5536 -4536 -3536 -2536
```

6. Press **Alt-X** to exit Borland C++ and return to the DOS prompt.
7. Continue the learning sequence with Module 12.

Module 59

LOGICAL EXPRESSIONS

DESCRIPTION

C++ logical expressions could also be considered under the discussions about conditionals. Logical expressions modify the meaning of a conditional. The *not* (!) operator reverses the meaning of a conditional test. *And* (&&) and *or* (| |) are used to explicitly combine two more conditionals.

```
if(conditional_1 && conditional_2){
     true_statements;
}else{
     false_statements;
}
```

&& is pronounced 'and.' Both conditional_1 and conditional_2 must evaluate to true before false_statements are executed.

```
if(!conditional){
     false_statements;
}
```

! is pronounced 'not.' It reverses the logical results of the conditional. The logical operators in C++ are:

Conditional	*Name*
&&	And
| |	Or
!	Not

The logical expressions should be used in conjunction with parentheses to modify the evaluation order of compound conditionals. Compound conditions are normally evaluated left to right starting from the innermost parenthesis pair.

```
if((x > y) && (y < z)){
     a = 0;
}
```

This *if* statement reads "If x is greater than y and y is less than z." The (x >y) is evaluated first. (y < z) is evaluated next. The results are logically anded to determine whether a = 0 will be executed.

APPLICATIONS

Use logicals to either reverse the meaning of a conditional or to connect two or more conditionals. The order of expression evaluation is modified via the logical expressions.

Enclosing compound conditionals in parentheses is not required by the compiler, but is good coding practice because a compound conditional is easier to read with explicit parentheses. The more complex the compound conditional, the more parentheses become necessary.

```
if((dollars < 0) && (cents > 0)){
     true_statements;
}
```

Parenthesis pairs must balance.

HANDS-ON ACTIVITY

The sample session illustrates compound conditional statements.

1. Type **BC** and press **Enter** to start up the compiler.
2. Press **Alt-FN** to pull down the File menu and create a new file.
3. Type the following code into the NONAME00.CPP edit window:

```
#include <iostream.h>

void main()
{
     long i;

     cout << "Module 59\n\n";
     cout << "Enter a number followed by Enter: ";
     cin >> i;
     if(!(i == 0)){
          cout << "The number is not ZERO.\n";
     }
     if((i != 0) && !(i > 0)){
          cout << "The number is negative.\n";
     }
```

```
        if(!(i < 1) || (i == 99)){
             cout << "The number is positive.\n";
        }
}
```

4. Press **Alt-RR** to compile and run the sample program.

```
Module 59
Enter a number followed by Enter:
```

5. Type **99** and press **Enter**.

```
Module 59
Enter a number followed by Enter: 99
```

6. The sample program completes execution then returns to Borland C++. Press **Alt-F5** to view the user screen.

```
Module 59
Enter a number followed by Enter: 99
The number is positive.
```

7. Continue the learning sequence with Module 11.

Module 60
LONG

DESCRIPTION

The *long* operator sets aside a 32-bit storage area for a variable to be used as an integer number. This is four bytes. Signed four-byte integers can represent –2,147,483,648 to 2,147,483,647. An unsigned long can represent 0 to +4,294,967,295.

The following example lists several ways to define a long int variable:

```
long int four_bytes;
static long sixteen_bits;
long wait;
static unsigned long int ridiculous;
unsigned int big_number;
```

APPLICATIONS

Use long variables when very large integer values are required. The long data type is frequently used for counters and indexes.

Some computer systems treat int as long by default instead of short. This can make a significant difference in the way passed arguments are represented, which in turn can lead to difficult-to-find program bugs. Using long for integer values passed to functions is a good habit to get into if there is any chance a program will be ported from the PC to a minicomputer such as the DEC VAX.

HANDS-ON ACTIVITY

The sample session illustrates long integers. The program defines two long integers, one signed and one unsigned. A very large integer value (429496700) is assigned to the signed variable, then printed to the screen. The value is then moved to an unsigned long integer and displayed again. The values shown are quite different. The program shows what happens when the result of adding two large integers causes an overflow.

1. Type **BC** and press **Enter** to start up the compiler from the DOS prompt.
2. Press **Alt-FN** to pull down the File menu and create a new file.
3. Type the following code into the NONAME00.CPP edit window:

```
#include <iostream.h>
#include <stdio.h>
#include <conio.h>

void main()
{
      long int neg_num = 429496700;
      long stuff;
      unsigned long big;

      cout << "\nModule 60\n";
      cout << "\nA very large positive number may be";
      cout << " negative when treated as signed.\n";
      printf("    neg_num: %d\n\n",neg_num);
      big = neg_num;
      cout << "The same value is positive when treated";
      cout << " as an unsigned integer\n";
      cout << "    big: " << big << "\n\n";

      cout << "Press any key to exit\n";
      do {;} while(!kbhit());
}
```

4. Press **Alt-RR** to compile the program, then run it.
5. Press **Alt-F5** to view the user screen.

```
Module 60

A very large positive number may be negative when treated as signed.
   neg_num: -26244

The same value is positive when treated as an unsigned integer.
   big: 429496700

Press any key to exit
```

6. Press **Alt-X** to exit Borland C++ and return to the DOS prompt.
7. Continue the learning sequence with Module 82.

Module 61

MAIN( )

DESCRIPTION

Every C++ program must have one function named main( ). C++ startup code is compiled into main( ). It is a special function. main( ) function arguments are restricted and cannot return a value. main( ) is assumed to return type void, meaning there is no return value.

The arguments are restricted to zero or two arguments. main( ) should not reference arguments unless command line parameters are expected.

APPLICATIONS

C++ startup code calls main( ) as the first function in a program. A program with a very simple main( ) with no arguments is:

```
#include <iostream.h>
     main()
     {
          cout << "Simple main";
     }
```

Command line arguments are easy to specify but more complicated to process. The first argument is *argc* for argument count. The second argument is *argv* for argument vector. argc is an integer count that contains the number of arguments on the command line. The program name is the first argument, so argc is one when there are no arguments to process. argc is two with one argument, etc.

argv is an array of character pointers to each argument. argv[0] is the program name. argv[1] is argument one. argv[2] is argument two. Command line arguments are generally used to specify processing options or filenames. An example of a main( ) that expects command line arguments is:

```
     #include <iostream.h>
     #include <string.h>
     main(int argc,char *argv[])
     {
```

```
        int  count;
        char pname[80];

        count = argc;
        strcpy(pname,argv[0]);
}
```

The function strcpy copies the program name from the command line to pname.

HANDS-ON ACTIVITY

The following session illustrates the use of command line arguments in a main( ) function.

1. Type **BC** and press **Enter** to begin Borland C++ from the DOS prompt.
2. Press **Alt-F** to pull down the File menu, then select **N** to edit a new file.

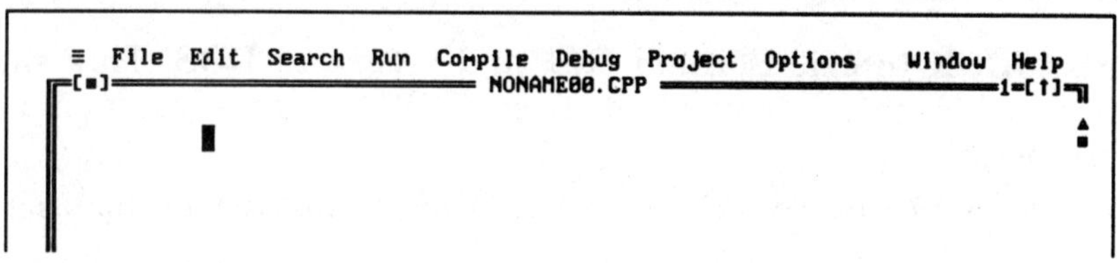

3. Type the following code into the edit window:

```
#include <iostream.h>
#include <string.h>
#include <conio.h>

void main(int argc, char *argv[])
{
      int count;
      int i;

      cout << "Module 61\n";
      count = argc;
      cout << "There are " << count - 1 << " args.\n";
      for(i=0;i<count;i++){
            cout << "Arg " << i << " is: " << argv[i] << "\n";
      }

      cout << "Press any key to exit\n";
      do {;} while(!kbhit());
}
```

4. Press **Alt-C** to pull down the Compile menu, then type **M** to compile the sample program.

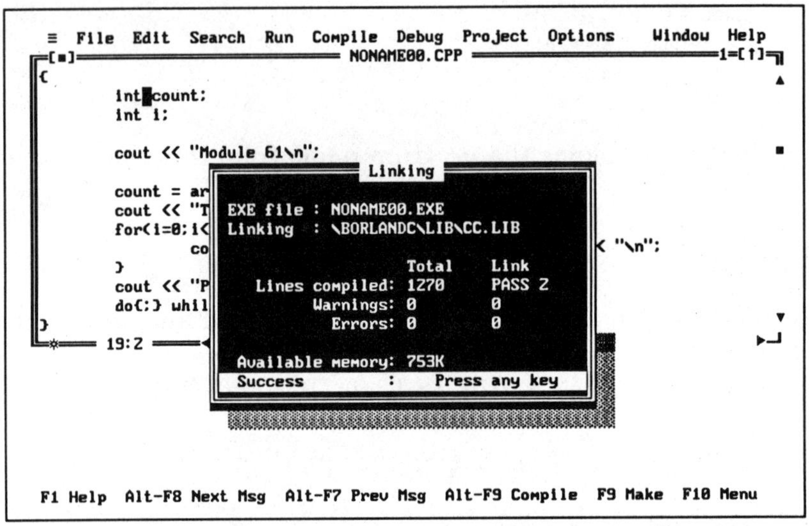

5. Press **Alt-X** to exit Borland C++ and return to DOS. This sample program is more convenient from DOS to pass command line parameters.
6. Type **MOD61 one two three** at the DOS prompt to run the program.

```
C:\NORM\TEST>mod61 one two three
Module 61
There are 3 args.
Arg 0 is: C:\NORM\TEST\MOD61.EXE
Arg 1 is: one
Arg 2 is: two
Arg 3 is: three
Press any key to exit
```

7. Continue the learning sequence with Module 53.

Module 62

METHODS

DESCRIPTION

Methods are functions attached to a class. Without methods, a class is little more than a struct in C. The terms method and function are sometimes used interchangeably since a method is a special type of function.

Methods may be classified according to usage and protection. The types of methods are:

- public
- private
- friend
- virtual

These represent possible protection level for methods. Any function can call a method declared public. The following class definition includes methods of each type identified above.

```
class SampleClass{
private:
      int status;
      char *string;
      void error_method();
public:
      SampleClass(){string = new char [80];};
      void a_method(void);
      void a_method(char*);
      virtual void  display_class();
      friend  void  show_status(SampleClass);
      friend  class AnotherClass;
};
```

The class followed by the scoping operator, ::, is prepended to the function name. For example:

```
SampleClass::display_class()
{
      statements;
}
```

Methods may be overloaded. That is, the same method name may have different argument lists. The compiler uses the calling sequence to determine which to call, so they are really unique functions even though they have the same name. a_method( ) in SampleClass is an example of this.

The syntax for invoking a method is:

```
object.method();
```

Where *object* is the name of an object and *method* is the method to call. The method must be a member of the object's class.

APPLICATIONS

Use methods to manipulate the data structures defined for a class. The following code segment illustrates declaring and using a method.

```
     ...
class MyClass{
private:
     int me;
public:
     void my_method(void);
};
void MyClass my_method(void)
{
     statements;
}
     ...
main()
{
          ...
     MyClass me;       // Define object
          ...
     me.my_method();  // Calls my_method
          ...
}
```

Each of the method types identified above are discussed in the following sections.

PUBLIC METHODS A public method can be called by any function in a C++ program, just as a public data element can be accessed in any function. Methods are usually declared public because they represent the interface between the class and the outside world. A method is declared public by placing its prototype in the public portion of the class definition. The SampleClass( ) constructor and show_status( ) are public in SampleClass.

PRIVATE METHODS Private methods can be called only by other methods in the class. Methods are declared private only rarely in practice. The primary use for a private method is for an internal error processing function. error_method( ) in SampleClass is a private method. Any method declared after the "private" keyword is private and therefore not accessable outside the class. Remember that items are private by default in a class definition.

FRIEND METHODS Both classes and individual methods may be declared friend. A friend method has access to the data structures of the class. Friend access provides selective protection. Friends should use the public methods to interface with the class to access data rather than directly manipulating fields.

Note that a friend function cannot also be virtual. A program with many friend functions is a sure sign that class selection is not quite right. The function prototype in a class definition must include the keyword "friend" for the method to be treated as a friend. show_status( ) in SampleClass is a friend function and AnotherClass is a friend class.

VIRTUAL METHODS Methods are actions or ideas to manipulate class data structures. Virtual methods allow the implementation of an idea to be different for different classes. For example, filling a polygon is an idea common to many shape classes. Yet each class requires a different implementation of that idea. Virtual methods are base class methods that may be redefined in a derived class.

display_class( ) in SampleClass is a virtual method. Another function with the same name and argument signature can be in a class derived from SampleClass. C++ executes the correct version based on the object type involved in the call. A method is virtual when the function prototype includes the keyword *virtual.*

Note that only member function may be declared virtual. Methods should be declared virtual only when different procedures are required later in the program to perform the same function. Virtual functions are a very powerful part of C++. When used correctly, they add to the simplification of the application by allowing a central concept or idea to have different implementation details.

HANDS-ON ACTIVITY

This sample program defines an integer stack class and methods to manipulate data in it. One stack is created, then values pushed onto it. The contents of the stack are displayed, then removed. The default constructor and destructor are used.

1. Type **BC** and press **Enter** to start up the compiler from the DOS prompt.
2. Press **Alt-FN** to pull down the File menu and create a new file.
3. Type the following code:

```
#include <iostream.h>
#include <stdio.h>
#include <string.h>
#include <conio.h>

class IntStack {
      int stack[10];
      int sp;                  // Stack Pointer
public:
      void push(int);
      int  pop(void);
      void show();
      IntStack(){ sp = 0; }
};
// ****************************************************
//               METHOD DEFINITIONS
// ****************************************************
void IntStack::push(int value)
{
      stack[sp++] = value;
}
int IntStack::pop(void)
{
      return(stack[--sp]);
}
void IntStack::show()
{
      int i;

      cout << "Stack contains:\n";
      for(i=sp-1;i;i--){
            cout << stack[i] << "\n";
      }
}
// ****************************************************
//               MAIN CODE
// ****************************************************
void main()
{
      int  i;
      int  value;

      clrscr();
```

```
        cout << "Module 62\n";
        cout << "This module uses methods\n\n";
        cout << "Create a stack object... \n";
        IntStack stack;
        cout << "Let's push some values...\n";
        for(i=0;i<5;i++){
              cout << "Type a number: ";
              cin  >> value;
              stack.push(value);
        }
        cout << "Now, show the stack.\n";
        stack.show();
        cout << "Pop the values...\n";
        for(i=0;i<5;i++){
              value = stack.pop();
              cout << value << " ";
        }

        cout << "\nPress any key to exit\n";
        do {;} while(!kbhit());
}
```

4. Press **Alt-RR** to compile and run the sample program.

```
Module 62
This module uses methods

Create a stack object...
Let's push some values...
Type a number:
```

5. The *Type a number:* query is performed five times. Start by typing **1** and pressing **Enter**. Then type **2** and press **Enter**. Continue by one until 1-5 are entered:

```
Module 62
This module uses methods

Create a stack object...
Let's push some values...
Type a number: 1
Type a number: 2
Type a number: 3
Type a number: 4
Type a number: 5
Now, show the stack.
Stack contains:
5
4
```

```
3
2
1
Pop the values...
5 4 3 2 1
Press any key to exit
```

6. Press any key to exit the sample program and return to Borland C++.
7. Press **Alt-X** to exit Borland C++ and return to DOS.

Several comments should be made about the sample program. A stack is a Last In-First Out data structure that is often useful in advanced applications. This means the values are returned from the stack in the reverse order that they were added.

The IntStack object used here is stack and is created by the following statement:

```
IntStack stack;
```

stack stores only integer numbers. Three methods are associated with the IntStack class, push( ), pop( ), and show( ). push( ) adds a value, pop( ) removes a value, and show( ) displays the current contents of a stack object.

8. Continue the learning sequence with Module 65.

Module 63
NAMING

DESCRIPTION

C++ has specific naming rules within the language. There are also naming conventions that most programmers follow to aid code readability. This module describes the rules for naming constants, variables, and functions.

APPLICATIONS

The general rules for naming identifiers are:

- Names can be up to 32 characters in length.
- Names must start with an alphabetic character.
- Case is significant.
- A name can contain the characters a-z, A-Z, 0-9, and '_'.
- Operator names, such as *if*, cannot be used.

In addition, generally accepted naming conventions are:

- Constants are all uppercase.
- Variables use all lowercase characters.
- Functions within a library frequently mix upper and lowercase to identify the library.

These naming rules apply to naming constants, variables, and functions. Examples of valid constant, function, and variable names are:

```
      // Constants
const ESCAPE          27
const MAX_WIDTH       100
const BLANK           32

      // Variables
int   count;
int   count_1;
int   line_length;
char  ch;
```

```
     // Functions
void NetOpen();
int  strlen(char*,char*);
void open_file();
```

Examples of invalid names include:

```
int   90_clock;                  // Starts with a number
const sys$open        88;  // $ is not allowed
void  if();                       // if is a C operator
```

The naming conventions described in this module apply to all C++ identifiers in a program. Choosing descriptive identifier names is important for program maintenance. C++ naming rules and conventions provide a sufficiently flexible base for using descriptive identifier names.

Continue the learning sequence with Module 47.

Module 64

NEW

DESCRIPTION

Memory allocation is controlled by the *new* operator in C++. new shows up most frequently in class constructors. The format of a new statement is:

```
type* = new type[n];
```

If the type* value is zero, the memory allocation failed. *type** is any C++ data type and *n* is the number of items to allocate space for. The [n] is necessary only for array allocation. Sample usage is:

```
char *string;
      ...
string = new char[80];
```

This statement allocates memory for an 80 byte character array and returns a pointer it. The delete operator deallocates memory allocated by new.

APPLICATIONS

Use the new operator to allocate memory. It is frequently used in constructors to allocate memory for data in the object. new is analogous to malloc in C. It is more efficient so should be used instead of malloc.

new essentially does a sizeof(data_type) then multiplies by the number of items in [ ], if any, to calculate the actual number of bytes of memory to allocate. Structures and classes can be used with new as well as the built-in data types.

HANDS-ON ACTIVITY

This sample program defines and manipulates a simple class.

1. Run Borland C++ from the DOS prompt.
2. Pull down the File menu and create a new file.

3. Type the following code into the NONAME00.CPP edit window:

```
#include <iostream.h>
#include <stdio.h>
#include <string.h>
#include <conio.h>

void main()
{
     char  *string;

     clrscr();
     cout << "Module 64\n";
     cout << "This module illustrates new\n\n";
     cout << "Reserve 80 bytes for a string...\n";
     string = new char [80];
     if(!string){
          cout << "Could not allocate memory.\n";
     }
     cout << "Type a string: ";
     gets(string);
     cout << "string now contains: " << string << "\n";
     cout << "Now give the memory back.\n";
     delete(string);
     cout << "\nPress any key to exit\n";
     do {;} while(!kbhit());
}
```

4. Press **Alt-RR** to compile and run the sample program.

```
Module 64
This module illustrates new

Reserve 80 bytes for a string...
Type a string:
```

5. Type **Finality is not the language of politics.** then press **Enter**. The following is displayed:

```
Module 64
This module illustrates new

Reserve 80 bytes for a string...
Type a string: Finality is not the language of politics.
string now contains: Finality is not the language of politics.
Now give the memory back.

Press any key to exit
```

6. Press any key to exit the sample program and return to Borland C++.
7. Press **Alt-X** to exit Borland C++ and return to DOS.
8. Continue the learning sequence with Module 29.

Module 65
OBJECTS

DESCRIPTION

Classes are the central concept that Object Oriented Programming (OOP) is built around. Objects are specific instances of a class. The class on the other hand defines the layout of a data structure and ties methods to the class. Every object is created by a constructor and removed by a destructor. Constructors and destructors are discussed in separate modules.

C++ automatically calls the constructor when an object is created to allocate memory for it. Objects follow the same scoping rules as other C++ data types. When an object goes out of scope, its destructor is called to deallocate memory and perform whatever cleanup is appropriate. C++ supplies default constructors and destructors or you may specify your own.

The syntax for defining an object is:

```
Class_name Object();
```

where *Class_name* is the name of a class and *Object* is the name of the object being defined. Object can be said to be of type Class_name. The ( ) are necessary only when passing arguments to the constructor.

Objects are at the heart of Object Oriented Programming. The data structures in an object may or may not be visible to the outside world. The "outside world" in this case means the rest of the program. An object's methods provide the pathway through which the rest of the application program accesses an object's data.

APPLICATIONS

Use objects to create an instance of a class. Methods associated with that class can be used to manipulate the object. Objects provide a safe access mechanism for its data structures. As long as the interface is via its class methods, the data structures may be completely changed with minimal impact on the overall reliability of the program.

Assume that you have a word processing program. It has a buffer class that uses a heap data structure limited to 64K. The buffer is implemented as a class with private data. Its interface to the rest of the program is the buffer class methods. At some point, the decision is made to change the buffer from a heap to a linked list using extended memory. The new buffer data structure can be implemented without affecting the rest of the program. As long as data access is hidden, its structure can change drastically without affecting the operation of the rest of the program. The new version of the buffer class is compiled into the program without having to worry about missing code that accessed the data directly.

Using objects for data hiding can pay huge dividends in reduced program maintenance over the long run because the interface is tied to methods, not data structures.

HANDS-ON ACTIVITY

This sample program defines and manipulates a simple class with objects. The class is named Queue. It implements a crude queue data structure. A queue is a First In-First Out data structure.

1. Run Borland C++ from the DOS prompt.
2. Press **Alt-FN** to pull down the File menu and create a new file.
3. Type the following code into the edit window:

```
#include <iostream.h>
#include <stdio.h>
#include <string.h>
#include <conio.h>

class Queue {
      void *que[10];
      int qps;                   // Queue Pointer Start
      int qpe;                   // Queue Pointer End
public:
      Queue(){ qps = qpe = 0; }
      void add(void*);
      void *fetch(void);
      void show();
};
// ****************************************************
//               METHOD DEFINITIONS
// ****************************************************
void Queue::add(void *anything)
{
      cout << "Adding anything to que\n";
      que[qpe++] = anything;
}
void *Queue::fetch(void)
{
```

```
        if(qps >= qpe){
             cout << "Queue is empty.\n";
             return(0);
        }
        return(que[qps++]);
   }
   void Queue::show()
   {
        int i;

        cout << "Queue contains:\n";
        for(i=qps;i<qpe;i++){
             cout << (int)que[i] << "\n";
        }
   }
   // ****************************************************
   //                MAIN CODE
   // ****************************************************
   void main()
   {
        int  value;

        clrscr();
        cout << "Module 65\n";
        cout << "This module manipulates objects\n\n";
        cout << "Create a queue object... \n";
        Queue numbers;
        cout << "Add some values...\n";
        numbers.add((void *)1);
        numbers.add((void *)42);
        cout << "Now, show the stack.\n";
        numbers.show();
        cout << "extract the values...\n";
        value = numbers.fetch();
        cout << value << " ";
        value = numbers.fetch();
        cout << value << " ";

        cout << "\nPress any key to exit\n";
        do {;} while(!kbhit());
   }
```

4. Press **Alt-RR** to compile and run the sample program.

```
Module 65
This module manipulates objects

Create a queue object...
```

```
Add some values...
Adding anything to que
Adding anything to que
Now, show the que.
Queue contains:
1
42
extract the values...
1 42
Press any key to exit
```

5. Press any key to exit the sample program and return to Borland C++.
6. Press **Alt-X** to exit Borland C++ and return to DOS.

The *Adding anything to que* message is generated by the constructor. The Queue object is created, then two values, 1 and 42, added. Notice that the values remained in order when extracted from numbers. This is the opposite behavior from the stack class used in Module 62, where values are extracted in reverse order.

7. Continue the learning sequence with Module 28.

Module 66

OPTIONS MENU

DESCRIPTION

Borland C++ is configurable to match many of the programmer's preferences. Everything from directories to the type of processor is selectable via the Options menu. Pressing Alt-O activates the Options menu.

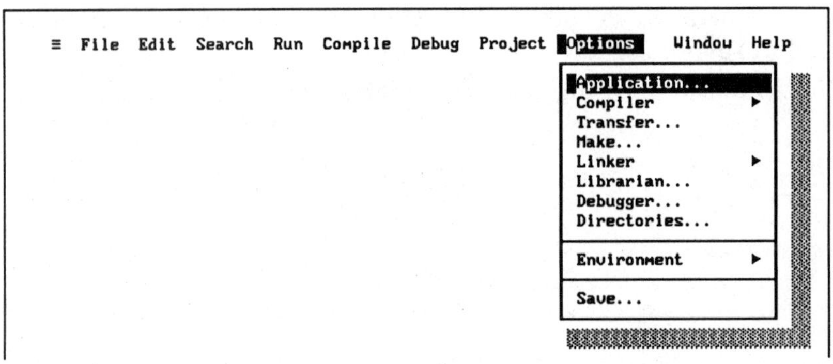

Submenu entries are listed separately after the main selections.

Application... This menu selection pops up the Set Application Options dialog box. You choose the type of application to generate. The choices are DOS Standard, DOS Overlay, Windows, and Windows DDL.

Compiler Options for the Borland C++ compiler are set by this selection.

Transfer... This option specifies external programs that can be run without exiting Borland C++. Programs listed in this option are available in the ≡ menu.

Make... This selection sets the error level to stop a compile using the make feature. The choices are warnings, errors, fatal errors, and link. Any combination may be specified.

Linker Options for the Borland C++ linker are specified via this menu item.

Librarian...	Options for the built-in IDE librarian that builds .LIB files are specified with this menu item.
Debugger...	Options for the debugger are specified by selecting this menu item. A submenu is displayed with the choices.
Directories...	Choose this item to specify the include directory, the library directory, and the output directory.
Environment	This option lets you choose Programmer's Platform preferences, editor configuration, and mouse options. Each selection has a separate submenu.
Save...	This option tells the Programmer's Platform what to save when you exit Borland C++. The choices are the environment, the desktop, and the project.

APPLICATIONS

The Borland C++ installation procedure sets up many of the default settings to match your computer. For example, the screen size will be set to 25 lines when a Hercules or CGA monitor is detected. Use Borland C++ with the default compiler settings until you become more experienced with the language. All of the examples and illustrations in this book have been developed using the default settings. Borland C++ option settings do not change unless installation is run again or you change options via the Options menu.

Each of the Options menu items listed in the Description section above use submenus to allow option selection. The following shows the hierarchy for all of the Borland C++ options and default settings.

- **Application...**
  - DOS Standard *
  - DOS Overlay
  - Windows App
  - Windows DDL

- **Compiler**
  - Code generation...
    - Options
      - Overlay support
      - Word alignment
      - Duplicate strings merged
      - Unsigned characters
      - Standard stack frame *
      - Test stack overflow
    - Model
      - Tiny
      - Small *
      - Medium
      - Compact
      - Large
      - Huge
    - Floating Point
      - None
      - Emulation *
      - 8087
      - 80287
    - Instruction Set
      - 8088/8086 *
      - 80186
      - 80286
    - Calling Convention
      - C *
      - Pascal

Compiler

- *Code generation... Cont.*
  - Options
    - Generate underbars *
    - Line numbers debug info
    - Debug info in OBJs *
    - Treat enums as ints *
    - Fast floating point *
    - Assume SS not equal DS
- C++ options...
  - C++ Virtual Tables
    - Smart *
    - Local
    - External
    - Public
  - Use C++ Compiler
    - CPP extension only *
    - C++ always
  - Out-of-line inline functions *
- Optimizations...
  - Optimization Options
    - Register optimization
    - Jump optimization
  - Register Variables
    - None
    - Register keyword
    - Automatic *
  - Optimize For
    - Size *
    - Speed
- Source...
  - Source Options
    - Nested comments
  - Keywords
    - Borland C++ *
    - ANSI
    - UNIX V
    - Kernighan and Ritchie
  - Identifier Length
    - 32
- Messages...
  - Compile Messages
    - Errors: Stop After 25
    - Warnings: Stop After 100
  - Display warnings *
  - Portability...
  - ANSI violations...
  - C++ warnings...
  - Frequent errors...
- Names...
  - Segment Names
    - Code Segment Name
    - Code Group Name
    - Code Class Name
    - Data Segment Name
    - Data Group Names
    - Data Class Name
    - BSS Segment Name
    - BSS Group Name
    - BSS Class Name

Transfer...

- Program Titles
  - Grep
  - Turbo Assembler
  - Turbo Debugger
  - Turbo Profiler

Make...

- Break Make On
  - Warnings
  - Errors *
  - Fatal Errors
  - Link
- Check auto-dependencies

Linker

- Map File
  - Off *
  - Segments
  - Publics
  - Detailed
- Initialize segments
- Default libraries *
- Graphics library *
- Warn duplicate symbols
- "No stack" warning *
- Case-sensitive link *
- Overlay EXE

Librarian...
- Generate list file
- Case sensitive library
- Purge comment records
- Create extended dictionary
- Library Page Size
  - 16

Debugger...
- Source Debugging
  - On *
  - Standalone
  - None
- Display Swapping
  - None
  - Smart *
  - Always
- Inspectors
  - Show inherited *
  - Show methods *
  - Program Heap Size
    - 64k
  - Show decimal
  - Show hex
  - Show both *

Directories...
- Include Directories
  - C:\TC\INCLUDE
- Library Directories
  - C:\TC\LIB
- Output Directory

Environment
- Preferences...
  - Screen Size
    - 25 lines *
    - 43/50 lines
  - Source Tracking
    - New window *
    - Current window
  - Auto Save
    - Editor files
    - Environment *
    - Desktop *
    - Project *
    - Save old messages
- Editor...
  - Editor Options
    - Create backup files *
    - Insert mode *
    - Autoindent mode *
    - Use tab character *
    - Optimal fill *
    - Backspace unindents *
    - Cursor through tabs *
  - Tab Size
    - 8
  - Default Extension
    - C
- Mouse...
  - Right Mouse Button
    - Nothing
    - Topic search *
    - Goto cursor
    - Breakpoint
    - Inspect
    - Evaluate
    - Add watch
  - Reverse mouse buttons
  - Mouse Double Click Speed

Save...
- Environment *
- Desktop *
- Project *

Options marked with a * show default settings.

HANDS-ON ACTIVITY

This activity illustrates changing an option by modifying the memory model from the default Small to Compact. This session assumes Borland C++ is already running.

1. Press **Alt-O** to pull down the Options menu.

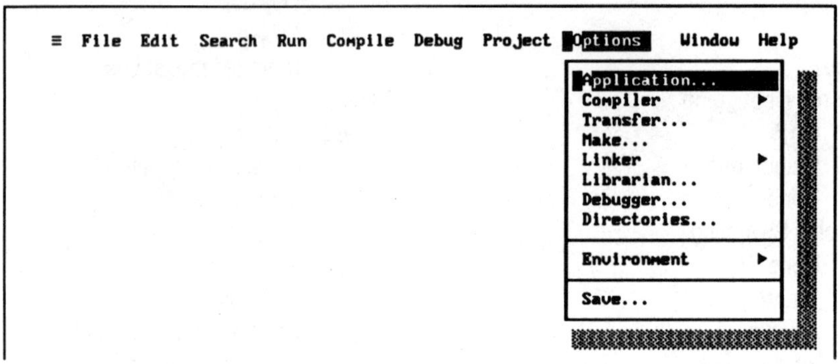

2. Highlight Compiler and press **Enter** to select the Compiler option.

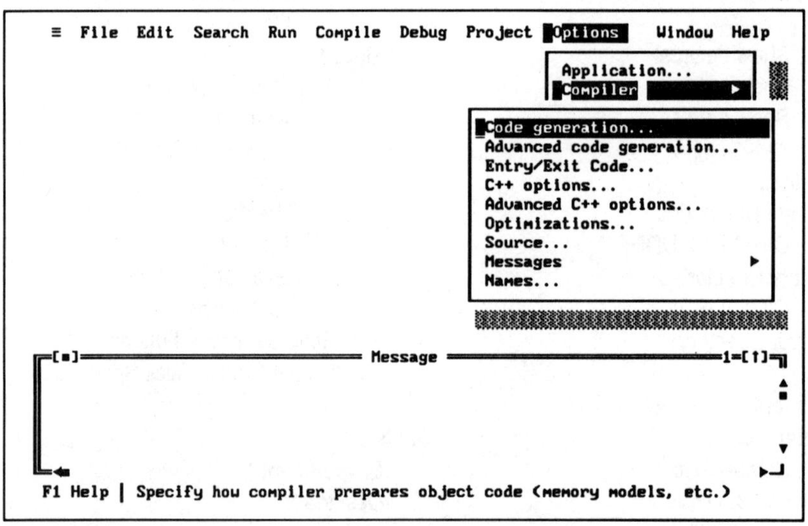

3. Highlight Code Generation and press **Enter** to activate the Code Generation dialog box.

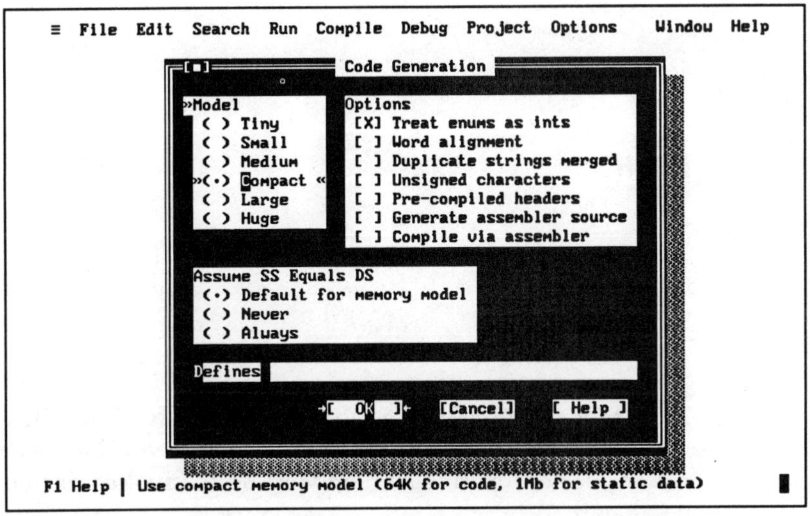

4. Press **Down Arrow** until Compact is selected.
5. Press **Enter** to accept the changes.
6. Press **Alt-X** to exit Borland C++ and return to DOS.
7. Continue the learning sequence with Module 101.

Module 67
OVERLOADING

DESCRIPTION

Overloading is a concept used in C++ to reduce the perceived complexity of a program. A function or an operator can have multiple versions with the same name. The compiler determines which version to invoke based on the argument list in the call.

Good examples of operator overloading are << and >>. The normal C action for << is shifting bits left and >> shifts bits right. C++ overloads << to output data to cout. >> reads the next string from the standard input (cin) stream.

There are a few restrictions on overloading operators. These are:

- New operators cannot be defined.
- Only existing C++ operators may be overloaded.
- Operator precedence is predefined and cannot be changed.
- Operator syntax cannot be changed.
- Operators may only be overloaded for classes.

The C++ operators that may be overloaded are +, –, *, /, %, ^, &, |, ~, =, <, >, +=, –=, *=, /=, %=, ^=, &=, |=, <<, >>, >>=, <<=, ==, !=, <=, >=, &&, ||, ++, —, [ ], ( ), new, and delete.

The syntax for declaring an overloaded operator is:

```
AnyClass& AnyClass::operator<< (char *);
```

Then write the routine as with any normal function.

Overloaded functions are a by-product of using classes. Assume a function adds integers, floating point numbers, and strings. A single function name *add( )* may be used for all three versions. Each is a separate version of add and has different argument types. For example:

```
int add(int n1, int n2);
float add(float n1, float n2);
char add(char *s1, char *s2);
```

The programmer calls a single function name and the compiler uses the data types in the argument list to call the correct version of add( ).

APPLICATIONS

Two of the primary advantages to overloading are:

- Simpler mental interface for the programmer
- More logical function naming

A simpler mental interface for the programmer or reducing the perceived complexity means fewer unique function names must be memorized.

In C, a function named *calcCIRarea* may be defined to calculate the area of a circle. *calcSQarea* calculates the area of a square and *calcTRIarea* calculates a triangle's area. Assume that each may be used with integer or real parameters. Two versions of each are required. The programmer has to become familiar with six function for calculating area, one for each shape type and argument combination.

The C++ alternative is a single overloaded function, *calcarea*. Six functions may still be required, but they can all have the same name. The function signatures provide information for the compiler to determine the correct function version to call. The C++ programmer expends less effort learning and remembering function names and more time developing the application.

More logical function naming is possible because a function name may be used more than once as long as the parameter sequence and class reference provide enough scoping information for the C++ compiler to resolve the call correctly.

The discussions above keep pointing out the C++ compiler uses scope information to determine the correct overloaded function/operator to invoke. This leads us to a word of caution; overloading should not be taken to the extreme. Too many overloaded functions/operators may cause the compiler to incorrectly resolve function calls. IT IS POSSIBLE FOR THE WRONG VERSION OF A HIGHLY OVERLOADED FUNCTION OR OPERATOR TO BE CALLED. This is true of any C++ compiler or translator. The solution is proper selection of functions to overload.

HANDS-ON ACTIVITY

The sample program illustrates operator and function overloading.

1. Type **BC** and press **Enter** to start up the compiler.

2. Press **Alt-FN** to pull down the File menu and create a new file.
3. Type the following code into the edit window:

```
#include <iostream.h>
#include <stdio.h>
#include <string.h>
#include <conio.h>

void list(char *string)
{
     cout << "list a string: " << string << "\n";
}
void list(int value)
{
     cout << "list an integer: " << value << "\n";
}
void main()
{
     char string1[80];

     clrscr();
     cout << "Module 67\n";
     cout << "Overloaded functions\n";

     cout << "Enter a string: ";
     gets(string1);
     list(string1);
     list(47);

     cout << "\n\nPress any key to exit";
     do {;} while(!kbhit());
}
```

4. Press **Alt-RR** to compile and run the sample program.

```
Module 67
Overloaded functions

Enter a string:
```

5. Type **There can be no economy where there is no efficiency** and press **Enter**. The following is displayed:

```
Module 67
Overloaded functions

Enter a string: There can be no economy where there is no efficiency
list a string: There can be no economy where there is no efficiency
list an integer: 47

Press any key to exit
```

6. Press any key to exit the sample program and return to Borland C++.
7. Continue the learning sequence with Module 68.

Module 68

PASSING OBJECTS

DESCRIPTION

There are three ways of passing an object to a function in C++. Objects are treated as a built-in data type when passing parameters to functions. An object can be passed by:

- Reference
- Value
- Pointer to an object

This module discusses passing objects as function parameters.

PASS BY VALUE C traditionally passes parameters to functions by value. The value of the parameter is received by the called function, not the actual variable. You can think of this as a separate copy of the parameter. The called function may change the value of a passed parameter without destroying the contents of a variable in the calling function. C++ uses pass by value as the default method of passing parameters.

Not being able to modify a passed parameter directly prevents some obscure bugs. Consider passing a constant integer 1 in parameter "1" in a call to a function, X:

```
X(1);
```

Here is a code segment for X:

```
void X(int One)
{
        ...
        One = 2;
        ...
}
```

From this point on, every time 1 is used, its value is really 2. This madness is prevented in C and C++ because parameters are normally passed by value.

The down side of pass by value argument passing is the occasion when the called function needs to modify a passed parameter. Pointers provide the mechanism for modifying a passed variable in C and C++.

POINTERS A parameter may be passed by specifying its address. This is a special case of pass by value parameter passing. The address is the passed value. This is the only way to modify the contents of a passed parameter. A pointer is specified by appending an '*' to the parameter type in the function declaration:

```
void Pass_Pointers(char* string)
{ ... }
```

string is defined as a pointer to a character variable. The address of the string must be used in the call to Pass_Pointers. There are two ways to specify an address in a calling sequence. For a character variable, specify the name without a subscript and the compiler supplies its address. The alternative is prepending an '&' to the variable name. For example:

```
char source[100];
     ...
Pass_Pointer(source);
     ...
Pass_Pointer(&source[0]);
     ...
```

Both calls to Pass_Pointer are identical; the address of the first byte of source is passed as the parameter. The second form (&) is required to pass the address other than the first byte.

PASS BY REFERENCE C++ goes a step past C by allowing parameters to be passed to a function by reference. The called function manipulates the actual variable as if it were defined locally rather than a pointer or value. Manipulating a variable directly can be much more convenient from a coding standpoint than working with pointers.

Append an '&' to the parameter type in the function declaration. For example:

```
void By_Reference(Cstring& ref)
{ ... }
```

The reference to a class type Cstring is expected in the calling sequence to By_Reference. The public portions of ref can be accessed and modified directly.

APPLICATIONS

Choose the method of passing objects that matches the intended use in the called function. If the object is not changed in the function, use normal pass by value referencing. The object can be used, but not changed. Use pointers to objects that will be changed by the called function. Use pass by reference to modify the object directly. This allows the program to reference arrays as vectors instead of the objects address. The pointer approach is more compatible with the way C allows structure manipulation.

HANDS-ON ACTIVITY

This program defines three classes and objects:

Class	*Object*
OneClass	one_object
TwoClass	two_object
ThreeClass	three_object

An object for each class is defined and initialized in its own constructor. The program displays the initial contents of the three objects. The objects are passed to functions and manipulated. The passing methods are:

Object	*Pass By*
one_object	Reference
two_object	Pointer
three_object	Value

The contents of each object is displayed before and after being passed to the function. Notice the differences in the way the objects are referenced within the called functions.

1. Type **BC** and press **Enter** to start the compiler.
2. Press **Alt-FN** to pull down the File menu and create a new file.
3. Type the following code into the NONAME00.CPP edit window:

```
#include <iostream.h>
#include <stdio.h>
#include <string.h>
#include <conio.h>

class OneClass{
public:
     int  one;
     char one_string[80];
     OneClass();
     void show_one();
};
```

```
OneClass::OneClass()
{
      one = 1;
      strcpy(one_string,"One");
}

void OneClass::show_one()
{
      cout << "one: " << one << "\n";
      cout << "one_string: " << one_string << "\n\n";
}

class TwoClass{
public:
      int  two;
      char two_string[80];
      TwoClass();
      void show_two();
};

TwoClass::TwoClass()
{
      two = 2;
      strcpy(two_string,"Two");
}

void TwoClass::show_two()
{
      cout << "two: " << two << "\n";
      cout << "two_string: " << two_string << "\n\n";
}

class ThreeClass{
public:
      int  three;
      char three_string[80];
      ThreeClass();
      void show_three();
};

ThreeClass::ThreeClass()
{
      three = 3;
      strcpy(three_string,"Three");
}

void ThreeClass::show_three()
{
```

```
    cout << "three: "        << three        << "\n";
    cout << "three_string: " << three_string << "\n\n";
}

void display_one(OneClass&);
void display_two(TwoClass*);
void display_three(ThreeClass);
void continue_demo();

main()
{
    clrscr();
    OneClass   one_object;
    TwoClass   two_object;
    ThreeClass three_object;
    cout << "Module 68\n";
    cout << "Passing Objects as parameters\n\n";
    cout << "Here are objects created so far...\n";
    one_object.show_one();
    two_object.show_two();
    three_object.show_three();
    continue_demo();

    cout << "Now passing the one_object by reference...\n";
    display_one(one_object);
    cout << "one_object was changed by display_one...\n";
    one_object.show_one();
    continue_demo();

    cout << "Now pass a class pointer...\n";
    display_two(&two_object);
    cout << "two_object was changed by display_two...\n";
    two_object.show_two();
    continue_demo();

    cout << "Now pass by value...\n";
    display_three(three_object);
    cout << "three_object was changed in display_three...\n";
    cout << "but not the one passed.\n";
    three_object.show_three();
    continue_demo();
}

void display_one(OneClass& got_one)
{
    cout << "one: " << got_one.one << "\n";
    cout << "one_string: " << got_one.one_string << "\n\n";
    cout << "Changing one: \n";
```

```
        got_one.one = 2;
        strcpy(got_one.one_string,"Not really one anymore...");
}
void display_two(TwoClass* got_two)
{
        cout << "two: " << got_two->two << "\n";
        cout << "two_string: " << got_two->two_string << "\n";
        got_two->two = 4;
        strcpy(got_two->two_string,"This may cause problems!");
}

void display_three(ThreeClass got_three)
{
        cout << "three: " << got_three.three << "\n";
        cout << "three_string: " << got_three.three_string << "\n";
        cout << "Changing the local copy of three_object...\n";
        got_three.three = 6;
        strcpy(got_three.three_string,"Three X two");
        cout << "three: " << got_three.three << "\n";
        cout << "three_string: " << got_three.three_string << "\n";
}
void continue_demo()
{
        char ch;
        cout << "\n\nPress any key to continue\n";
        do {;} while(!kbhit());
        ch = getch();
        clrscr();
}
```

4. Press **Alt-RR** to compile and run the sample program.

```
Module 68
Passing Objects as parameters

Here are objects created so far...
one: 1
one_string: One

two: 2
two_string: Two

three: 3
three_string: Three

Press any key to continue
```

5. Press **Enter** for the next screen.

```
Now passing the one_object by reference...
one_object was changed by display_one...
one: 1
one_string: One

Changing one:
one_object was changed by display_one...
one: 2
one_string: Not really one anymore...

Press any key to continue
```

6. Press **Enter** for the next screen.

```
Now pass a class pointer...
two_object was changed by display_two...
two: 2
two_string: Two

two_object was changed by display_two...
two: 4
two_string: This may cause problems!

Press any key to continue
```

7. Press **Enter** for the last screen.

```
Now pass by value...
three_object was changed in display_three...
but not the one passed.
three: 3
three_string: Three

Changing the local copy of three_object...
three: 6
three_string: Three X two

three_object was changed in display_three...
but not the one passed.
three: 3
three_string: Three

Press any key to continue
```

8. Press any key to exit the program.
9. Press **Alt-X** to exit Borland C++ and return to DOS.
10. Continue the learning sequence with Module 38.

Module 69
POINTERS

DESCRIPTION

One of the most powerful and widely used features of both C and C++, pointers are frequently considered as the most difficult part of the language to learn. Pointers are variables that contain the address of a data structure. Several operators are specific to pointers and others have special meaning when used with pointers.

Operator	*Meaning*
*	Flags a variable as a pointer when used in the variable declaration.
*	Contents of when used with an assignment statement.
&	Address of - used on the right side of an assignment statement.
->	Points to - used with a structure pointer

Here is the syntax for defining and referencing a pointer:

`char *string;`	Define a character pointer.
`char buffer[80];`	Character array of 80 bytes.
`char ch;`	Character.
`string = buffer;`	Load the address of the first byte of buffer into the character pointer *string*.
`string = &buffer[0];`	Equivalent to string = buffer.
`ch = *string;`	Move the contents of the character pointed to by the address in string into ch.
`string = &buffer[27];`	Load the address of buffer[27] into string.
`*string = '\0';`	Load NULL into the character pointed to by the address in string.
`cstring->length = 0;`	*cstring* is a structure pointer. *length* is a field in cstring.

Any data type can be declared a pointer. Pointers can be nested. A pointer to a pointer is valid, although hard to follow:

```
char **double_indirection;
```

APPLICATIONS

Use pointers as an alternate method of manipulating arrays described in Module 5. Many people have trouble knowing when to use * and when to use & when first dealing with pointers. This becomes easier the more pointers are used. In fact, the more you use pointers, the less natural referencing arrays by subscript ([ ]) seems.

There are two important rules for using pointers. These are initialize pointers before using them and be sure memory is allocated for the data item pointed to. Failure to do either will cause program bugs that can cause a program to crash and lock up your PC.

One area of confusion is passing an array to a function. Assume you have defined the following character array:

```
char string[80] = "ABCDEF";
```

A function that accepts a character pointer is also necessary for this illustration:

```
void emit(char *string)
{
      char ch;
      while(ch = *string++){
            putchar(ch);
      }
}
```

This function demonstrates several pointer operations. emit types the string passed to it on the screen. The *string++ refers to the contents of the address in string, then increments string to point to the next character. Save the pointer in a temporary variable before manipulating it if the start of the string is needed later in the function. Once string has been incremented; the original starting address of the string is lost.

Calling emit using string is done with the following statement:

```
emit(string);
```

The string is an array in the calling function and a character pointer in the called function emit( ). Referencing an array name implies the address of element [0]. Thus:

```
emit(&string[0]);
```

is identical to the previous call. This is the correct form to use when other than the first byte is passed. For example:

```
emit(&string[3]);
```

passes the address of the "D" in the string to emit.

Another powerful use of pointers is storing the address of a function. A function pointer is defined by:

```
void (*funct)();
```

This declaration defines a pointer to a function with no return value and no parameters. A normal assignment operator loads a function address into funct.

```
funct = any_function;
```

Where any_function( ) can be any C++ function. any_function can then be executed by executing the contents of funct:

```
(*funct)();
```

This usage of pointers can be used to build a finite state table or implement vectored execution. The execution characteristics of a program can be altered by loading different function addresses into the function pointer.

The last major use of pointers is structures. Observe the following structure and function call:

```
struct CountedString {
      int len;
      char string[80];
} my_string;
      ...
some_function(&my_string);
```

A pointer to the structure can be passed to a function. The function is:

```
void some_function(struct *string)
{
      string->len = 99;
      cout << string->string;
}
```

The -> operator means pointer to. It points to the field within the structure.

HANDS-ON ACTIVITY

Pointer usage is demonstrated in this program. The examples in the text are used as the starting point for this code.

1. Type **BC** and press **Enter** to start up the compiler from the DOS prompt.

2. Press **Alt-FN** to pull down the File menu and create a new file.
3. Type the following code into the NONAME00.CPP edit window:

```
#include <iostream.h>
#include <stdio.h>
#include <string.h>
#include <conio.h>

void emit(char *string)
{
     char ch;
     while(ch = *string++){
          putchar(ch);
     }
}
struct CountedString {
     int len;
     char Cstring[80];
};

void main()
{
     struct CountedString my_string;
     char  string[80];

     clrscr();
     cout << "Module 69\n";
     cout << "This module exercises pointers\n\n";
     cout << "Type a string: ";
     gets(string);
     cout << "emit &string[0]\n";
     emit(&string[0]);
     cout << "\nNow, emit string\n";
     emit(string);
     cout << "\nThey are the same...\n\n";
     cout << "emit &string[3]\n";
     emit(&string[3]);

     cout << "\nPress any key to exit\n";
     do {;} while(!kbhit());
}
```

4. Press **Ctrl-F9** to compile and run the sample program.

```
Module 69
This module exercises pointers

Type a string:
```

5. Type **We are as near to heaven by sea as by land!** and press **Enter**. The following is displayed:

```
Module 69
This module exercises pointers

Type a string: We are as near to heaven by sea as by land!
emit &string[0]
We are as near to heaven by sea as by land!
Now, emit string
We are as near to heaven by sea as by land!
They are the same...
emit &string[3]
re as near to heaven by sea as by land!
Press any key to exit
```

6. Press any key to exit the sample program and return to Borland C++.
7. Press **Alt-X** to exit Borland C++ and return to DOS.
8. Continue the learning sequence with Module 90.

Module 70

PREPROCESSOR

DESCRIPTION

The C++ preprocessor is a powerful tool that allows the programmer to perform string substitution, conditional compilation, and many other operations. Preprocessor statements begin with # in column 1. The preprocessor statements supported by Borland C++ are:

Statement	*Description*
#include	Read another file
#if	Test a condition
#else	False portion of #if test
#elif	Else If
#endif	End an #if
#ifdef	If symbol defined
#ifndef	Test for a symbol not defined
#define	Define symbol and macro substitution
#undef	Undefine a symbol
#line	Supply line number and filename for debugging
#error	Generate error message at compile time
#pragma	Specify compile time directives to compiler

One commonly used preprocessor statement in C was #define to create constants. C++ eliminates the necessity of this use in most cases because of the *const* operator. Another important use of the preprocessor is conditional compilation.

Program portability can be aided via preprocessor statements. Define a symbol, such as UNIX to flag Unix specific code. Test for the existence of UNIX with #ifdef to include specific code. The same approach can be used for generating different versions of a program. Simply use the correct #define for the version being compiled.

All preprocessor statements execute at compile time. The most commonly used preprocessor statements are described in separate modules.

Continue the learning sequence with Module 26.

Module 71

PRINTF

DESCRIPTION

printf( ) is the C formatted print function. It outputs values based on a format specifier. The general form for printf( ) is:

```
#include <stdio.h>
int printf(const char*format[,arguments]);
```

The return value is either the number of characters output for a successful call or EOF on error. The argument list is optional and based on the format. The format specifier is generally a constant string containing formatting information for each argument. Example printf( ) calls are:

```
status = printf("This call has no arguments.");
status = printf("Program name is: %s\n", argv[0]);
```

There are several related printf( ) functions:

printf — Outputs the formatted string to stdout. The function prototype is:

```
int printf(char *format,args);
```

fprintf — Outputs a formatted string to an output file. The function prototype is:

```
int fprintf(FILE* stream,char *format,args);
```

sprintf — Writes the formatted output to a string. The function prototype is:

```
int sprintf(char*buff,char*format,args);
```

vprintf — Outputs a formatted string using a variable number of arguments. The function prototype for vprintf( ) is:

```
int vprintf(const char*format,args);
```

vfprintf — Writes a formatted string to an output stream. This function is similar to fprintf except a variable length argument list is accepted. The function prototype is:

```
int vfprintf(FILE*stream,
             const char*format,args);
```

cprintf	Outputs formatted values to the console. This is a DOS only function.

```
int cprintf(const char*format,args);
```

The format specifier, *const char*format,* is a string containing characters or values to format and output. The format has the following parts:

```
%[flags][width][.prec][size]type
```

Where:

%	Signals special format
flags	Marks justification, signs, decimal point, etc.
width	Minimum number of characters to output, padded with blanks or zeros
.prec	For integers, minimum number digits to output; otherwise the maximum number characters to output. The '.' is required.
size	Overrides default size of argument
type	Conversion type. The argument will be converted from the internal binary format into character form on output.

Items enclosed in [ ] are optional.

The following table identifies the flag characters and their usage:

Flag	*Meaning*
–	Left justify field; pad right with blanks.
+	Right justify field; pad left with blanks.
#	Use alternative form conversion.
blank	Pad output with a blank for a positive value. Start negative values with a minus sign.

The size modifiers are:

Modifier	*Meaning*
F	Far pointer
N	Near pointer
h	Short integer
l	Long integer
L	Long double

The conversion types are:

Type	*Meaning*
c	Character
d	Signed decimal integer
i	Signed decimal integer
o	Unsigned octal integer
u	Unsigned decimal integer
x	Unsigned hexadecimal integer using lowercase

X	Unsigned hexadecimal integer using uppercase
f	Signed floating point number in form [-]dddd.dddd
g	Signed floating point using e or f form depending on value and precision
e	Signed floating point form [-]d.dddd or e[+-]ddd
E	Signed floating point form [-]d.dddd or E[+-]ddd
G	Signed floating point form E or f depending on value and precision
s	Prints contents of string pointer
%	Prints % if no argument is specified
n	Store count of bytes output so far in corresponding argument
p	Outputs pointer in either XXXX:YYYY or YYYY format depending on current memory model

An illustration is in order:

```
status = printf("Integer Trash %-4.2d\n",TRASH);
```

The format specifier, *%-4.2d,* outputs *i* as a decimal number, left justified within the field, with a maximum of four digits and a minimum of two digits. If TRASH contains 123456, the value is not truncated. If TRASH contains 9, then 09 will be output.

The standard C character constants, such as \t and \n, can be used in the format string to generate the Tab or Newline character respectively. The character constants are:

Constant	*Meaning*
\0	NULL
\a	Alarm or beep character
\b	Backspace
\f	Formfeed
\n	Newline (CR-LF)
\r	Carriage return
\t	Tab
\v	Vertical tab
\\	Backslash
\'	Single quote
\"	Double quote
\?	Question mark
\ooo	Output the octal number in character form
\xhhh	Output the hexadecimal number in character form

APPLICATIONS

Use printf( ) or one of its variants to produce formatted ASCII output. printf( ) is not used in C++ as often as in C. The C++ *cout* class is frequently used for simple output instead of printf( ) because of its convenience. printf( ) still has a place in C++ for complex output formatting.

HANDS-ON ACTIVITY

The sample session illustrates compound conditional statements.

1. Type **BC** and press **Enter** to start up the compiler.
2. Press **Alt-FN** to pull down the File menu and create a new file.
3. Type the following code into the NONAME00.CPP edit window:

```
#include <iostream.h>
#include <stdio.h>
#include <conio.h>

void main()
{
      long  i;
      float x;
      char  ch;

      printf("Module 71\n\n");
      printf("Type a character followed by Enter: ");
      cin  >> ch;
      printf("\nThe character is: %c\n",ch);
      printf("ch has a decimal value too: %d\n\n",ch);
      printf("Enter a large (>65535) number: ");
      cin  >> i;
      printf("\nThe integer is: %d\n",i);
      printf("Oops! That is the integer form...\n");
      printf("This is the correct value: %ld\n",i);
      printf("The difference is d requires the l size\n");
      printf("   modifier- ld to format a long integer\n\n");
      printf("Any number can be formatted in a variety of ways.\n");
      printf("This is i as an E floating point: %5.4E\n",
                  (float)i);
      x = i;            // Conversion is done automatically
      printf("This is g floating point %5.4g\n",x);
      printf("Press Any Key to continue");
      do {;} while(!kbhit());
}
```

4. Press **Alt-RR** to compile and run the sample program.

```
Module 71

Type a character followed by Enter:
```

5. Type **X** and press **Enter**. The following is displayed:

```
Module 71

Type a character followed by Enter: X
The character is: X
ch has a decimal value too: 88

Enter a large (>65535) number:
```

6. Type a number, such as **99000**, then press **Enter**.

```
Module 71

Type a character followed by Enter: X
The character is: X
ch has a decimal value too: 88

Enter a large (>65535) number: 99000

The integer is: -32072
Oops! That is the integer form...
This is the correct value: 99000
The difference is d requires the l size
   modifier- ld to format a long integer

Any number can be formatted in a variety of ways.
This is i as an E floating point: 9.9000E+04
This is g floating point 9.9e+04
Press Any Key to continue
```

This code illustrates a common formatting mistake of using %d to format a large integer number. Use %ld for proper operation when the number is defined as a long. The program also shows that the output format of a number is not tied directly to its data type.

7. Press any key to exit the sample program and return to Borland C++. Press **Alt-F5** to view the user screen if you wish to view the run again.
8. Continue the learning sequence with Module 88.

Module 72
PRIVATE

DESCRIPTION

Private is one of three access protection levels used for classes, data structures, and methods. The other two are public and protected.

Items within a class marked as private can only be accessed by methods defined in the class. Data is most often defined as private.

The syntax for private protection within the *class* statement is:

```
class ClassName{
private:
     data_structures;
public:
     methods;
};
```

The default protection is private. The private: keyword can occur anywhere within the class definition.

The format for defining a derived class with public base class protection is:

```
class BaseClass{
private:
     data_structures;
public:
     methods();
};
class DerivedClass: public BaseClass{
private:
     data_structures;
public:
     methods();
};
```

The derived class cannot access Base Class data items because they are declared as private in the Base Class definition.

APPLICATIONS

Use private protection for methods, classes, or data that cannot be accessed outside the class. Methods are rarely protected because methods are the interface to the data from the rest of the program.

Using private protection for any class, whether base or derived protects the items from access any further up the class hierarchy. Assume three classes, Base, Derived1, and Derived2.

```
class Base{
protected:
     data_structures;
public:
     methods;
};

class Derived1 : private Base{
protected:
     data_structures;
public:
     methods;
};

class Derived2 : public Derived1{
     data_structures;
public:
     methods;
};
```

The Derived2 class can refer to protected items in Derived1, but not Base because the Derived1 class definition declares the Base Class private. Derived1 methods can access protected items from Base.

HANDS-ON ACTIVITY

The following program defines a base class and two derived classes. The base class is declared private in the first derived class so access from the next derived class is restricted. Data from the base class cannot be manipulated from the top level derived class.

1. Run Borland C++ from DOS and open a new file window.
2. Type the following code into the NONAME00.CPP edit window:

```
#include <iostream.h>
#include <stdio.h>
#include <string.h>
#include <conio.h>
```

```
class Base{
protected:
     char B_string[80];
public:
     void B_show(void);
};
class Derived1 : private Base{
protected:
     char D1_string[80];
public:
     Derived1(void);
     void D1_show(void);
};
class Derived2 : public Derived1{
     char D2_string[80];
public:
     Derived2(char*);
     void D2_show(void);
     void show_all(void);
};
Derived1::Derived1(void)
{
     strcpy(B_string,"B_string");
}
Derived2::Derived2(char *string)
{
     strcpy(D2_string,string);
     strcpy(D1_string,"D1_string");
//         The next line generates a compile error
//   strcpy(B_string,"B_string");
}
void Base::B_show(void)
{
     cout << "B_string:  " << B_string << "\n";
}
void Derived1::D1_show(void)
{
     cout << "A Derived1 method\n";
     cout << "B_string:  " << B_string << "\n";
     cout << "D1_string: " << D1_string << "\n";
}
void Derived2::D2_show(void)
{
     cout << "A Derived2 method\n";
     cout << "D1_string: " << D1_string << "\n";
     cout << "D2_string: " << D2_string << "\n";
}
void Derived2::show_all(void)
```

```
{
     cout << "Show all data\n";
     this->D1_show();
     cout << "D2_string: " << D2_string << "\n";
}

void main()
{
     char  string1[80] = "";

     clrscr();
     cout << "Module 72\n";
     cout << "Private Protection Demonstration\n\n";
     cout << "Type a string: ";
     gets(string1);
     cout << "Define an object for Derived2... ";
     Derived2 PubObject(string1);
     cout << "\nAccess Base class from Derived1 method \n";
     PubObject.D1_show();

     cout << "\nNext, access D1 from D2 class\n";
     PubObject.D2_show();

     cout << "\nNow access all 3 classes\n";
     PubObject.show_all();

     cout << "\nPress any key to exit\n";
     do {;} while(!kbhit());
}
```

3. Press **Ctrl-F9** to compile and run the sample program.

```
Module 72
Private Protection Demonstration

Type a string:
```

4. Type **Protection is not a principle, but an expedient.** and press **Enter**. The following is displayed:

```
Module 72
Private Protection Demonstration

Type a string: Protection is not a principle, but an expedient.
Define an object for Derived2...

Access Base class from Derived1 method
A Derived1 method
B_string:  B_string
```

```
D1_string: D1_string

Next, access D1 from D2 class
D1_string: D1_string
D2_string: Protection is not a principle, but an expedient.

Now access all 3 classes
Show all data
B_string:  B_string
D1_string: D1_string
D2_string: Protection is not a principle, but an expedient.

Press any key to exit
```

5. Press any key to exit the sample program and return to Borland C++.
6. Press **Alt-X** to exit Borland C++ and return to DOS.

The sample program defines three classes, a base and two derived classes. Items in the base class can be accessed only from the first derived class. The second derived class cannot directly manipulate the data in the base class. The line that is commented out in Derived2::Derived2( ):

```
//    strcpy(B_string,"B_string");
```

accesses the base class data directly. It generates a compiler error because this access attempts to use private data. The second derived class must use the publicly defined methods to indirectly access data in the base class.

7. Continue the learning sequence with Module 74.

Module 73
PROJECT MENU

DESCRIPTION

This module describes the selections available from the Project menu. A Borland C++ project is a collection of modules that compile into a single program. The Project menu maintains a project file. The project file contains the list of modules (.H, .C, and .CPP files) that are used to build the program. Compiling a project produces a single object or executable file.

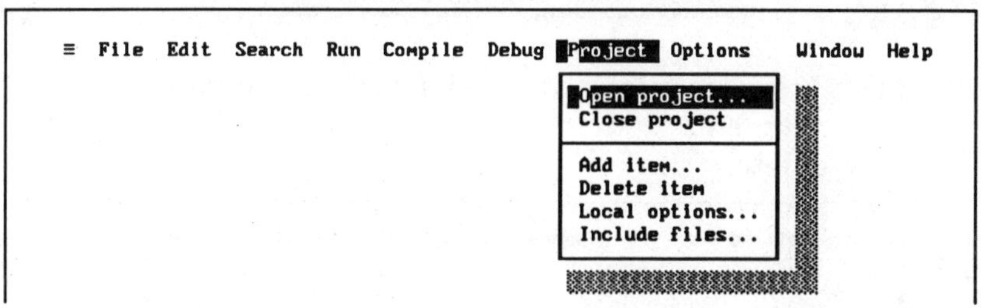

Open project... — Open a new project file. A submenu is displayed with the .PRJ files shown. Enter the filename at the prompt or select the project file by moving the menu bar to the filename and pressing Enter. The primary source file is loaded into the edit window.

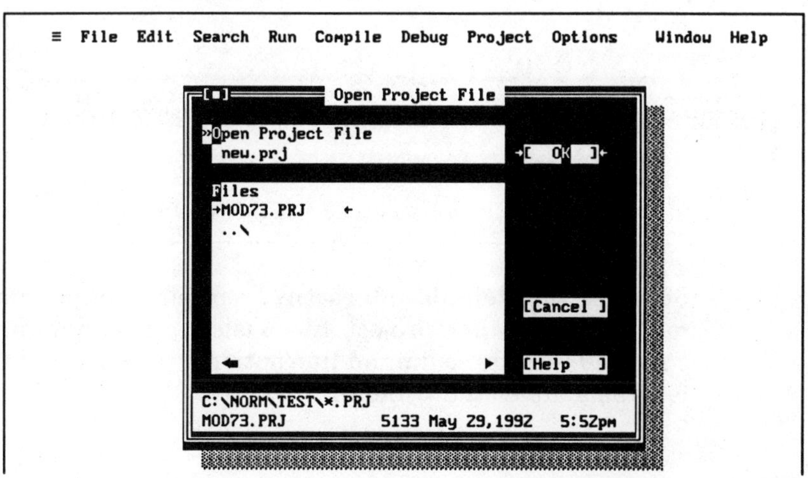

Close project — Close the current project file. Any open edit windows are closed and source files updated.

Add item... — This item displays a submenu for adding a filename to the current project file.

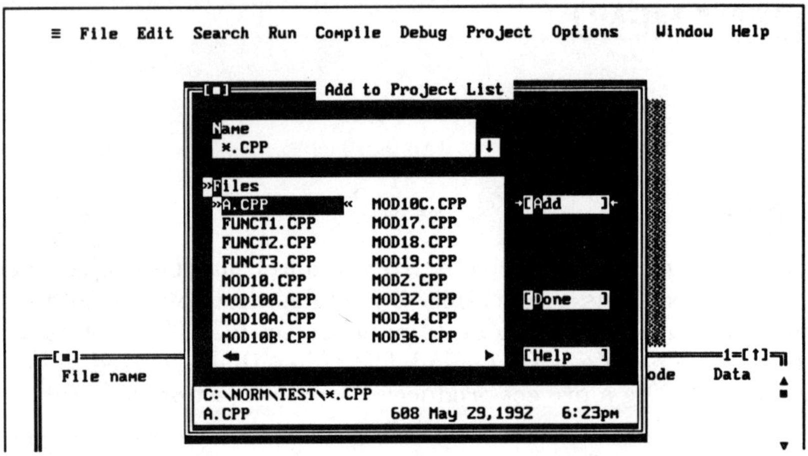

Delete item — A source file is deleted from the current project file. A submenu is displayed for selection of the source file to delete.

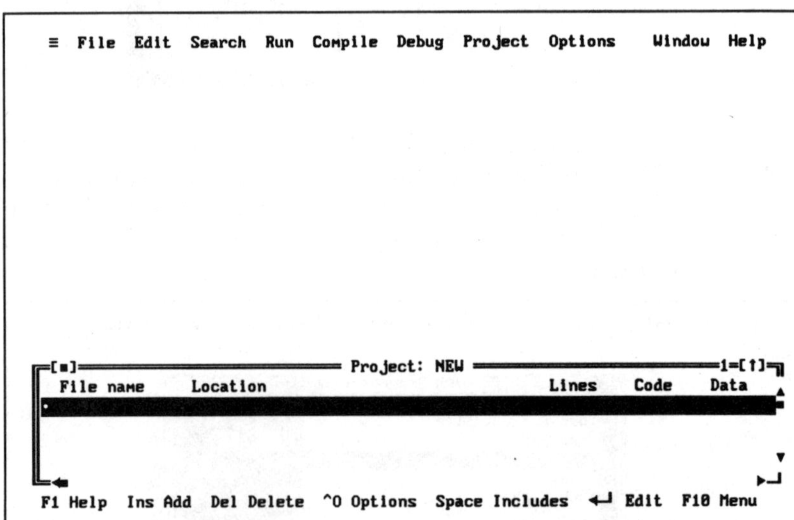

Local options... — Some of the default interactive compiler option may be modified on a per project file basis. Items that may be specified include command line options, the choice of transfer items under the ≡ menu.

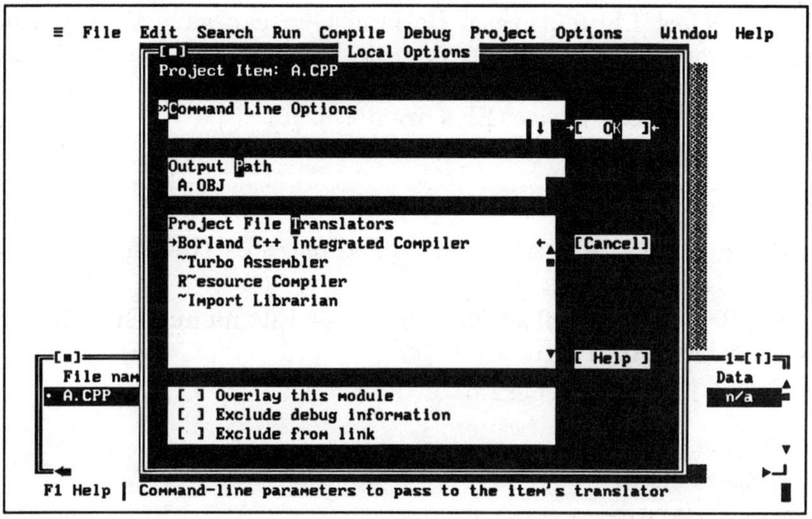

Include files... This selection pops up the Include Files dialog box. This shows the files included in the current project file.

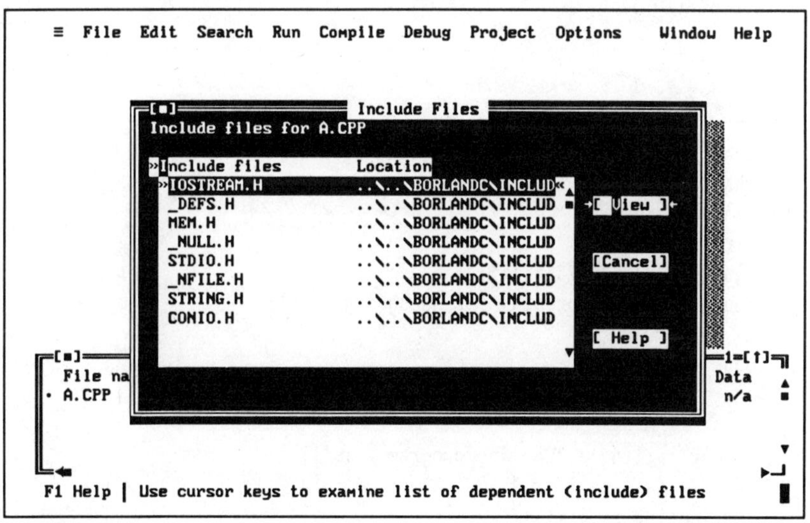

APPLICATIONS

Use the Project menu to create and maintain project files for multiple module programs. Project files are one of the Borland C++ facilities that aid constructing large programs. The project file identifies all of the pieces of the program to the compiler, so files are automatically compiled when source code is modified.

Using the project file feature of Borland C++ can save time developing large programs because all source code changes get compiled into the program automatically. Forgetting to compile a single module can cause debugging problems if project files are not used.

HANDS-ON ACTIVITY

This session sets up a project file and illustrates the benefits of using project files for large programs.

1. Start Borland and select **New** from the File menu. The edit window is NONAME00.CPP.
2. Type the following program.

```
#include <iostream.h>
#include <stdio.h>
#include <string.h>
#include <conio.h>

int program1();
int program2(int);

main()
{
      int status;
      char  calling_1[]="Calling program 1...\n";
      char* calling_2;

      clrscr();
      cout << "Module 73A\n\n";
      cout << "Simple program for debugging \n\n";

      cout << calling_1;
      status = program1();

      strcpy(calling_2,"Calling program 2...");
      cout << calling_2 << "\n";
      for(int i=0;i<10;i++){
            status = program2(i);
      }
      cout << "\n\nPress any key to exit";
      do {;} while(!kbhit());
}
```

3. Press **Alt-F** and select **Save as...** to save the file. Use MOD73A.CPP as the filename.
4. Press **Alt-FN** to open a new edit window, then type the code for MOD73B:

```
// FILE: MOD73B.CPP
#include <iostream.h>
int program1()
{
      cout << "This is the original Program1\n";
      return(0);
}
```

5. Select **Save as...** from the File menu to save the file. Use MOD73B.CPP as the filename.
6. Press **Alt-FN** to open a new edit window, then type the code for MOD73C:

```
// FILE: MOD73C.CPP
#include <iostream.h>
int program2(int num)
{
      if (num<1){
            cout << "First call to Program2\n";
      }else{
            cout << "Program2 again: " << num << "\n";
      }
return(num);
}
```

7. Press **Alt-F** and select **Save as...** to save the file. Use MOD73C.CPP as the filename.

At this point, there are three files in this program. The next steps build a project file, compile the program, and execute the program.

8. Press **Alt-P** to pull down the Project menu, then select **Open project**.
9. Type **MOD73.PRJ** and press **Enter** in the Open Project dialog box. An empty project file is created.
10. Press the **Ins** to open the Add Item dialog box.
11. Move the cursor to **MOD73A.CPP** and press **Enter** to add MOD73A.CPP to the project file. Perform the same steps for MOD73B.CPP AND MOD73C.CPP.
12. Press **Esc** to close the Add Item dialog box.

13. Press **F6** to move from the Project window back to an edit window.
14. Press **Alt-RR** to compile and run MOD73.EXE.

```
Module 73A

Simple program for debugging

Calling program 1...
This is the original Program1

Calling program 2...
First call to Program2
Program2 again: 1
Program2 again: 2
Program2 again: 3
Program2 again: 4
Program2 again: 5
Program2 again: 6
Program2 again: 7
Program2 again: 8
Program2 again: 9

Press any key to exit
```

15. Press any key to exit the program and return to the compiler.
16. Press **Alt-X** to exit Borland C++.
17. Rename MOD73.PRJ to MOD73.PXX. Type **REN MOD73.PRJ MOD73.PXX** at the DOS prompt to perform this operation. Borland C++ automatically loads any project file so every program will begin by compiling MOD73, which causes compile errors.
18. Continue the learning sequence with Module 66.

Module 74
PROTECTED

DESCRIPTION

Protected is one of three access protection levels used for data structures and methods. The other two are public and private. Classes cannot be declared protected.

Items within a class marked as protected can be accessed by methods defined for the class and any derived classes.

The syntax for protected items within the *class* statement is:

```
class ClassName{
protected:
     data_structures;
public:
     methods;
};
```

The format for defining a derived class with a protected base is:

```
class BaseClass{
protected:
     data_structures;
public:
     methods();
};
class DerivedClass: private BaseClass{
private:
     data_structures;
public:
     methods();
};
```

Derived Class may access protected data in Base Class but later classes cannot access Base Class data in this example.

APPLICATIONS

Use protected for methods, or data that can be accessed in any later class derived from the class. Methods are rarely marked as protected because they are the interface between the class and the rest of the program.

Assume three classes, Base, Derived1, and Derived2.

```
class Base{
protected:
     data_structures;
public:
     methods;
};

class Derived1 : public Base{
protected:
     data_structures;
public:
     methods;
};

class Derived2 : private Derived1{
     data_structures;
public:
     methods;
};
```

The Derived2 class can refer to protected items in both Base and Derived1. Classes that are derived from Derived2 do not have access to data in Derived1 or Base classes because the class protection for Derived1 is private. Protection can be increased as new derived classes are defined, but levels cannot be reduced.

HANDS-ON ACTIVITY

The following program defines a base class and two derived classes. The base class is declared public in the first derived class so the next derived class can access data from the base class directly.

1. Run Borland C++ from DOS and open a new file window.
2. Type the following code into the NONAME00.CPP edit window:

```
#include <iostream.h>
#include <stdio.h>
#include <string.h>
#include <conio.h>

class Base{
```

```
protected:
      char B_string[80];
};
class Derived1 : public Base{
protected:
      char D1_string[80];
};
class Derived2 : private Derived1{
      char D2_string[80];
public:
      Derived2(char*);
      void D2_show(void);
};
Derived2::Derived2(char *string)
{
      strcpy(D2_string,string);
      strcpy(D1_string,"D1_string");
      strcpy(B_string,"B_string");
}
void Derived2::D2_show(void)
{
      cout << "A Derived2 method\n";
      cout << "B_string:  " << B_string << "\n";
      cout << "D1_string: " << D1_string << "\n";
      cout << "D2_string: " << D2_string << "\n";
}

void main()
{
      char  string1[80] = "";

      clrscr();
      cout << "Module 74\n";
      cout << "Protected Classes \n\n";
      cout << "Type a string: ";
      gets(string1);
      cout << "Define an object for Derived2...\n";
      Derived2 PubObject(string1);

      cout << "Now access all 3 classes from Derived2\n";
      PubObject.D2_show();

      cout << "\nPress any key to exit\n";
      do {;} while(!kbhit());
}
```

3. Press **Ctrl-F9** to compile and run the sample program.

```
Module 74
Protected Classes

Type a string:
```

4. Type **Almost everything that is great has been done by youth.** and press **Enter**. The following is displayed:

```
Module 74
Protected Classes

Type a string: Almost everything that is great has been done by youth.
Define an object for Derived2...
Now access all 3 classes from Derived2
A Derived2 method
B_string:  B_string
D1_string: D1_string
D2_string: Almost everything that is great has been done by youth.

Press any key to exit
```

5. Press any key to exit the sample program and return to Borland C++.
6. Press **Alt-X** to exit Borland C++ and return to DOS.

The sample program defines three classes, a base and two derived classes. Items in the base class are accessed from both derived classes.

7. Continue the learning sequence with Module 97.

Module 75
PUBLIC

DESCRIPTION

Public is one of three access protection levels used for classes, data structures, and methods. The other two are private and protected.

Items within a class marked as public can be accessed directly by any function in the whole program. Methods are most often defined as public. Public data offers no protection and defeats much of the purpose for using classes in the first place. Public items are essentially unprotected.

The general syntax for public protection within the *class* statement is:

```
class ClassName{
     data_structures;
public:
     methods;
};
```

The position of the *public:* protection modifier marks the beginning of the public items.

The format for defining a derived class with public base class protection is:

```
class BaseClass{
     data_structures;
public:
     methods();
};
class DerivedClass: public BaseClass{
     data_structures;
public:
     methods();
};
```

APPLICATIONS

Use public protection for methods, classes, or data that can be accessed from any point in a program. Public data can be considered global.

Methods are almost always public because they are the interface between the rest of the program and the data structures within the class.

Using public protection for a base class in derived class makes the protection for the base class carry forward. Assume three classes, Base, Derived1, and Derived2. The Derived2 class can refer to items in Base only if Base is declared public in the definition of Derived1.

```
class Base{
     data_structures;
public:
     methods;
};

class Derived1 : public Base{
     data_structures;
public:
     methods;
};

class Derived2 : public Derived1{
     data_structures;
public:
     methods;
};
```

Derived2 methods can access data items in Base.

HANDS-ON ACTIVITY

The following program defines a base class and two derived classes. The derived classes specify public protection allowing access down the class hierarchy. Data from the base class is manipulated from the top level derived class.

1. Type **BC** and press **Enter** to start up the compiler from the DOS prompt.
2. Press **Alt-FN** to pull down the File menu and create a new file.
3. Type the following code:

```
#include <iostream.h>
#include <stdio.h>
#include <string.h>
#include <conio.h>

class Base{
protected:
     char B_string[80];
public:
```

```
    void B_show(void);
};
class Derived1 : public Base{
protected:
    char D1_string[80];
public:
    void D1_show(void);
};
class Derived2 : public Derived1{
    char D2_string[80];
public:
    Derived2(char*);
    void D2_show(void);
};
Derived2::Derived2(char *string)
{
    strcpy(D2_string,string);
    strcpy(D1_string,"D1_string");
    strcpy(B_string,"B_string");
}
void Base::B_show(void)
{
    cout << "B_string:  " << B_string << "\n";
}
void Derived1::D1_show(void)
{
    cout << "D1_string: " << D1_string << "\n";
}
void Derived2::D2_show(void)
{
    cout << "B_string:  " << B_string << "\n";
    cout << "D1_string: " << D1_string << "\n";
    cout << "D2_string: " << D2_string << "\n";
}

void main()
{
    char  string1[80] = "";

    clrscr();
    cout << "Module 75\n";
    cout << "Public Protection Demonstration\n\n";
    cout << "Type a string: ";
    gets(string1);
    cout << "Define an object for Derived2... ";
    Derived2 PubObject(string1);
    cout << "\nNow access all 3 classes from top level\n";
    PubObject.D2_show();
```

```
        cout << "\nPress any key to exit\n";
        do {;} while(!kbhit());
    }
```

4. Press **Ctrl-F9** to compile and run the sample program.

```
Module 75
Public Protection Demonstration

Type a string:
```

5. Type **The depositary of power is always unpopular.** and press **Enter**. The following is displayed:

```
Module 75
Public Protection Demonstration

Type a string: The depositary of power is always unpopular.
Define an object for Derived2...
Now access all 3 classes from top level
B_string:  B_string
D1_string: D1_string
D2_string: The depositary of power is always unpopular.

Press any key to exit
```

6. Press any key to exit the sample program and return to Borland C++.
7. Press **Alt-X** to exit Borland C++ and return to DOS.
8. Continue the learning sequence with Module 72.

Module 76

PUTC( ),FPUTC( )

DESCRIPTION

The functions *putc( )* and *fputc( )* write a character to a file. Their syntax is:

```
#include <stdio.h>
int putc(int,FILE*);
int fputc(int,FILE*);
```

The return value is the character written for a successful call. EOF is returned on error. The file descriptor (FILE*) is the result of calling fopen( ) with a mode of write or append. putc( ) and fputc( ) are functionally identical. A typical call to fputc( ) is:

```
#include <stdio.h>
     ...
int  status;
FILE *descriptor
char ch;
     ...
descriptor = fopen("FILE","w");
     ...
status = fputc(ch,descriptor);
```

Many C compilers implement putc( ) as a preprocessor macro that is equivalent to fputc( ).

APPLICATIONS

Use fputc( ) to write a character to an output file stream. The file must be opened using fopen( ) prior to being written to. fputc( ) is frequently used to write unformatted output to a file. The file descriptors, stdout and stderr, may be used with fputc( ). For example:

```
char message[] = "This is a message";
     ...
for(i=0;message[i];i++){
     fputc(message[i],stdout);
}
```

This code segment writes the *message* to the computer screen. This technique of writing to the screen is useful when a program writes to a file under some conditions and to the screen under others.

HANDS-ON ACTIVITY

The sample program demonstrates both fgetc( ) and fputc( ) to copy a file. A '.' is output for every 100 characters copied.

1. Type **BC**, then press **Enter** at the DOS prompt to start Borland C++.
2. Press **Alt-F** and select **New**, then type the following code:

```
#include <iostream.h>
#include <stdio.h>
#include <string.h>
#include <conio.h>

void main()
{
      long  i = 0;
      int   status;
      FILE  *fd_in;
      FILE  *fd_out;
      char  ch;
      char  file_in[80];
      char  file_out[80];

      clrscr();
      cout << "Module 76\n";
      cout << "This module uses fputc to copy a file\n\n";
            /*
            | Read filenames
            */
      cout << "Enter input filename : ";
      gets(file_in);
      cout << "Enter output filename: ";
      gets(file_out);
            /*
            | Open files
            */
      fd_in = fopen(file_in,"r");
      if(!fd_in){
            cout << "Could not open file: " << file_in <<"\n";
      }
      fd_out = fopen(file_out,"w");
      if(!fd_out){
            cout << "Could not open file: " <<file_out<<"\n";
      }
```

```
        /*
        | Copy file_in to file_out using fgetc and fputc
        */
    do{
        ch          = fgetc(fd_in);
        status      = fputc(ch,fd_out);
        if(status == EOF){
            cout << "Error writing output file\n";
        }
        i++;
        if(!(i%100)){ putchar('.'); }
    }while(ch != EOF);
    cout << "\nCopied " << i << " characters.\n";

    cout << "\nPress any key to exit";
    do {;} while(!kbhit());
}
```

3. Save the code as MOD76.CPP.
4. Press **Alt-RR** to compile and run the sample program.

```
Module 76
This module uses fputc to copy a file

Enter input filename:
```

5. Type **MOD76.CPP** and press **Enter**. Any filename in the current directory will work if you have not saved the MOD76.CPP source code.

```
Module 76
This module uses fputc to copy a file

Enter input filename:  MOD76.CPP
Enter output filename:
```

6. Type **TRASH.DAT** then press **Enter**. This file will be written.

```
Module 76
This module uses fputc to copy a file

Enter input filename:  MOD76.CPP
Enter output filename: TRASH.DAT
..................
Copied 1823 characters.

Press any key to exit
```

7. Press any key to exit the sample program and return to Borland C++.
8. Press **Alt-X** to exit Borland C++ and return to DOS.
9. Continue the learning sequence with Module 40.

Module 77

PUTCHAR( )

DESCRIPTION

The I/O function *putchar* writes a character to stdout. stdout is the computer screen by default. It may be redirected to a file from the command line. The usage syntax is:

```
#include <stdio.h>
int putchar(int);
```

The return value is the character written to stdout for a successful call. EOF is returned on error. putchar( ) uses stdout as the output file descriptor. A typical call to putchar( ) is:

```
#include <stdio.h>
     ...
int  status;
char ch;
     ...
status = putchar(ch);
```

This call is equivalent to:

```
status = putc(ch,stdin);
```

Many C compilers implement putchar(ch) as a preprocessor macro that is compiled as the putc(ch,stdout) call.

APPLICATIONS

Use putchar when a character is written to the standard output stream, which may be either the screen or a file. The main advantage of using putchar( ) is convenience. stdout is automatically opened by the compiler during startup and closed during program termination; the programmer does not have to explicitly open or close the file.

Command line I/O redirection applies to stdout as it does to stdin. File names may be specified on the command line with a leading **>** and putchar( ) writes to the file rather than the screen. For example:

```
C:\> APROGRAM >OUTPUT.FIL
```

This command runs APROGRAM and redirects stdout to OUTPUT.FIL rather than the screen.

HANDS-ON ACTIVITY

The sample program uses putchar( ) to write to the computer screen.

1. Type **BC** and press **Enter** at the DOS prompt to start Borland C++.
2. Press **Alt-F** and select **New**, then type the following code:

```
#include <iostream.h>
#include <stdio.h>
#include <string.h>
#include <conio.h>

void main()
{
      int   len;
      int   i;
      int   status;
      char  ch;
      char  string[80];

      cout << "Module 77\n";
      cout << "This module uses putchar\n\n";
      cout << "Type a string: ";
      gets(string);
      cout << "The string has been read; ";
      cout << "use putchar to type it:";

      len = strlen(string);
      for(i=0;i<len;i++){
            ch     = string[i];
            status = putchar(ch);
            if(status == EOF){
                  cout << "Error writing to stdout\n";
            }
      }

      cout << "\n\nPress any key to exit";
      do {;} while(!kbhit());
}
```

3. Press **Alt-RR** to compile and run the sample program.

```
Module 77
This module uses putchar

Type a string:
```

4. Type **This is a string** and press **Enter**. The following is displayed:

```
Module 77
This module uses putchar

Type a string: This is a string
The string has been read; use putchar to type it: This is a string

Press any key to exit
```

5. Press any key to exit the sample program and return to Borland C++.
6. Press **Alt-X** to exit Borland C++ and return to DOS.
7. Continue the learning sequence with Module 78.

Module 78

PUTS( )

DESCRIPTION

The function *puts( )* writes a character string to stdout. stdout is normally the computer screen. It may be redirected on the command line to write to a file instead of the screen. The usage is:

```
#include <stdio.h>
int puts(const char*);
```

puts( ) returns the EOF on failure, otherwise the return value is an undetermined nonnegative value. Each call to puts( ) appends a newline character to the end of the string. Thus, each call is displayed on the next line on the screen. stdout is the output file descriptor for puts( ). A typical call is:

```
#include <stdio.h>
     ...
int  status;
char string[80];
     ...
status = puts(string);
```

The puts( ) call writes the string to standard output. The above call to puts( ) is equivalent to:

```
status = fputs(string,stdout);
```

Some C compilers implement puts( ) as a preprocessor macro that calls fputs( ) with a file descriptor of stdout.

APPLICATIONS

Use puts( ) to write a string to the standard output (stdout) stream. The main advantage of using puts( ) is convenience. The compiler automatically opens stdout as part of program startup. The programmer does not have to explicitly open or close the file nor specify the error handling code associated with opening a file.

Command line I/O redirection works for puts( ). Files specified on the command line with a leading **>** are written to rather than the screen. For example:

```
C:\> APROGRAM >FILE.OUT
```

This command runs APROGRAM and redirects stdout. puts( ) writes to the file FILE.OUT rather than the screen.

HANDS-ON ACTIVITY

This program uses puts( ) to write strings to the screen.

1. Start Borland C++.
2. Open a new file window by pressing **Alt-FN**.
3. Type the following code in the NONAME00.CPP window:

```
#include <iostream.h>
#include <stdio.h>
#include <string.h>
#include <conio.h>

void main()
{
      int  status;
      char string[80];

      cout << "Module 78\n";
      cout << "This module uses puts\n\n";
      cout << "Type a string: ";
      gets(string);
      status = puts("\nThe string is: ");
      if(status == EOF){
            cout << "Error writing stdout.\n";
      }
      status = puts(string);
      if(status == EOF){
            cout << "Error writing stdout.\n";
      }
      putch('\n');

      cout << "\nPress any key to exit";
      do {;} while(!kbhit());
}
```

4. Press **Ctrl-F9** to run the program.

```
Module 78
This module uses puts

Type a string:
```

5. Type **Little things affect little minds** and press **Enter.** The following is displayed:

```
Module 78
This module uses puts

Type a string: Little things affect little minds

The string is:
Little things affect little minds

Press any key to exit
```

6. Press any key to exit the sample program and return to Borland C++.
7. Press **Alt-X** to exit Borland C++ and return to DOS.

puts( ) can be used in place of cout when writing strings to the screen. cout has the advantage of automatically writing any built-in C data type. puts( ) only handles strings.

8. Continue the learning sequence with Module 41.

Module 79

RUN MENU

DESCRIPTION

This module describes the Run menu and its options. The Run menu is used during program testing to compile and debug the C++ program currently in the edit window. The Run menu also provides access to several Programmer's Platform debugging facilities.

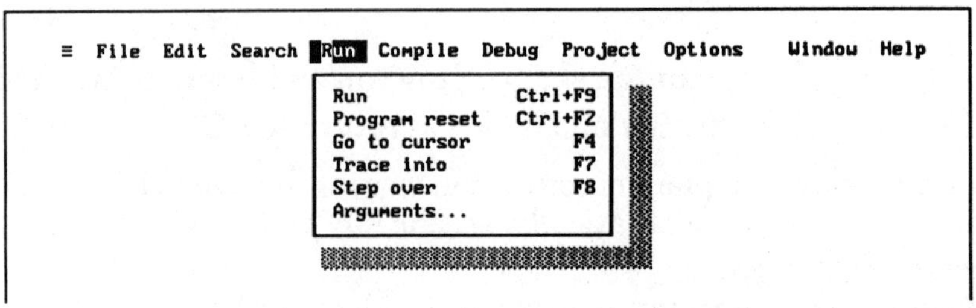

Run — Compile the source code currently in the edit window and begin execution. The source code is not compiled unless changed since the last Run command. Executions continues if compilation is not necessary. Ctrl-F9 is the shortcut key for this command.

Program reset — Use this command to reset the program to the initial state. The next time Run is selected, the program is rerun from the beginning. Program Reset can be selected by pressing Ctrl-F2.

Goto cursor — Program execution starts from the current location and continues until the line that contains the cursor is encountered. This feature allows you to stop program execution at specific points and examine the contents of variables. The F4 key executes this command directly.

Trace into — Toggles whether program tracing operates in the current function or traces into called C++ functions. Tracing executes one program line at a time. main( ) is the initial trace function.

Step over — Executes the next command or function call without tracing each line. The shortcut command for Step over is F7.

Arguments... — Selecting Arguments... pops up a submenu to specify calling arguments for the next function call. The F8 key can be used to access Arguments... directly, bypassing the Run menu.

APPLICATIONS

The Run menu provides a convenient and powerful facility to speed up the debugging process significantly over compilers that do not contain integrated debugging facilities. Borland C++'s debugging features can be extended significantly with the addition of the optional Borland Debugger. (Details of the operation of Borland Debugger are covered in a separate book, *Illustrated Turbo Debugger.*)

Program Reset reinitializes the program so that a section of code can be executed again. Restarting a program without recompiling is a very useful capability if a program aborts. You can run the program again up to the point of the crash and examine variables to determine the reason for the abort.

Go to cursor is useful for getting to a specific location in the code without having to single step to it. Executing up to the cursor position can be a real time saver in a large program.

Single step execution normally operates within the function main( ). Selecting Trace into causes single step execution to continue into called C++ functions to find problems in lower level functions.

Step over saves time by executing through function calls when single stepping. When Trace into is on, there is no need to single step functions that are correct.

Arguments... lets you specify arguments to a function before calling it. This can be done when testing a function to see how it behaves with a variety of values without having to recompile the program for every value.

HANDS-ON ACTIVITY

This session is an introduction to debugging Borland C++ programs. Additional debugging capabilities are covered in the module on the Debug menu. The example program includes variables and functions to examine to show a typical debugging session.

1. Type **BC** at the DOS prompt and press **Enter** to run Borland C++.
2. Press **Alt-F** to pull down the File menu. Select **New** to start a new file.
3. Type the following program into the edit window. The program is used in later steps to illustrate debugging features of Borland C++.

```
#include <iostream.h>
#include <stdio.h>
#include <string.h>
#include <conio.h>

int incr_integer(int);                  // function prototype

main()
{
      int var1;                         // uninitialized variable
      int var2=0;                       // initialized to 0
      int i;                            // work variable

      char string[]="CHAR";             // really 5 bytes

      clrscr();
      cout << "Module 79\n";
      cout << "This module examines the Run Menu\n\n";

      for(i=0;i<10;i++){                // loop will execute 10 times
            var1 = incr_integer(var2);  // call function
            var2 = var1;                // get ready for next loop
            cout << "var1= " << var1 << "\n"; // to screen
      }

      cout << "\nPress any key to exit\n";
      do {;} while(!kbhit());

}
int incr_integer(int xxx)
{
      xxx++;                            // increment funct argument
      return(xxx);
}
```

4. Save the text using the Save as... option of the File menu. Begin by pressing **Alt-F** to activate the File menu, then move the selection bar down to Save as... by pressing **Down Arrow** three times. Make the selection by pressing **Enter**.
5. Type **MOD79.CPP** at the prompt in the Save as... submenu, and press **Enter**. This saves MOD79.CPP for additional debugging experimentation.
6. Press **Alt-R** to pull down the Run menu.
7. Select Run by pressing **Enter**. Borland C++ will compile and execute the code in the edit window. The output will flash up on the screen too fast to read. You can press **Alt-F5** to display the user window.

8. Press **Alt-R** and type **T** to pull down the Run menu and select the Trace command. The compiler highlights the first executable line of the main( ) function. Variable initialization executes during startup, so the line highlighted is:

```
int var2=0;                    // initialized to 0
```

9. Press **F7** two times to trace to the first line within main( ) that executes. The next line to be executed is highlighted.
10. Press **F8** to execute the call to function *clrscr( )*.

F7 traces into the function and F8 executes it. Thus tracing into every function is not required but an option depending on whether you press F7 or F8.

11. Press **Alt-R** then type **P** to select program reset. Program execution begins again. This allows you to trace the program from the beginning without having to exit to the compiler and run it again.
12. Press **Alt-X** to exit Borland C++ and return to the DOS prompt. MOD79.CPP can be used for additional experimentation with debugging a program in Borland C++.
13. Continue the learning sequence with Module 15.

Module 80

SCANF( ), FSCANF( )

DESCRIPTION

scanf( ) is the C formatted input function. It reads values based on a format specifier from the stdin stream. fscanf( ) reads fields from a file. The general form for the scanf( ) function family is:

```
#include <stdio.h>
int scanf(const char*format[,address,...]);
int fscanf(FILE*,const char*format[,address,...]);
```

The possible return values are:

- Number of fields successfully read
- EOF when end of file is reached
- Zero when no fields are read

The address list is optional and based on the format. The format specifier is a constant string containing format information for each field. Example scanf( ) calls are:

```
status = scanf("%s", &string);
status = scanf("%d", &i);
```

scanf( ) treats blank, tab, and newline as whitespace characters to delimit fields. Whitespace characters are ignored from an input conversion standpoint.

There are several functions in the scanf( ) family:

scanf — Reads the formatted fields from stdin. The function prototype is:

```
int scanff(char *format,&args);
```

fscanf — Inputs formatted fields from an input file. The function prototype is:

```
int fscanf(FILE* stream,char *format,&args);
```

sscanf — Reads the formatted fields from a string. The function prototype is:

```
int sscanf(char*buff,char*format,&args);
```

vscanf — Reads formatted fields using a variable number of arguments. The function prototype for vscanf( ) is:

```
int vscanf(const char*format,*arglist);
```

vfscanf — Reads and formats input from a stream. This function is similar to fscanf except a variable length argument list is accepted. The function prototype is:

```
int vfscanf(FILE*stream,
                    const char*format,*args);
```

cscanf — Inputs formatted values from the console. This is a DOS only function.

```
int cscanf(const char*format,*args);
```

The format specifier, *const char*format*, is a string containing characters or values to read and format. The format has the following parts:

```
%[flags][width][size]type
```

Where:

%	Signals special format
flags	Marks justification, signs, decimal point, etc.
width	Minimum number of characters to output, padded with blanks or zeros
size	Overrides default size of argument
type	Conversion type. The argument will be converted from the internal binary format into character form on output.

Items enclosed in [ ] are optional.

scanf( ) size modifiers are:

Modifier	*Meaning*
F	Far pointer
N	Near pointer
h	Short integer
l	Long integer
L	Long double

The conversion types are:

Type	*Meaning*
c	Character
d	Signed decimal integer
i	Signed decimal integer
o	Unsigned octal integer
u	Unsigned decimal integer
x	Unsigned hexadecimal integer using lower case
f	Signed floating point number in form [-]dddd.dddd

g	Signed floating point using e or f form depending on value and precision
e	Signed floating point form [-]d.dddd or e[+-]ddd value and precision
s	Prints contents of string pointer
%	Prints % if no argument is specified

APPLICATIONS

Use scanf( ) or one of its variants to read formatted data. scanf( ) is not used frequently in C++. The C++ *cin* class is used for simple input instead of scantf( ) because of its convenience.

When a string is read by scanf( ), characters up to the next whitespace character are read. The effect is that scanf( ) reads a word at a time rather than the whole line as a string.

HANDS-ON ACTIVITY

The sample session illustrates simple scanf( ) function call statements.

1. Type **BC** and press **Enter** to start up the compiler.
2. Press **Alt-FN** to pull down the File menu and create a new file.
3. Type the following code:

```
#include <iostream.h>
#include <stdio.h>
#include <string.h>
#include <conio.h>

void main()
{
      int value;
      char string[80];

      clrscr();
      cout << "Module 80\n";
      cout << "This module demonstrates scanf\n\n";
      cout << "Type a number: ";
      scanf("%d",&value);
      cout << "value is : " << value << "\n";
      cout << "Type a string: " ;
      scanf("%s",&string);
      cout << "string is: " << string << "\n";
      cout << "Type a number and a string: ";
      scanf("%d %s",&value,string);
      cout << "value is : " << value << "\n";
      cout << "string is: " << string << "\n\n";
```

```
      cout << "Press any key to exit";
      do {;} while(!kbhit());
}
```

4. Press **Alt-RR** to compile and run the sample program.

```
Module 80
This module demonstrates scanf

Type a number:
```

5. Type **27** and press **Enter**. The following is displayed:

```
Module 80
This module demonstrates scanf

Type a number: 27
value is : 27
Type a string:
```

6. Type **Trash** then press **Enter**.

```
Module 80
This module demonstrates scanf

Type a number: 27
value is : 27
Type a string: Trash
string is: Trash
Type a number and a string:
```

7. Type **87 Stuff** and press **Enter**.

```
Module 80
This module demonstrates scanf

Type a number: 27
value is : 27
Type a string: Trash
string is: Trash
Type a number and a string: 87 Stuff
value is : 87
string is: Stuff

Press any key to exit
```

8. Press any key to exit the sample program and return to Borland C++. Press **Alt-F5** to view the user screen if you wish to view the run again.
9. Continue the learning sequence with Module 30.

Module 81

SEARCH MENU

DESCRIPTION

This module describes the operation of the Programmer's Platform Search menu. Menu choices allow fast movement around the source code.

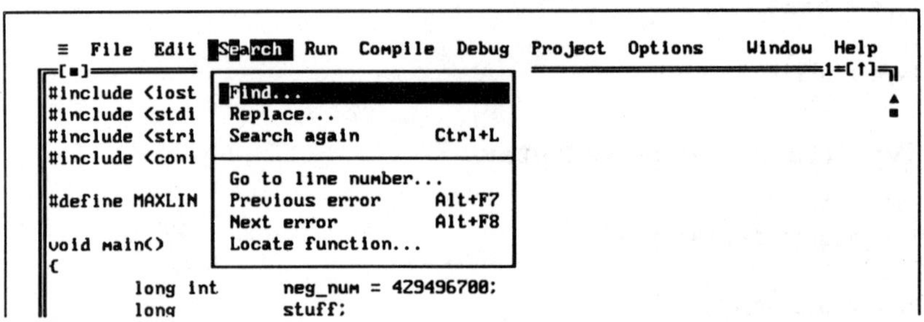

APPLICATIONS

The options available from the Search menu are:

Find... This menu selection allows you to search for a specified string. There are several search options available via sub-menus. The hierarchy of search options is:

OPTIONS
- Case Sensitive *
- Whole Words
- Regular Expression

SCOPE
- Global *
- Selected Text

DIRECTION
- Forward *
- Backward

ORIGIN
- From cursor *
- Entire scope

NOTE The items marked with an '*' are the default values.

The entries listed under OPTIONS are on/off selections. All other selections are a choice between the two lowest level items. The shortcut command for find is Ctrl-QF.

Replace...	You can search for a string and replace it with a new string. Replace... has the same search options as Find... Ctrl-QA is the short command for Replace...
Search again	This menu selection searches for the string specified in the last Find... or Replace... command. This item can be selected by pressing Ctrl-L.
Go to line number...	Jump to a specific line number by selecting this menu item.
Previous error	Select this item to jump to the previous error when editing after a compile. Use Alt-F7 as the shortcut to select this command.
Next error	Select Next error to jump to the next error after a compile. The short command for Next error is Alt-F8.
Locate function...	This menu selection searches the current edit window for the specified function.

HANDS-ON ACTIVITY

This session shows the details of using the Find... Search menu selection. You can apply the example to the rest of the items in the Search menu. The steps assume that the current directory contains the example C++ source file from Module 2.

1. Start Borland C++ by typing **BC** and pressing **Enter**.
2. Press **F3** to pop up the Load a File submenu and select MOD2.CPP.
3. Move the cursor to the beginning of the program.
4. Press **Alt-S** to activate the Search menu, then type **F** to pop up the Find... submenu.

5. Type **cout** and press **Enter** to begin the search for the string cout. The cursor stops on the sixth line.

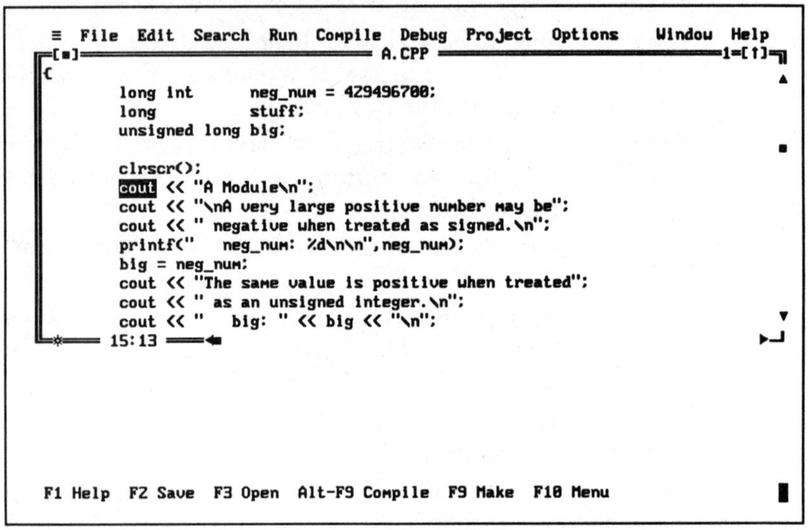

6. Press **Ctrl-L** to search for 'cout' again. A message box will pop up to inform you that the find string was not found.

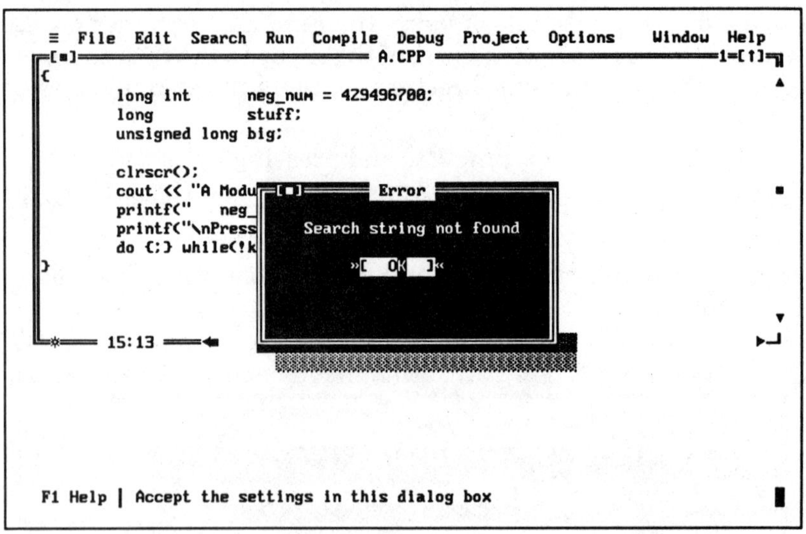

7. Press **Alt-X** to exit back to DOS.

Try this search again from the beginning. This time select the Case sensitive suboption. The find string 'COUT' will not be found by the initial search operation.

8. Continue the learning sequence with Module 79.

Module 82

SHORT

DESCRIPTION

The *short* operator sets aside two bytes of storage for a variable to be used as an integer number. The size, 16 bits, limits the value range that a short variable can represent. The range for a signed short is –32,768 to +32,767. An unsigned short can represent 0 to +65,535.

short is short for short integer. The following example lists several ways to define a short variable:

```
auto short sixteen_bits;
static short integer two_bytes;
short int stuff;
static unsigned short trash;
unsigned short int zero_to_65535;
```

APPLICATIONS

short is short for *short integer*. int and short are both 16-bit number variables. Refer to Module 58 for the discussion of int variables.

Continue the learning sequence with Module 5.

Module 83
STRCAT( ) and STRNCAT( )

DESCRIPTION

String concatenation is a common string operation. The contents of one string are appended to the end of another string. Both strings must be NULL terminated. C++ provides library functions *strcat( )* and *strncat( )* for this purpose. The usage synopsis is:

```
#include <string.h>
int strcat(char*, const char *);
int strncat(char*, const char*, int);
```

An example call is:

```
#include <string.h>
     ...
int  len;
char *status;
char destination[80];
char source[] = "This is a string with some stuff";
     ...
status = strcat(destination,source);
```

The return value of the strcat( ) call is the address of the concatenated string. The new length of *destination* is the original length plus the length of *source*.

APPLICATIONS

Use strcat( ) to combine two strings. The contents of the source string is appended to the contents of the destination string. Both strings must be terminated with a NULL. The destination string must be large enough to hold both strings.

strncat( ) requires the number of bytes to concatenate.

HANDS-ON ACTIVITY

The sample program uses strcat( ) to append one string to another. It also performs the concatenation process manually using strlen( ) and a loop.

1. Type **BC** and press **Enter** to start up the compiler.
2. Press **Alt-FN** to pull down the File menu and create a new file.
3. Type the following code into the NONAME00.CPP edit window:

```
#include <iostream.h>
#include <stdio.h>
#include <string.h>
#include <conio.h>

void main()
{
      int   i;
      int   j;
      int   len;
      char  ch;
      char  source[80];
      char  destination[80] = "The Destination";

      clrscr();
      cout << "Module 83\n";
      cout << "This module uses strcat\n\n";
      cout << "Type a string: ";
      gets(source);
      cout << "The string is in source: " << source << "\n";
      cout << "Using strcat() to concatenate strings...\n";
      cout << "destination before: " << destination << "\n";
      strcat(destination,source);
      cout << "destination now contains: " << destination << "\n\n";
      cout << "Now do concatenation for ourselves...\n";
      destination[15] = '\0';      // Restore original string
      len = strlen(destination);
      for(i=0,j=len;;i++){
            ch              = source[i];
            destination[j++] = ch;
            if(ch == 0){ break; }
      }
      cout << "Our concatenation is: " << destination << "\n";

      cout << "Press any key to exit\n";
      do {;} while(!kbhit());
}
```

Notice the multiple include statements at the beginning of the code. Each is required because of the C++ library functions referenced in the code.

Include	*Function*
iostream.h	cout( )
conio.h	kbhit( ), clrscr( )
stdio.h	gets( )
string.h	strcat( ), strlen( )

4. Press **Alt-RR** to compile and run the sample program.

```
Module 83
This module uses strcat()

Type a string:
```

5. Type **The Source** and press **Enter**. The following is displayed:

```
Module 83
This module uses strcat()

Type a string: The Source
The string is in source: The Source

Using strcat() to concatenate strings...
destination before: The Destination
destination now contains: The DestinationThe Source

Now do concatenation for ourselves...
Our concatenation is: The DestinationThe Source

Press any key to exit
```

6. Press any key to exit the sample program and return to Borland C++.
7. Press **Alt-X** to exit Borland C++ and return to DOS.

This code illustrates using the string function, strcat( ), to concatenate two strings. It also shows that you can write code that does this same string manipulation. Use built-in string functions rather than duplicating them because the supplied functions are generally more efficient.

8. Continue the learning sequence with Module 84.

Module 84

STRCHR

DESCRIPTION

There are no explicit substring functions in the C++ string library. C++ uses character pointers (discussed in another module) to allow string functions to manipulate substrings. A function is provided to find a particular character within a string, strchr( ). strchr( ) searches a string for a character and returns the address where the character is found. The return value is zero if the character is not found. The usage synopsis is:

```
#include <string.h>
char *strchr(const char *, int);
```

An example call is:

```
#include <string.h>
     ...
int  len;
char *sub_string;
char source[] = "This is a string with some text";
     ...
sub_string = strchr(source,'w');
if(!sub_string){
     cout << "strchr search failed\n";
}else{
     cout << sub_string;
}
```

APPLICATIONS

Use strchr( ) to find the first character of a substring within a string. The NULL character that terminates a string is included in the character search. This makes it possible to find the address of the end of a string strchr( ):

```
end_ptr = strchr(string,0);
```

end_ptr will contain a pointer to the end of string.

HANDS-ON ACTIVITY

The sample program uses strchr( ) to find the start of a substring within a string. It also performs the process manually using a loop.

1. Type **BC** and press **Enter** to start up the compiler.
2. Press **Alt-FN** to pull down the File menu and create a new file.
3. Type the following code into the NONAME00.CPP edit window:

```
#include <iostream.h>
#include <stdio.h>
#include <string.h>
#include <conio.h>

void main()
{
      int   i;
      char  *sub_string;
      char  ch;
      char  source[80];

      clrscr();
      cout << "Module 84\n";
      cout << "This module uses strchr()\n\n";
      cout << "Type a string: ";
      gets(source);
      cout << "The string is in source: " << source << "\n";
      cout << "Using strchr() to find start sub-string..\n";
      sub_string = strchr(source,'d');
      if(sub_string){
            cout << "Found sub-string: " << sub_string << "\n";
      }else{
            cout << "Search failed\n";
      }

      cout << "Now do it ourselves...\n";
      sub_string = 0;
      for(i=0;ch!=0;i++){
            ch           = source[i];
            if(ch == 'd'){
                  sub_string = &source[i];     // Save the address
                  break;
            }
      }
      if(sub_string){
            cout << "Found sub-string: " << sub_string << "\n";
      }else{
            cout << "Search failed\n";
      }
```

```
        cout << "Press any key to exit\n";
        do {;} while(!kbhit());
    }
```

Notice the multiple include statements at the beginning of the code. Each is required because of the C++ library functions referenced in the code.

Include	*Function*
iostream.h	cout( )
conio.h	kbhit( ), clrscr( )
stdio.h	gets( )
string.h	strchr( )

4. Press **Alt-RR** to compile and run the sample program.

```
Module 84
This module uses strchr()

Type a string:
```

5. Type **abcdefghijklmnopqrstuvwxyz** and press **Enter**. The following is displayed:

```
Module 84
This module uses strchr()

Type a string: abcdefghijklmnopqrstuvwxyz
The string is in source: abcdefghijklmnopqrstuvwxyz

Using strchr() to find start sub-string..
The sub-string is: defghijklmnopqrstuvwxyz

Now do it ourselves...
Found sub-string: defghijklmnopqrstuvwxyz

Press any key to exit
```

6. Press any key to exit the sample program and return to Borland C++.
7. Press **Alt-X** to exit Borland C++ and return to DOS.

This code illustrates using the string function, strchr( ), to find the start of a substring.

8. Continue the learning sequence with Module 85.

Module 85
STRCMP( ) and STRNCMP( )

DESCRIPTION

C++ does not have a string compare operator. Instead, string library functions *strcmp( )* and *strncmp( )* compare two strings. Both must be NULL terminated. *strncmp( )* compares the first 'n' characters of two strings. strcmp( ) usage synopsis is:

```
#include <string.h>
int strcmp(const unsigned char*, const unsigned char *);
int strncmp(const unsigned char*, const unsigned char *,int);
```

An example call is:

```
#include <string.h>
     ...
int  nchars;
int  status;
unsigned char string1[80] = "ABCD";
unsigned char string2[]   = "abcd";
     ...
status = strcmp(string1,string2);
status = strncmp(string1,string2,nchars);
```

strcmp( ) returns three possible results:

Return	*Meaning*
Zero	Strings are equal.
Positive	String 1 greater than string 2.
Negative	String 1 less than string 2.

APPLICATIONS

Use strcmp( ) to compare two strings using their natural length. The strncmp( ) variation explicitly specifies the number of characters to compare.

strcmp( ) can be confusing. Most C++ library functions return a success/fail value. Success is equated to TRUE, which is usually 1. The fail value is

FALSE (zero). strcmp( ) uses FALSE to mean success. This is confusing and can lead to program bugs unless you are very careful.

HANDS-ON ACTIVITY

This sample program uses strcmp( ) to compare strings.

1. Type **BC** and press **Enter** to start up the compiler.
2. Press **Alt-FN** to pull down the File menu and create a new file.
3. Type the following code into the NONAME00.CPP edit window:

```
#include <iostream.h>
#include <stdio.h>
#include <string.h>
#include <conio.h>

void main()
{
     int   status;
     char  string1[80];
     char  string2[80] = "XYZ";

     clrscr();
     cout << "Module 85\n";
     cout << "This module uses strcmp()\n\n";
     cout << "Type a string: ";
     gets(string1);
     cout << "string1 is: " << string1 << "\n";
     cout << "Using strcmp() to compare strings...\n";
     status = strcmp(string1,string2);
     if(status == 0){
          cout << "string1 == string2\n";
     }else{
          cout << "The strings do not match.\n";
     }
     cout << "\nNow use strncmp()...\n";
     cout << "Type another string: ";
     gets(string1);
     cout << "string1 is: " << string1 << "\n";
     status = strncmp(string1,string2,5);
     if(status == 0){
          cout << "string1 == string2\n";
     }
     if(status < 0){
          cout << "string1 < string2\n";
     }
     if(status > 0){
          cout << "string1 > string2\n";
```

```
        }

        cout << "Press any key to exit\n";
        do {;} while(!kbhit());
}
```

4. Press **Alt-RR** to compile and run the sample program.

```
Module 85
This module uses strcmp()

Type a string:
```

5. Type **XYZ** and press **Enter**. The following is displayed:

```
Module 85
This module uses strcmp()

Type a string: XYZ
string1 is: XYZ
Using strcmp() to compare strings...
string1 == string2

Now use strncmp()...
Type another string:
```

6. Type **ABCDEFGHIJK** and press **Enter**. The following is displayed:

```
Module 85
This module uses strcmp()

Type a string: XYZ
string1 is: XYZ
Using strcmp() to compare strings...
string1 == string2

Now use strncmp()...
Type another string: ABCDEFGHIJK
string1 is: ABCDEFGHIJK
string1 < string2
```

7. Press any key to exit the sample program and return to Borland C++.
8. Press **Alt-X** to exit Borland C++ and return to DOS.

This code illustrates using the string functions strcmp( ) and strncmp( ) to compare two strings. Don't forget that a zero return means the strings match.

9. Continue the learning sequence with Module 86.

Module 86

STRCPY( ) and STRNCPY( )

DESCRIPTION

C++ does not have a string assignment operator. String library functions *strcpy( )* and *strncpy( )* compare strings. *strcpy( )* copies the contents of one NULL terminated string to another. *strncpy( )* copies 'n' characters from the source string to the destination string. strcpy( ) usage synopsis is:

```
#include <string.h>
int strcpy(char*, const char*);
int strncpy(char*, const char*,int);
```

Sample usage is:

```
#include <string.h>
     ...
int  nchars;
char *status;
char destination[80];
char source[80];
     ...
status = strcpy(destination,source);
status = strncpy(destination,source,nchars);
```

The return status value is the pointer to the destination string.

APPLICATIONS

Use strcpy( ) and strncpy( ) to copy the contents of one string to another string. The contents of the destination string are overwritten by the source string. If the source and destination strings overlap, the results of the copy operation is unpredictable. There is no checking to see if the destination string array is large enough to hold the source string.

The source string must be NULL terminated when using strcpy( ). The trailing NULL is copied automatically.

The source string does not have to be NULL terminated for strncpy( ). The number of characters parameter overrides the natural string length. strncpy( ) does not append a trailing NULL.

HANDS-ON ACTIVITY

This sample program uses strcpy( ) to copy strings.

1. Type **BC** and press **Enter** to start up the compiler.
2. Press **Alt-FN** to pull down the File menu and create a new file.
3. Type the following code into the NONAME00.CPP edit window:

```
#include <iostream.h>
#include <stdio.h>
#include <string.h>
#include <conio.h>

void main()
{
     int  len;
     char string1[80] = "";
     char string2[80] = "";
     char string3[80] = "";

     clrscr();
     cout << "Module 86\n";
     cout << "This module uses strcpy\n\n";
     cout << "Type a string: ";
     gets(string1);
     cout << "\nstring1 is: " << string1 << "\n";
     cout << "string2 is: " << string2 << "\n";
     cout << "string3 is: " << string3 << "\n\n";

     cout << "Using strcpy() to copy string1 to string2...\n";
     strcpy(string2,string1);
     cout << "string1 is: " << string1 << "\n";
     cout << "string2 is: " << string2 << "\n";
     cout << "string3 is: " << string3 << "\n\n";

     cout << "\nNow use strncpy()...\n";
     len = strlen(string2);
     len = len / 2;              // only copy half the string
     strncpy(string3,string2,len);
     string3[len+1] = '\0'; // must add null
     cout << "string1 is: " << string1 << "\n";
     cout << "string2 is: " << string2 << "\n";
     cout << "string3 is: " << string3 << "\n\n";
```

```
      cout << "Press any key to exit\n";
      do {;} while(!kbhit());
}
```

4. Press **Alt-RR** to compile and run the sample program.

```
Module 86
This module uses strcpy()

Type a string:
```

5. Type **1234567890** and press **Enter**. The following is displayed:

```
Module 86
This module uses strcpy

Type a string: 1234567890
string1 is: 1234567890
string2 is:
string3 is:

Using strcpy() to copy string1 to string2...
string1 is: 1234567890
string2 is: 1234567890
string3 is:

Now use strncpy()...
string1 is: 1234567890
string2 is: 1234567890
string3 is: 12345

Press any key to exit
```

6. Press any key to exit the sample program and return to Borland C++.
7. Press **Alt-X** to exit Borland C++ and return to DOS.

This code illustrates using the string functions strcpy( ) and strncpy( ) to copy a string.

8. Continue the learning sequence with Module 91.

Module 87

STREAM I/O

DESCRIPTION

C++ automatically opens several I/O stream descriptors at startup. These are analogous to stdin, stdout, and stderr. Many of the sample programs have used stream I/O throughout this book. The stream I/O prototypes and data structures are included from IOSTREAM.H. They are logically connected to the computer screen and keyboard. The streams are:

Descriptor	*Meaning*
cin	Standard Input
cout	Standard Output
cerr	Standard Error
clog	Buffered version of cerr

cin, cout, and cerr may be redirected to/from files on the command line.

Streams are a data abstraction where data flows from a source, the input file, and to a sink, the output file. C++ implements the stream concept via classes.

C++ provides both formatted and unformatted stream I/O capabilities. The most commonly used I/O is unformatted, which is implemented using the overloaded operators << and >>. These operators are more convenient to use for typing informational messages and prompts to the screen than printf( ).

```
cout << "The contents of X is: " << X << "\n";

printf("The contents of X is: %d\n",X);
```

Preparing a file for access (read, write, or both) is conceptually similar to normal C file I/O, but the mechanisms involved are different. Several steps are required to access files in C. A file is assigned a file descriptor (FD) by calling one of the open functions such as open( ) and fopen( ). The file is read or written by calling an I/O function, such as fgets( ) or fwrite( ), using the file descriptor. When the program has finished accessing the file, it is flushed and closed by a call to fclose( ). A typical C code sequence to process an input file is:

```
FILE* input_fd;
     ...
input_fd=fopen("some.fil","r");
     ...
while(ch=fgetc(input_fd)){  /* Read until EOF */
     ...}
fclose(input_fd);
```

File access in C++ begins by establishing an input or output file stream. The file is then opened. Reading the file is done by referring to the stream name rather than a file descriptor. Methods are provided in the stream class for reading and writing the stream. The stream is closed by calling the close method for that stream. A typical C++ code sequence to open and read a file is:

```
ifstream input_file;            // Define the stream
     ...
input_file.open("some.fil",ios::nocreate);
     ...
while(input_file.get(ch)){      // Read until EOF
     ...};
input_file.close;               // Close stream
```

The conceptual manipulation of files closely parallel between C and C++. As you can see, the details are quite different.

Borland C++ provides a rich selection of stream I/O classes and operators. There are two base and several derived stream classes. These are discussed in this section.

BASE STREAM CLASSES There are two base classes for streams, streambuf and ios. All of the user level stream classes are derived from these two classes.

Class streambuf provides I/O buffering. Buffers for stream are allocated automatically. Data is read into and written from these buffers. There is very little I/O formatting inherent in streambuf. streambuf members are generally very low level and are declared inline to maximize run-time performance.

Class ios contains flags, format, and state variables relating to a streambuf. Hence, ios methods are called to set file attributes, control formatting, and report errors. The following table identifies the ios file attribute modifiers:

Attribute	*Description*
app	APPend to end of existing file
ate	AT End; Seek to end of file on open
in	INput; Implied for ifstreams

nocreate	An error if file does not exist
noreplace	An error if files exists, unless app or ate also specified
trunc	Delete existing file, then open for write
out	OUTput; Implied for ofstreams

The ios file attribute is specified when a file stream is defined. For example:

```
ifstream ifile("input.fil",ios::nocreate);
```

sets the file attribute flag and sets an error flag if input.fil does not already exist.

The format flags specify how data is written to or read from a stream. For example, whether whitespace is automatically skipped or not can be specified via a format flag. Each flag corresponds to a bit in a long int variable. The format flags are:

- dec — Decimal format conversion
- fixed — Fixed point notation for floating point
- hex — Hex format conversion
- internal — Internal padding
- left — Left-adjust output
- oct — Octal format conversion
- right — Right-adjust output
- scientific — Scientific notation for floating point
- showbase — Base indicator on output
- showpoint — Show decimal point on output
- showpos — Output '+' for positive integers
- skipws — Skip whitespace
- stdio — Flush stdout and stderr after output
- unitbuf — Flush all streams after output
- uppercase — Uppercase hex output

The member functions setf and unsetf are provided to set and clear the format flags.

Status bits are set by I/O operations. These can be tested, set, or cleared by ios member functions:

- bad — Returns zero unless badbit or hardfail is set
- clear — Clear the specified status flags
- eof — Tests end of file flag; zero means !eof
- fail — Returns zero unless failbit, badbit, or hardfail bits are set
- good — Returns true (nonzero) if any status flag is set
- rdstate — Read error state

The status flag names are:

- badbit — True when last I/O was invalid. The I/O can be retried after clearing the bit.
- eofbit — True when end of file occurs. Additional I/O requests for this stream are ignored.
- failbit — True when last I/O conversion or extraction failed. The I/O may be re-tried after clearing the bit.
- goodbit — Zero means no error flags are set.
- hardfail — True means stream has unrecoverable I/O error.

It is good programming practice to test the status flags after I/O operations such as after opening a file.

DERIVED STREAM CLASSES The C++ application programmer generally does not use the base stream classes directly. C++ includes a number of stream classes derived from streambuf and ios for application program level use. The derived stream classes are:

- istream
- ostream
- iostream
- withassign
- fstream
- ifstream
- ofstream

A stream is an object or instance of one of the above classes. Each stream class has specific functionality that is discussed below.

istream is a basic input stream class. Data is buffered via class streambuf. Both formatted and unformatted I/O are supported by istream. cin is an istream object. Member functions and operators associated with istream include:

- get — Gets the next character from the input stream, even if it is a white space character.
- putback — Puts the specified character back into the input stream.
- read — Read multiple objects from the stream.
- >> — Overloaded 'get from' operator. White space is automatically skipped.

ostream is an output stream class that allows formatted and unformatted output. This class is derived from streambuf. cout, cerr, and clog are ostream objects. Member functions and operators associated with ostream include:

- put — Puts a single character to the output stream.

- write — Writes multiple objects to the output stream.
- << — Overloaded 'put to' operator.

iostream is derived from istream and ostream. It adds bidirectional I/O such that a single stream may be both input and output at the same time. Including the iostream header file, iostream.h, automatically provides the standard streams cin, cout, cerr, and clog in a program.

withassign adds the assignment operator to istream and ostream. This is how the standard streams are actually created. This class is included via iostream.h.

fstream is a stream class with files attached. It is derived from iostream, ifstream, and ofstream. Use fstream for files that are both input and output. Member functions and operators associated with fstream include:

- open — Associates a stream with a file.
- close — Closes the specified stream.
- closeall — Closes all open streams.
- seekg — Sets current 'get' position in a file stream.
- seekp — Sets current 'put' position in a file stream.
- tellg — Returns the 'get' position of a file stream.
- tellp — Returns the 'put' position of a file stream.

ifstream is the input file stream class. ifstream derives from istream.

ofstream is the output file stream class. It is derived from ostream.

Using streams for I/O is covered in separate modules.

Continue the learning sequence with Module 13.

Module 88
STRINGS

DESCRIPTION

Strings are a very important part of C/C++ application programming. C++ has no specific string data type. Rather, a string is an array of characters. Strings are typically variable length data elements, while array memory is allocated in fixed amounts. The character array must be sized to hold the largest string expected. The NULL character, \0, is used to mark the end of the string within the fixed array bounds. Strings in C++ are termed "null terminated" strings.

Typical string declarations include:

```
char string[81];
char buffer[128];
char junk[]     = "This is a junk string";
char trash[128] = "A lot of trash";
```

The variable *string* can contain a string up to 80 characters in length. Don't forget the trailing NULL character must be accounted for too. Always add one to the array length when calculating the maximum length to declare.

The length of *junk* is determined by the length of the string constant, "This is a junk string," plus one (22 bytes) because the empty brackets tell the compiler to automatically size the array to hold the constant. *trash*, on the other hand, is 128 bytes long. It is initialized with "A lot of trash."

APPLICATIONS

Use character strings to represent variable length arrays of characters. C++ includes an entire library of string manipulation functions. These include:

Function	*Description*
strcat	Append a string to another string
strchr	Search a string for a specified character
strcmp	Compare two strings
strcpy	Copy a string

strcspn	Calculate the number characters at beginning of a string1 not in string2
strcmpi	Compare two strings with case insensitivity
strcoll	Compare two strings taking local character set into consideration, e.g., accent marks
strdup	Allocate, then copy a string into the allocated memory
strerror	Return pointer to error associated with errnum variable
stricmp	Case insensitive compare of two strings
strlen	Calculate the length of a string
strlwr	Convert string to lowercase
strncat	Append n characters from one string to another string
strncmp	Compare n characters of two strings
strncmpi	Case insensitive compare n characters of two strings
strncpy	Copy n characters of one string to another
strnicmp	Case insensitive compare first n characters of two strings
strnset	Set first n bytes of a string to a specified character
strpbrk	Search string for first occurrence of any character from a given set
strrchr	Search string for last occurrence of a specified character
strrev	Reverse order of characters in a string
strset	Set all characters in a string to specified character
strspn	Search string for starting substrings that match in two strings
strstr	Scan string for a substring
strtod	Convert string to a double value
strtok	Search a string for specified tokens
strtol	Convert string to long value
strtoul	Convert string to unsigned long value
strupr	Convert string to uppercase
strxfrm	Copy no more than n characters from one string to another

The most commonly used string functions are discussed in individual modules.

Using character strings as arrays of characters will be natural to anyone with experience in other programming languages such as Fortran. The big difference is C++ arrays are zero-based rather than one-based. Zero-based means the first element of the array is [0]. One-based uses [1] to reference the first array element.

Character strings can also be manipulated as array pointers and addresses. When the name of an array is referenced, the address of the first byte is used. Both *string* and *&string[0]* refer to the address of the first character of string.

HANDS-ON ACTIVITY

The sample program is roughly equivalent to the C++ function strcpy, which copies one string to another.

1. Type **BC** and press **Enter** to start up the compiler.
2. Press **Alt-FN** to pull down the File menu and create a new file.
3. Type the following code into the NONAME00.CPP edit window:

```
#include <iostream.h>
#include <stdio.h>
#include <conio.h>

void main()
{
      long  i;
      char  ch;
      char  buffer[80];
      char  junk[80];
      char  stuff[10];
      char  trash[] = "ABCDEFGHIJKLMNOPQRSTUVWXYZ";

      cout << "Module 88\n\n";
      cout << "This module manipulates strings\n";
      cout << "Type a string: ";
      gets(buffer);
      cout << "The string is in buffer: " << buffer << "\n";
      cout << "Move buffer to junk: ";
      cout << "\n\n";
      cout << "trash now contains: " << trash << "\n";

      cout << "Now move junk to stuff: ";
      for(i=0;;i++){
            ch       = junk[i];
            if(!ch){ break; }
            stuff[i] = ch;
            cout    << ch;
      }
      cout << "\n";
      cout << "This could overwrite trash: " << trash << "\n";

      cout << "Press any key to exit";
      do {;} while(!kbhit());
}
```

4. Press **Alt-RR** to compile and run the sample program.

```
Module 88

This module manipulates strings
Type a string:
```

5. Type **This is a test!** and press **Enter**. The following is displayed:

```
Module 88

This module manipulates strings
Type a string: This is a test!
The string is in buffer: This is a test!
Move buffer to junk: This is a test!

trash now contains: ABCDEFGHIJKLMNOPQRSTUVWXYZ
Now move junk to stuff: This is a test!
This could overwrite trash: ABCDEFGHIJKLMNOPQRSTUVWXYZ
Press any key to exit
```

6. Press any key to exit the sample program and return to Borland C++.

This code shows two loop variations for copying one string to another. There is no protection for fetching or writing past the end of an array. Some compilers allocate space for strings in contiguous blocks of memory. If stuff[ ] and trash[ ] are allocated together, the second loop would write over the beginning of trash[ ]. That is not the case in this example.

The next modules in the learning sequence discuss several of the most commonly used string functions.

7. Continue the learning sequence with Module 89.

Module 89
STRLEN

DESCRIPTION

A string operation performed frequently is calculating the length of a string. The C++ library function *strlen()* performs this task. The usage synopsis is:

```
#include <string.h>
int strlen(const char *);
```

An example call is:

```
#include <string.h>
     ...
int  len;
char stuff[] = "This is a string with some stuff";
     ...
len = strlen(stuff);
```

The result of the strlen( ) call is 32. The NULL marks the end of the string and is not included in the length. So, stuff really occupies 33 bytes of memory.

APPLICATIONS

Use strlen( ) when the current length of a string is required. Typical uses include testing a buffer for overflow, checking for an empty string, and calculating the number of bytes to allocate for a string.

HANDS-ON ACTIVITY

The sample program uses strlen( ) to get the length of a string. It also calculates the string length in a loop to verify the results of the strlen( ) call.

1. Type **BC** and press **Enter** to start up the compiler.
2. Press **Alt-FN** to pull down the File menu and create a new file.

3. Type the following code into the NONAME00.CPP edit window:

```
#include <iostream.h>
#include <stdio.h>
#include <string.h>
#include <conio.h>

void main()
{
      long  i;
      int   len;
      char  ch;
      char  buffer[80];

      cout << "Module 89\n";
      cout << "This module uses strlen\n\n";
      cout << "Type a string: ";
      gets(buffer);
      cout << "The string is in buffer: " << buffer << "\n";
      cout << "Using strlen() to calculate its length...\n";
      len = strlen(buffer);
      cout << "buffer length is: " << len << "\n\n";
      cout << "Now calculate the length for ourselves...\n";

      for(i=0;;i++){
            ch       = buffer[i];
            if(ch == 0){ break; }
      }
      cout << "Our length calculation is: " << i << "\n";

      cout << "Press any key to exit";
      do {;} while(!kbhit());
}
```

4. Press **Alt-RR** to compile and run the sample program.

```
Module 89
This module uses strlen()

Type a string:
```

5. Type **ABCDEFGHIJKLMNOPQRSTUVWXYZ** and press **Enter**. The following is displayed:

```
Module 89
This module uses strlen()

Type a string: ABCDEFGHIJKLMNOPQRSTUVWXYZ
The string is in buffer: ABCDEFGHIJKLMNOPQRSTUVWXYZ
```

```
Using strlen() to calculate its length...
buffer length is: 26

Now calculate the length for ourselves...
Our length calculation is: 26

Press any key to exit
```

6. Press any key to exit the sample program and return to Borland C++.
7. Press **Alt-X** to exit Borland C++ and return to DOS.

This code illustrates using the string function, strlen( ), to find the length of a string. It also shows that you can write code that does this same string manipulation. Always use built-in string functions rather than duplicating them. The supplied string functions are highly optimized.

8. Continue the learning sequence with Module 83.

Module 90
STRUCT

DESCRIPTION

C++ treats struct as a class with a default protection of public. This is a big departure from C where structs only contain data. In practice, struct usage can be interchanged between C and C++ as long as no methods are declared. The traditional *struct* is a data structure which contains related data items. The general syntax for struct is:

```
struct StructName{
protection:
      data_structures;
      methods();
}Instance;
```

Where: *struct* is the keyword to start a structure definition.

StructName is the name of the struct being defined.

protection declares access protection, usually private for data and public for methods.

data_structures are any normal C++ data structures.

methods are methods.

Instance defines an instance of StructName.

The instance name is optional. The ";" is required. A typical struct for a calendar program might be:

```
struct Calendar{
      int month;
      int day;
      int year;
      char day_of_week[10];
};
```

This statement declares the structure but does not allocate memory.

```
struct Calendar today;
```

defines an instance of Calendar named today. This statement allocates memory for one occurrence of the Calendar struct.

APPLICATIONS

Use *struct* to define C++ data structures. The data items in a struct are considered public by default. This is the opposite of the class statement where the default protection is private. Data in a struct is not restricted.

Data items in a struct can be referred to in two ways, as members and via pointers. The following code segment illustrates both:

```
     ...
struct payroll{
     int  emp_num;
     int  hours;
     int  rate;
     char name[80];
};
     ...
struct payroll programmer;
struct payroll *senior;
     ...
programmer.emp_num = 999;
senior = &programmer;
senior->rate = 99;
```

A structure named *payroll* is defined. An instance, programmer, and a pointer to a payroll structure, senior, are defined. The instance name followed by a '.' and the field name is the proper way to reference a structure. The "points to", ->, operator is used when referring to a field using pointer notation.

HANDS-ON ACTIVITY

This sample program defines and manipulates a simple class.

1. Type **BC** and press **Enter** to start Borland C++ from the DOS prompt.
2. Press **Alt-FN** to pull down the File menu and create a new file.
3. Type the following code into the edit window:

```
#include <iostream.h>
#include <stdio.h>
#include <string.h>
#include <conio.h>

struct computer{
     char brand[40];
     int  ram;
     int  disk;
};
```

```
void main()
{
      int    value;
      struct computer mine;          // define struct
      struct computer *mine_too;
      char   string1[80] = "";

      clrscr();
      cout << "Module 90\n";
      cout << "This module illustrates struct\n\n";
      mine_too = &mine;
      cout << "Type computer brand: ";
      gets(string1);
      strcpy(mine.brand,string1);
      cout << "How much RAM? ";
      cin  >> value;
      mine.ram = value;
      cout << "How many disks? ";
      cin  >> mine.disk;
      cout << "The computer structure contains: \n";
      cout << "  Computer: " << mine_too->brand    << "\n";
      cout << "  RAM     : " << mine_too->ram      << "\n";
      cout << "  Disks   : " << mine_too->disk     << "\n";

      cout << "\nPress any key to exit\n";
      do {;} while(!kbhit());
}
```

4. Press **Alt-RR** to compile and run the sample program.

```
Module 90
This module illustrates struct

Type computer brand:
```

5. Type **Cheap Clone** then press **Enter**. The following is displayed:

```
Module 90
This module illustrates struct

Type computer brand: Cheap Clone
How much RAM?
```

6. Respond with **640**.

```
Module 90
This module illustrates struct

Type computer brand: Cheap Clone
```

```
How much RAM? 640
How many disks?
```

7. Type **2** and press **Enter** to continue.

```
Module 90
This module illustrates struct

Type computer brand: Cheap Clone
How much RAM? 640
How many disks? 2
The computer structure contains:
  Computer: Cheap Clone
  RAM     : 640
  Disks   : 2

Press any key to exit
```

8. Press any key to exit the sample program and return to Borland C++.
9. Press **Alt-X** to exit Borland C++ and return to DOS.
10. Continue the learning sequence with Module 95.

Module 91

STRUPR( ) and STRLWR( )

DESCRIPTION

Converting a string to all uppercase characters, *strupr( ),* or all lowercase characters, *strlwr( ),* is a useful string manipulation operation.

The strupr( ) and strlwr( ) usage synopsis is:

```
#include <string.h>
char *strlwr(char*);
char *strupr(char*);
```

Sample usage is:

```
#include <string.h>
      ...
char *status;
char string[80];
      ...
status = strupr(string);
status = strlwr(string);
```

The return status value is the pointer to the source string. The case conversion happens in place.

APPLICATIONS

Use strupr( ) and strlwr( ) to convert the contents of a string to all upper and all lowercase characters respectively. Only the characters a-z and A-Z are modified. Other characters, such as digits or punctuation, are unchanged. The string must be terminated with the NULL character. Converting a string to all upper or all lowercase is useful for constructing retrieval keys to guarantee case consistency.

HANDS-ON ACTIVITY

1. Type **BC** and press **Enter** to start up the compiler.

2. Press **Alt-FN** to pull down the File menu and create a new file.
3. Type the following code into the NONAME00.CPP edit window:

```
#include <iostream.h>
#include <stdio.h>
#include <string.h>
#include <conio.h>

void main()
{
      char  string1[80] = "";

      clrscr();
      cout << "Module 91\n";
      cout << "This module uses strupr and strlwr\n\n";
      cout << "Type a string: ";
      gets(string1);
      cout << "\nstring1 is: " << string1 << "\n";
      strupr(string1);
      cout << "Converted to upper case: " << string1 << "\n";
      strlwr(string1);
      cout << "Converted to lower case: " << string1 << "\n";

      cout << "Press any key to exit\n";
      do {;} while(!kbhit());
}
```

4. Press **Alt-RR** to compile and run the sample program.

```
Module 91
This module uses strupr and strlwr

Type a string:
```

5. Type **This is TEST 91!** and press **Enter**. The following is displayed:

```
Module 91
This module uses strupr and strlwr

Type a string: This is TEST 91!
string1 is: THIS IS TEST 91!
string1 is: this is test 91!

Press any key to exit
```

6. Press any key to exit the sample program and return to Borland C++.
7. Press **Alt-X** to exit Borland C++ and return to DOS.
8. Continue the learning sequence with Module 6.

Module 92
SWITCH

DESCRIPTION

The *switch* statement is a structured programming construct that eliminates the need for most nested if statements. The general syntax is:

```
switch(expression){
case 1:
     statements_case1;
     break;
case 2:
     statements_case2;
case 3:
     statements_case3;
     break;
default:
     statements_default;
}
```

The expression may be either a variable or the result of a function call. It must be an integer value. The following nested if construct is equivalent to the above case statement.

```
if(expression == 1){
     statements_case1;
}else{
     if(expression == 2){
          statements_case2;
          if(expression == 3){
               statements_case3;
          }
     }else{
          statements_default;
     }
}
```

The switch statement is much easier to read and understand. The case, break, and default statements are part of the switch statement. Each is discussed in detail in its own module.

APPLICATIONS

Use the switch statement where possible to eliminate nested if statements. *switch* does not remove the need for a nested if construct completely. The switch value must be an integer number. There are times when the different string values represent each case. The switch statement cannot be used.

C compilers generally construct a jump table at the start of the switch. Each case is resolved to an offset. The proper branch is calculated and taken at run-time based on the value of the switch expression.

A good switch statement example is processing an error return from a function call.

```
error = some_function();
switch(error){
case INFO:
     cout << "No real problem, just some information";
case SUCCESS:
     cout << "Really successful processing";
     break;
case RETRY:
     cout << "Play it again Sam...";
     error = some_function();
     break;
case FATAL:
     cout << "A fatal error occurred";
     break;
case WARNING:
     cout << "This is just a warning message";
     break;
default:
     cout << "An unknown error occurred";
}
```

This switch statement uses a variable, *error,* as the switch expression. The case values (INFO, SUCCESS, etc.) are constants defined earlier in the code. The break statements are a secondary control mechanism in switch. The code branches to the end of the switch when break is encountered. Thus if error is equal to the INFO case, the statements associated with INFO will execute. Processing falls through to the SUCCESS case and execution continues until the break is encountered.

Anytime the expression evaluates to an undefined case value, the code for the *default* case is executed. default is generally the last case in the switch statement.

HANDS-ON ACTIVITY

The sample program illustrates a typical switch statement.

1. Type **BC** and press **Enter** to start up the compiler.
2. Press **Alt-FN** to pull down the File menu and create a new file.
3. Type the following code into the NONAME00.CPP edit window:

```
#include <iostream.h>
#include <stdio.h>
#include <string.h>
#include <conio.h>

#define SUCCESS  0
#define INFO          1
#define WARNING  2
#define FATAL         3
#define RETRY         4

int some_function()
{
      return(INFO);
}

void main()
{
      int value;

      clrscr();
      cout << "Module 92\n\n";
      cout << "The switch statement\n";

      cout << "Enter a value between 0 and 4: ";
      cin  >> value;
      cout << "\nvalue     is: " << value << "\n";

      switch(value){
      case INFO:
           cout << "No real problem, just some information";
      case SUCCESS:           // No error, so do nothing
           break;
      case RETRY:
           cout << "Let's try again";
           value = some_function();
           break;
      case FATAL:
           cout << "A fatal error occurred";
           break;
      case WARNING:
```

```
            cout << "This is just a warning message";
            break;
        default:
            cout << "An unknown error occurred";
        }
        cout << "\n\n";
        cout << "Press any key to exit";
        do {;} while(!kbhit());
    }
```

4. Press **Alt-RR** to compile and run the sample program.

```
Module 92

The switch statement
Enter a value between 0 and 4:
```

5. Type **1** and press **Enter**. The following is displayed:

```
Module 92

The switch statement
Enter a value between 0 and 4: 1

value     is: 1
No real problem, just some information

Press any key to exit
```

6. Press any key to exit the sample program and return to Borland C++.
7. Continue the learning sequence with Module 10.

Module 93
TYPEDEF

DESCRIPTION

typedef creates a shorthand name representation of a data type. The data type may be a structure, union, or a built-in data type such as int or char. The syntax for typedef is:

```
typedef declaration t_name;
```

where declaration is a data definition and t_name is the type of name. The following code segment illustrates a typedef statement:

```
typedef char *STRING;
     ...
STRING char_array;
```

This is equivalent to:

```
char *char_array;
```

APPLICATIONS

Use typedef to create shorthand representation of often used complex data declarations. typedef is most used with structures.

```
typedef struct{
     int  value;
     char ch;
     char array[80];
} My_defs;
typedef void (*funct)();
     ...
main()
{
     My_defs stuff;
     funct any_function;
          ...
}
```

The statement "My_defs stuff;" is equivalent to:

```
struct{
     int  value;
     char ch;
     char array[80];
} stuff;
```

or

```
struct My_defs{
     int  value;
     char ch;
     char array[80];
};
struct My_defs stuff;
```

typedef is a convenient way to shorten code. Some code complexity can be hidden by giving data declarations meaningful names, such as *funct* or STRING in the above examples.

There is one important thing to remember here. typedef is like struct; memory is not actually allocated to the item described until it is defined in the program. *My_defs* is declared by the struct statement, but not defined. Memory for a single instance of a *My_defs* structure is allocated when *stuff* is defined in the above example.

HANDS-ON ACTIVITY

This program illustrates one approach to error handling.

1. Type **BC** and press **Enter** to start the compiler.
2. Press **Alt-FN** to pull down the File menu and create a new file.
3. Type the following code:

```
#include <iostream.h>
#include <stdio.h>
#include <stdlib.h>
#include <string.h>
#include <conio.h>

typedef void (*funct)();
typedef struct {
     int  len;
     char string[80];
}Cstring;

void some_function()
{
     cout << "In some_function\n";
```

```
}
void main()
{
      Cstring counted;
      funct any_function;
      char string[80];

      clrscr();
      cout << "Module 93\n";
      cout << "This module uses typedef\n";
      printf("Enter a string: ");
      gets(counted.string);
      counted.len = strlen(counted.string);
      cout << "string in the Cstring struct typedef is: ";
      cout << counted.string << "\n\n";
      cout << "Load any_function with the address of some_function\n";
      any_function = some_function;
      cout << "Now, execute any_function...\n";
      (any_function)();

      cout << "\n\nPress any key to exit";
      do {;} while(!kbhit());
}
```

4. Press **Alt-RR** to compile and run the program.

```
Module 93
This module uses typedef

Enter a string:
```

5. Respond by typing **Testing typedef**, then press **Enter**.

```
Module 93
This module uses typedef

Enter a string: Testing typedef
string in the Cstring struct typedef is: Testing typedef

Load any_function with the address of some_function
Now, execute any_function...
In some_function

Press any key to exit
```

6. Press any key to exit the sample program and return to Borland C++.
7. Press **Alt-X** to exit Borland C++ and return to DOS.
8. Continue the learning sequence with Module 69.

Module 94

UNGETC( )

DESCRIPTION

ungetc( ) places a character back into the input file stream. This function is useful to implement a one character look ahead in the input stream. The syntax is:

```
#include <stdio.h>
int ugetc(int,FILE*);
```

The character is returned on success and EOF returned on error. The int parameter contains the character to be pushed back onto the input file. FILE* is a file descriptor obtained from a fopen( ) call. Typical calls are:

```
#include <stdio.h>
     ...
int ch;
FILE *descriptor;
     ...
ch = getc(descriptor);
     ...
ch = ungetc(ch,descriptor);
```

Any valid ASCII character except EOF can be used with ungetc.

APPLICATIONS

Use ungetc( ) when the character just read from the input file is not needed and will be read again elsewhere in the program. The file must be opened and read using one of the getc( ) related functions before calling ungetc( ). File positioning calls, such as fseek( ), affect the operation of ungetc( ).

HANDS-ON ACTIVITY

This program illustrates ungetc( ). These instructions assume you previously saved the code from Module 48 as MOD48.CPP and that module is in the current directory. Use any valid filename if MOD48.CPP does not exist. The results will vary slightly with a different file.

1. Type **BC** and press **Enter** to start up the compiler.
2. Press **Alt-FN** to pull down the File menu and create a new file.
3. Type the following code into the NONAME00.CPP edit window:

```
#include <iostream.h>
#include <stdio.h>
#include <string.h>
#include <conio.h>

void main()
{
     int  i;
     int  status;
     FILE *descriptor;
     char ch;
     char filename[80];

     clrscr();
     cout << "Module 94\n";
     cout << "This module uses ungetc\n\n";
     cout << "Enter filename: ";
     gets(filename);
     descriptor = fopen(filename,"r");
     if(!descriptor){
          cout << "File not found.\n";
     }
     cout << "Read and echo 20 characters from the file: ";
     for(i=0;i<20;i++){
          ch = fgetc(descriptor);
          if(ch == EOF){
               cout << "\nGot EOF from fgetc()\n";
          }else{
               cout << ch;
          }
     }
     cout << "\nCall ungetc...\n";
     cout << "The last character read was: " << ch << "\n";
     status = ungetc(ch,descriptor);
     if(status == EOF){
          cout << "Error in ungetc()\n";
     }
     cout << "\nRead the character again: ";
     ch = getc(descriptor);
     cout << ch;

     cout << "\n\nPress any key to exit";
     do {;} while(!kbhit());
}
```

4. Press **Ctrl-F9** to compile and run the program.

```
Module 94
This module uses ungetc

Enter filename:
```

5. Type **MOD48.CPP**, then press **Enter**.

```
Module 94
This module uses ungetc

Enter filename: mod48.cpp
Read and echo 20 characters from the file: #include <iostream.h>

Call ungetc...
The last character read was: h

Read the character again: h

Press any key to exit
```

6. Press **Alt-X** to exit Borland C++ and return to DOS.
7. Continue the learning sequence with Module 76.

Module 95
UNION

DESCRIPTION

A *union* defines a special data structure that allows a memory location to reference more than one variable. Only a single value may be stored at any given time. However, the value type may be different from one reference to the next.

```
union UnionName{
      data_type1;
      data_type2;
}Instance;
```

Where: *union* is the keyword to start the union definition.
UnionName is the name of the union being defined.
data_type is any normal C++ data type.
Instance defines an instance of UnionName.

The instance name is optional. The ";" is required. A typical union is:

```
union Flags{
      int   truth;
      float zero;
      char  flag;
};
```

This statement declares the union. No memory is allocated.

```
union Flags status;
```

defines a union of type Flags named status. This statement allocates memory for one occurrence of the Flags union. The amount of memory allocated to the union is determined by the largest data item in the definition. A union may occur within a struct.

APPLICATIONS

Use *union* to define a C++ data structure that holds different data types at different times.

Union data items can be referred to in two ways, as members and as pointers. The following code shows each:

```
     ...
union Cell{
     int   i;
     short s;
     float f;
     char  c;
};
     ...
union Cell item;
     ...
item.i = 999;
item.s = 1;
item.c = 'A';
item.f = 99.0;
```

The instance name followed by a '.' and the field name references a union. The "points to", ->, operator is also used to reference a pointer to a union. All of the fields in a union start at the same memory location.

HANDS-ON ACTIVITY

This program demonstrates using the union statement.

1. Start Borland C++ and use the File menu to create a new source window.
2. Type the following code into the edit window:

```
#include <iostream.h>
#include <stdio.h>
#include <string.h>
#include <conio.h>

union Any_type{
     int   i;
     long  l;
     char  c;
};

void main()
{
     union Any_type value;

     clrscr();
     cout << "Module 95\n";
     cout << "This module uses a union\n\n";
     cout << "Type a number: ";
```

```
        cin  >> value.i;
        cout << "value.i: " << value.i << "\n";
        cout << "value.l: " << value.l << "\n";
        cout << "value.c: " << value.c << "\n";

        cout << "\nPress any key to exit\n";
        do {;} while(!kbhit());
}
```

3. Press **Ctrl-F9** to compile and run the sample program.

```
Module 95
This module uses a union

Type a number:
```

4. Type **64040** and press **Enter**. The following is displayed:

```
Module 95
This module uses a union

Type a number: 64040
value.i: -1496
value.l: 64040
value.c: (

Press any key to exit
```

5. Press any key to exit the sample program and return to Borland C++.
6. Press **Alt-X** to exit Borland C++ and return to DOS.
7. Continue the learning sequence with Module 7.

Module 96
VARIABLES

DESCRIPTION

One of the principle data structures in C++ is the variable. Variables come in many shapes and sizes. This module provides a general overview of variables. Subsequent modules address individual types of variable.

A variable creates a symbol that can be referenced in C++ functions. Memory space is allocated by a variable declaration. The contents of a variable can be modified by assignment operators. Variables have the following characteristics:

- A variable may be manipulated via its address.
- Contents are not guaranteed upon entry into a function.
- Users should follow naming conventions described in Module 63.
- Users should follow C++'s scoping rules.
- Memory is allocated when the variable is declared.
- The compiler automatically converts between data types in calculations.

There are two types of variables, automatic and static. A variable declaration has the following form:

```
{scope} type name {= value};
```

for single value variables, or

```
{scope} type name[occurrences] {= value};
```

for arrays of variables. Scope and value are optional. The value portion of a variable definition is not allowed with some scope declarations.

Variable examples are:

```
static long count;
int  i = 0;
char ch;
register x;
extern unsigned char uch;
```

Variable Scope

The valid types of scope are:

- auto
- static
- register
- extern

Automatic is implied so is used very rarely. Automatic variables are considered local when defined within a function. They are automatically allocated each time a function is executed and deallocated upon function exit. The majority of all variables are automatic.

Static variables have a permanent memory allocation and values remain from the previous execution. Scoping rules apply. Static variables are useful for retaining counters or indexes from one function call to the next. A static variable may not be assigned a value.

Register variables use processor registers as temporary storage. Execution speed is increased by placing frequently used variables in registers. There are a very small number of registers available, so the compiler will make register assignments only when there is one available. Borland C++ automatically makes loop indexes register variables. Declaring a register variable was much more important in the early days of C when compiler technology was in its early stages of development.

A variable may be defined only once. Large programs with multiple modules may define a variable in one module then refer to it in another. Extern solves the problem of allocating space twice for the same variable. Declaring a variable extern tells the compiler to set up an identifier, but space has been allocated somewhere else in the program. The linker, tlink, resolves the external references while building the executable, .EXE, image file.

Scope defines the portion of the program that may access a variable. Where a variable is defined in a program controls its scope. A variable defined within a function is local to that function. No other part of the program may access it. A variable defined outside a function is accessible from the point of definition to the end of the current source file. Variables defined this way are global. Global variables may be referenced in other modules by adding extern to the declaration.

Variable Types

The valid type clause entries are:

- short
- int
- long
- double
- char
- float
- void
- enum

In addition, each short, int, long, and char may also be *signed* or *unsigned*. Unsigned is implied. The amount of storage remains the same for each. The range of values represented by the variable changes. A signed int can represent –32768 to +32767 and unsigned int ranges from 0 to +65,535. An example of each is:

```
short two_bytes;
unsigned int two_bytes;
long four_bytes;
double eight_bytes;
char one_byte;
float four_bytes;
void *four_bytes;
enum two_or_four_bytes;
```

int is the implied data type whenever the scope declaration is used. For example:

```
extern count;
static index;
```

Both count and index are treated as int values. extern and static can be used with all types except enum:

```
extern char ch;
static void *any_type;
```

Arrays of data types are discussed in a separate module.

Variable Names

Variable names can be up to 32 characters, must start with an alpha character, and can contain letters, digits, and the underscore. Variables are identifiers and therefore follow the naming rules described in Module 63.

Variable Value

Variable values may be changed by any of the assignment operators, initialized upon function entry, or by the return from a function call. A variable can be initialized at the start of a function using the following syntax:

```
int truth = 1;
```

Modifying a variable using an assignment operator such as = uses this form:

```
truth = 99;
```

A variable modified by a function return value is:

```
truth = is_it_true();
```

Continue the learning sequence with Module 98.

Module 97
VIRTUAL FUNCTIONS

DESCRIPTION

Virtual functions are special functions defined in a base class, then overloaded in later derived functions. For example, a graphics base class defines a method named draw( ). Classes derived from the graphics base class may also have a draw( ) method. The definition of draw( ) in the derived class overloads or redefines draw( ) in the base class. Such a function is called a virtual function or method. Use the *virtual* keyword with the function declaration to make the function virtual:

```
class BaseClass{
     data_structures;
public:
     virutal void any_method(void);
};
class DerivedClass : public BaseClass{
     data_structures;
public:
     virtual void any_method(void);
};
```

The idea behind virtual functions is the compiler cannot determine which version of a function to call at compile time because the function names and argument lists are identical. Instead, the version of the virtual function to call is determined at run-time based on the type of object referenced.

Virtual functions are the mechanism used by C++ to implement late binding. Early binding is the normal C++ way of resolving which function to execute based on the combination of class name, function name, and parameter list.

APPLICATIONS

Use virtual functions to overload functions. The program determines at run-time which version of a function to execute based on the object associated with the call. Virtual functions are also called dynamic functions in some texts.

Virtual functions are used in situations where the objects used in a progarm are not known at compile-time. A program that uses pop-up windows is a good example. The number of windows a user may open cannot be known at compile-time. So, the run-time function resolution of virtual functions can be used to solve the problem.

Only functions originally defined in the base class can be virtual. Even if the base class function is never called, it still must be defined in the base class. A useful debugging aid is including an error message in the base class definition of virtual functions when they are not referenced. That way the error message prints when the base virtual function is called by mistake.

```
class BaseWinClass{
      int status;
public:
      virtual void WhoAmI(void){ cout << "I'm BaseWinClass\n"; }
};
class DerivedPopupClass : public BaseClass{
      char string[80];
public:
      virtual void WhoAmI(void){
            cout << "I'm DerivedPoupuClass\n";
      }
};

BaseWinClass first_window;
DerivedPopupClass help_menu;
```

When the program runs with the above class definitions, the program determines whether to call DerivedPopupClass::WhoAmI( ) or BaseWin-Class::WhoAmI( ) based on the object type associated with the call.

```
help_menu.WhoAmI();
```

will call DerivedPopupClass::WhoAmI( ) and

```
first_window.WhoAmI();
```

calls BaseWinClass::WhoAmI( ).

Several other items to remember about virtual function are:

- A virtual function cannot be used as a friend function.
- A constructor cannot be a virtual function.
- A destructor can be virtual.

HANDS-ON ACTIVITY

This sample program defines and manipulates a simple class with objects. The class is named Queue. It implements a crude queue data structure. A queue is a First In-First Out data structure.

1. Run Borland C++ from the DOS prompt.
2. Press **Alt-FN** to pull down the File menu and create a new file.
3. Type the following code:

```
#include <iostream.h>
#include <stdio.h>
#include <string.h>
#include <conio.h>

class AircraftClass{
      int status;
public:
      virtual void WhoAmI(void){ cout << "I'm Aircraft\n"; }
};
class PiperClass : public AircraftClass{
      char string[80];
public:
      virtual void WhoAmI(void){
            cout << "I'm PiperClass\n";
      }
};

void main()
{
      clrscr();
      cout << "Module 97\n";
      cout << "This module uses virtual functions\n\n";
      cout << "Create a aircraft object... \n";
      AircraftClass prop;
      cout << "Create a Piper aircraft...\n";
      PiperClass Aztec;
      cout << "Now, call WhoAmI for prop object.\n";
      prop.WhoAmI();
      cout << "Now for Aztec...\n";
      Aztec.WhoAmI();

      cout << "\nPress any key to exit\n";
      do {;} while(!kbhit());
}
```

4. Press **Alt-RR** to compile and run the sample program.

```
Module 97
This module uses virtual functions\n\n";

Create a aircraft object... \n";
Create a Piper aircraft...\n";
Now, call WhoAmI for prop object.\n";
```

```
I'm Aircraft
Now for Aztec...\n";
I'm PiperClass

Press any key to exit
```

5. Press any key to exit the sample program and return to Borland C++.
6. Press **Alt-X** to exit Borland C++ and return to DOS.
7. Continue the learning sequence with Module 46.

Module 98
VOID

DESCRIPTION

The *void* operator has several meanings depending upon usage context. void can be used in the following ways:

- As a data type
- To indicate a function expects no return value
- To indicate a function expects no arguments

APPLICATIONS

void as a data type is a void pointer. It defines storage for a generic pointer data object. * in a variable declaration means "pointer to."

```
void (*function_ptr)();
void *any_ptr;
```

define pointer variables to void data types. The name, function_ptr, indicates that the variable will be used to store the address of a function. Any value stored in function_ptr must be explicitly cast to/from void* in an assignment statement:

```
function_ptr = (void*) any_function;
value        = (long) function_ptr;
```

A function that expects no return value is declared void. For example:

```
void generic_function();
```

A function that expects no arguments uses void in the calling sequence:

```
void generic_function(void);
```

void is used more often in function declarations than as variables.

HANDS-ON ACTIVITY

The sample session which illustrates void presents an advanced concept; storing and using a function pointer.

1. Start Borland C+.
2. Press **Alt-FN** to create a new file.
3. Type the following code into the NONAME00.CPP edit window:

```
#include <iostream.h>

      // function prototypes
void any_function();
void generic_function(void);

void main()
{
      long i;
      void (*function_ptr)();
      void *a_long;

      function_ptr = any_function;
      cout << "The function pointer is: " << function_ptr;
      cout << "\n";
      i      = 99;
      a_long = (void*) i;
      cout << "A long is: " << a_long << "\n";
      cout << "Calling generic_function\n";
      generic_function(1);  // This is an error..
      cout << "Calling any_function\n";
      (*function_ptr)();
}
void any_function()
{
      cout << "In any_function\n";
}
void generic_function(void)
{
      cout << "In generic_function\n";
}
```

4. Press **Alt-C** and type **C** to compile the sample program.

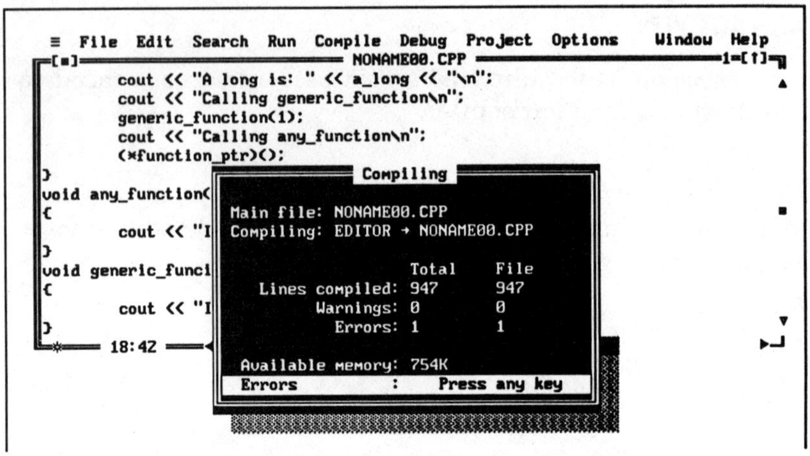

5. The call to generic_function included an argument. The function declaration tells the compiler that no arguments are allowed, so the call generates an error. Change the line:

```
generic_function(1);   // This is an error..
```

to

```
generic_function();
```

6. Press **Alt-RR** to compile the program, then run it.
7. Press **Alt-F5** to view the user screen.

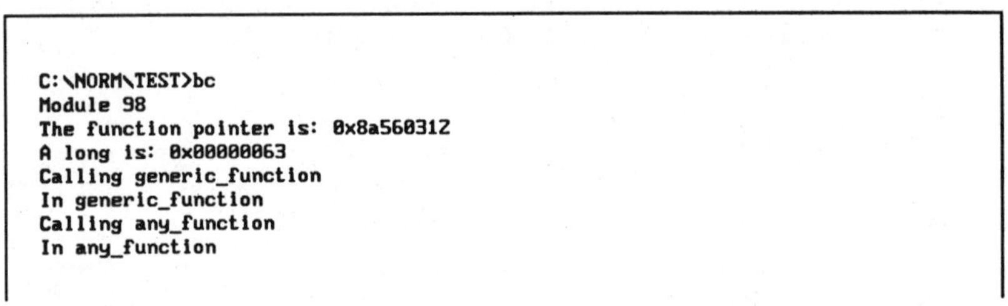

8. Press **Alt-X** to exit Borland C++ and return to the DOS prompt.

The line:

```
(*function_ptr)();
```

calls the function whose address is contained in the void pointer variable function_ptr. Storing a function address in a variable then executing the contents of the variable can be a very useful technique in some applications.

9. Continue the learning sequence with Module 58.

Module 99
WHILE

DESCRIPTION

The while statement has two uses in C++, one is as a separate looping construct and the second is the end of a do loop. Each is discussed in separate modules to clearly distinguish the different usages. The syntax for while is constant between the two usages:

```
while(condition)
```

The statement tests some condition or expression that resolves to a True or False to determine whether to continue or exit the loop that while is part of.

See Module 100 for the discussion of the while loop and Module 31 for while used in the do loop.

Turn to Module 100 to continue the learning sequence.

Module 100

WHILE( ){ }

DESCRIPTION

The while loop implements a structured looping construct that continues to execute as long as the expression is True. The exit condition test is performed at the top of the loop. The usage syntax is:

```
while(expression){
     statements;
}
```

The expression may be a comparison, or a variable, or the result of a function call. The { } are optional when there is a single statement to execute, but required with multiple statements. The break statement can be used to exit the loop early.

APPLICATIONS

Use the while loop when:

- The number of loop iterations is not known
- The exit condition needs to be tested at the beginning of the loop

It is possible that the statements within the while never execute because the exit condition is tested for at the top of the loop. A typical while statement is:

```
i  = 0;
ch = string[i++];
while(ch != 0){
     cout << ch;
     ch = string[i++];
}
```

The while exits the loop when ch becomes zero. This loop types the contents of string to stdout.

HANDS-ON ACTIVITY

The sample program uses a while loop to step through a string, then shows the same operation using one of the other looping constructs to illustrate contrasting ways of looping.

1. Type **BC** and press **Enter** to start up the compiler.
2. Press **Alt-FN** to pull down the File menu and create a new file.
3. Type the following code into the NONAME00.CPP edit window:

```
#include <iostream.h>
#include <stdio.h>
#include <conio.h>
#include <string.h>
#include <ctype.h>

void main()
{
     int  i;
     char ch;
     char string[80];
     char destination[80];

     clrscr();
     cout << "Module 100\n\n";
     cout << "The while loop\n\n";
     cout << "Enter a string: ";
     gets(string);
     cout << "Copy string into destination: ";
     i   = 0;
     ch  = string[i];
     while(ch){
          destination[i] = ch;
          cout << ch;
          ch = string[++i];
     }
     destination[i] = ch;
     cout << "\ndestination: " << destination;
     cout << "\nNow copy destination back to string: ";
     for(i=0;i<=(strlen(destination));i++){
          ch        = destination[i];
          string[i] = toupper(ch);
          cout << string[i];
     }
     cout << "\nPress any key to exit\n";
     do{ ; } while(!kbhit());
}
```

4. Press **Alt-RR** to compile and run the sample program.

```
Module 100

The while loop

Enter a string:
```

5. Type **just some text** and press **Enter**. The following is displayed:

```
Module 100

The while loop

Enter a string: just some text
Copy string into destination:
destination: just some text
Now copy destination back to string: JUST SOME TEXT

Press any key to exit
```

6. Press any key to exit the sample program and return to Borland C++.

The sample program copies the contents of one string to another using a while loop. A contrasting for loop is used to perform the same operation, converting the string to uppercase to show it working.

7. Continue the learning sequence with Module 31.

Module 101

WINDOW MENU

DESCRIPTION

The Programmer's Platform is a window based program development environment. The Window menu provides the capabilities to manipulate those windows.

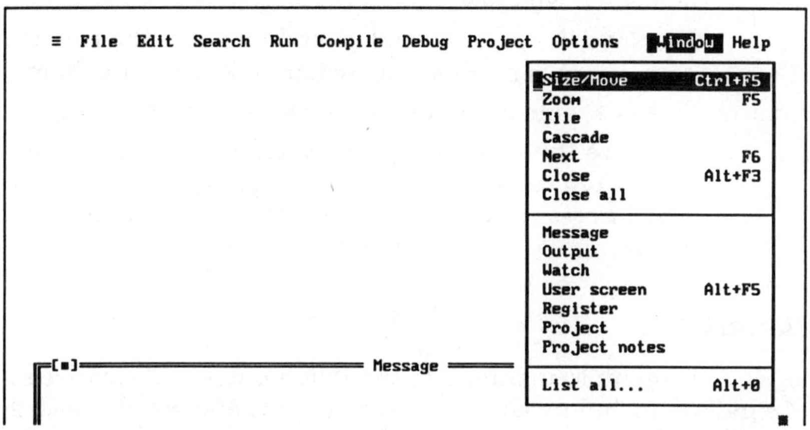

Size/Move	Select this item to move or resize the current window. Ctrl-F5 also performs this operation.
Zoom	Resize the current window to fill the whole screen. If the window has already been zoomed, the window is set back to its original size. Use F5 to zoom the window.
Tile	Rearrange all of the open windows so they are the same size on the screen. Windows are placed side by side on the screen. Tiled windows are useful for examining source code in multiple edit windows.
Cascade	Rearrange the windows from top to bottom on the screen. Windows are cascaded by default by the Programmer's Platform.

Next	Move to the next window. The window is redrawn if necessary. Use F6 to go to the next window without accessing the Window menu.
Close	Close the current window. The window remains in the window list and can be reopened later. Alt-F3 is the short command to close a window.
Close all	Close all open windows. The history list of close windows is also cleared.
Message	Displays and makes the message window active.
Output	Displays and makes active the output window.
Watch	Displays the watch window. It becomes the current window.
User screen	Displays the user window. Press Alt-F5 to access the user window directly.
Register	Displays the contents of the PC processor registers in a dedicated window.
Project	Displays the project window and makes it the current window. There is no shortcut command key for this item.
Project notes	Opens a window that lets you enter notes about file.
List...	Displays the window list. All open and closed windows are listed. You can reopen a closed window via this menu selection. Press Alt-0 to display the window list without accessing the Window menu.

APPLICATIONS

Use the Window menu to manipulate the IDE windows. There are several types of windows including edit, message, output, and watch. Each serves a specific function.

The windows can be manipulated faster using the shortcut keys for changing or closing windows (F5 and Alt-F3). Window manipulation is one area that is especially suited to mouse control. Windows can be zoomed, resized, and moved around the screen easily using a mouse. Using function keys or a mouse speeds window manipulation significantly over accessing the Window menu.

WINDOWS The state of a window can be determined visually. The current or active window is outlined with double lines. All inactive windows are outlined using single lines. The current window also has other visual features:

- Horizontal scroll bar
- Vertical scroll bar
- A solid square in [ ]
- A single or double ended up arrow in [ ]

All of these are used in the mouse interface. Only the current window can be resized and zoomed.

WINDOW MANIPULATION WITH A MOUSE The Programmer's Platform can be controlled equally well with a mouse or function keys. However, window manipulation is especially suited to mouse control. The following procedures can be performed directly using a mouse.

- Switch windows
- Zoom current window
- Resize current window
- Close current window
- Move the position of the current window on the screen
- Scroll the current window horizontally
- Scroll the current window vertically
- Position cursor within an edit window
- Mark text within an edit window

Borland C++ checks for the presence of a mouse driver at startup. A separate cursor is generated when a mouse is found. The mouse cursor is a square block that moves whenever the mouse moves. The normal underline cursor in the edit window remains present. The mouse cursor can be moved anywhere on the screen.

Switching windows is a matter of moving the mouse cursor to the new window and clicking the left button once. This window becomes the current window. You can switch windows in any order with the mouse.

Clicking the left button with the mouse cursor on the arrow in the [ ] on the top line of the window zooms the current window. When the arrow is single ended, the window is zoomed up to fill the entire screen. When the arrow is double ended, the window is returned to its normal size.

The current window size can be set using the following steps:

1. Positions the mouse cursor on the bottom right-hand corner of the window.
2. Press and hold down the left mouse button.
3. Move the mouse to change the window size.
4. Release the mouse button to set the window size.

Positioning the current window is accomplished using the following steps.

1. Move the mouse cursor to the top line of the window.
2. Press and hold the left mouse button.
3. Move the mouse to position the window in the desired location on the screen.
4. Release the mouse button.

Scroll bars are provided for both horizontal and vertical scrolling. The square block within the scroll bar indicates the relative position of what is displayed on the screen. The square blocks move as you move through the file. The steps to scroll the screen using a mouse are:

1. Move the mouse cursor to the scroll arrow that points in the desired scroll direction.
2. Press and hold the left mouse button to begin scrolling.
3. Release the button when the text has scrolled to the desired location.

The current window can be closed using the following steps:

1. Move the mouse cursor to the square block in [ ] on the top line of the window.
2. Click the left mouse button.

The Programmer's Platform does not require a mouse to operate efficiently. However, if you do have one attached to your PC, a mouse will save window manipulation time.

HANDS-ON ACTIVITY

The sample session illustrates several of the Window menu capabilities using shortcut command keys and menu selections.

1. Execute Borland C++ by typing **BC** then pressing **Enter**.
2. Press **Alt-F** to activate the File menu.
3. Press **Enter** to select the open file function.
4. Type **MOD2.CPP** to load the file into the edit window.
5. Compile and run MOD2.CPP by pressing **Ctrl-F9**. Compiling the program generates output to the output window. The edit and message windows are cascaded on the screen when a compile error occurs.

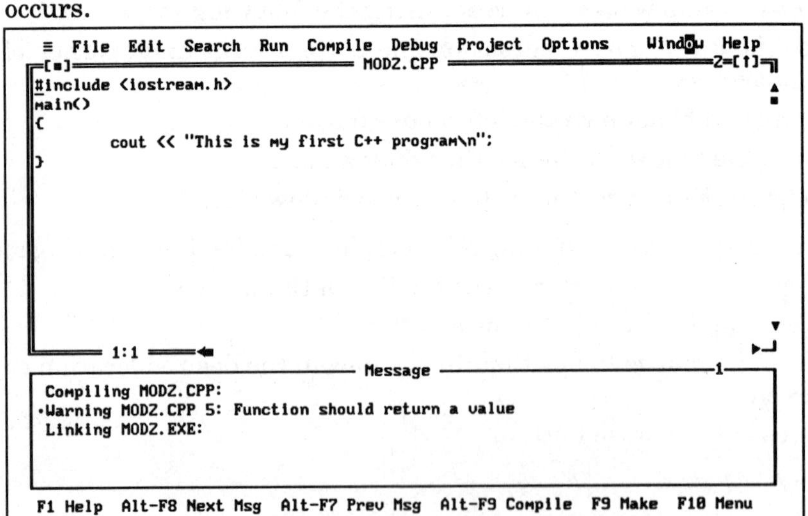

6. Press **Alt-F5** to show the user screen. This screen contains the output from running MOD2.
7. Press **Esc.**
8. Press **Alt-FN** to open a new file edit window.
9. Press **Alt-W** to activate the Window menu.
10. Highlight **Tile** and press **Enter.** The three windows on the screen are displayed in tiled format.

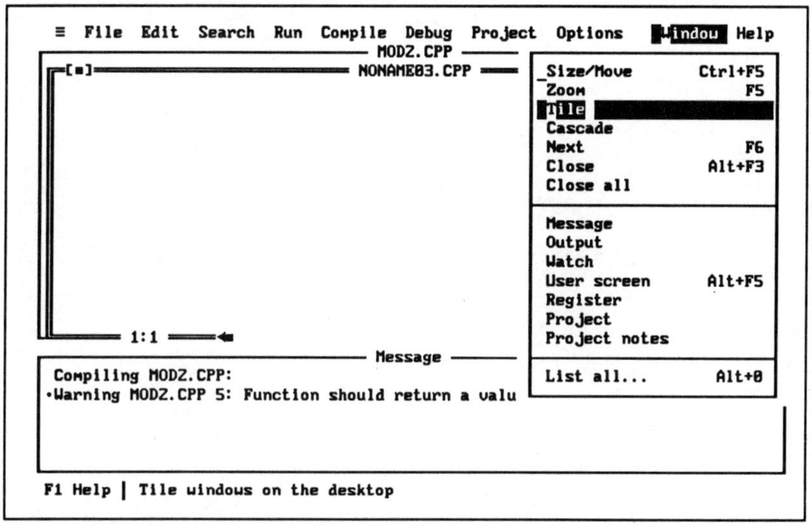

11. Press **Esc** and then **Alt-FN** to open an edit window.
12. Highlight **Tile** and press **Enter.** There are three windows on the screen.
13. Scroll through the windows by pressing **F6** until the Message window is current.
14. Press **Alt-F3** to close the Message window.
15. Press **Alt-W** to pull down the Window menu.
16. Highlight **Cascade** and press **Enter** to change the window display format to cascade.
17. Press **Alt-0** to activate the list window option.
18. Move the selection bar to **user screen** and press **Enter** to reopen the user window.
19. Press **Esc** and then press **Alt-X** to exit Borland C++ and return to the DOS prompt.
20. Continue the learning sequence with Module 52.

Appendix A
RESERVED WORDS

This appendix contains listings of identifiers and terms reserved as keywords for Borland C++. Each entry consists of the keyword and whether the word is reserved by Borland C++, the ANSI C standard, or C++ 2.0.

Keyword	*Reserved By*	*Keyword*	*Reserved By*
auto	ANSI C	new	C++
break	ANSI C	operator	C++
case	ANSI C	overload	C++
catch	C++ (Reserved for future use.)	pascal	Borland C++
		private	C++
char	ANSI C	public	C++
class	C++	register	ANSI C
const	ANSI C, C++	return	ANSI C
continue	ANSI C	short	ANSI C
default	ANSI C	signed	ANSI C, C++
delete	C++	sizeof	ANSI C
do	ANSI C	static	ANSI C
double	ANSI C	struct	ANSI C
else	ANSI C	switch	ANSI C
enum	ANSI C	this	C++
else	ANSI C	try	C++ (Reserved for future use.)
extern	ANSI C		
float	ANSI C	typedef	ANSI C
for	ANSI C	union	ANSI C
friend	C++	unsigned	ANSI C
goto	ANSI C	virtual	C++
if	ANSI C	void	ANSI C
inline	C++	volatile	ANSI C, C++
int	ANSI C	while	ANSI C
long	ANSI C		

Appendix B
TURBO C++ EDITOR KEY BINDING

DESCRIPTION

This appendix presents the commands available in the Borland C++ editor. The commands are sorted in keystroke order.

Action	*Keystroke*
Word to left	Ctrl-A or Ctrl-Left Arrow
Next screen	Ctrl-C or PgDn
Right one character	Ctrl-D or Right Arrow
Previous line	Ctrl-E or Up Arrow
Word to right	Ctrl-F or Ctrl-Right Arrow
Delete character under cursor	Ctrl-G or Del
Delete character to left of cursor	Ctrl-H or Backspace
Tab 8 characters	Ctrl-I or Tab
Mark start of text block	Ctrl-KB
Copy marked text block	Ctrl-KC
Hide marked text block	Ctrl-KH or Ctrl-KI
Mark end of text block	Ctrl-KK
Set place marker	Ctrl-Kn or Ctrl-KP
Read file, place at cursor	Ctrl-KR or Ctrl-KS
Mark word	Ctrl-KT or Ctrl-KU
Move marked text block	Ctrl-KV
Write marked text block to disk	Ctrl-KW
Delete marked text block	Ctrl-KY
Search again	Ctrl-L
Insert blank line	Ctrl-N
Toggle auto-indent mode	Ctrl-OI or Ctrl-OT
Insert control character	Ctrl-P
Search and replace	Ctrl-QA
Jump to bottom of file	Ctrl-QC
Jump to end of line	Ctrl-QD
Jump to top of screen	Ctrl-QE
Find	Ctrl-QF
Undo last delete	Ctrl-QL
Jump to place marker	Ctrl-Qn

Action	*Keystroke*
Jump to top of file	Ctrl-QR
Jump to start of line	Ctrl-QS
Jump to bottom of screen	Ctrl-QX
Delete to end of line	Ctrl-QY
Previous screen	Ctrl-R
Move one character to left	Ctrl-S or Left Arrow
Delete word	Ctrl-T
Toggle Insert/overstrike mode	Ctrl-V or Ins
Scroll screen up one line	Ctrl-W
Next line	Ctrl-X or Down Arrow
Delete line	Ctrl-Y
Scroll screen down one line	Ctrl-Z
Next line	Down Arrow or Ctrl-X or End
Help	F1
Save file	F2
New file	F3
Exit BC	F10
Beginning of line	Home
Toggle insert/overstrike mode	Ins or Ctrl-V
Move one character to left	Left Arrow or Ctrl-S
Next Screen	PgDn or Ctrl-C
Previous Screen	PgUp or Ctrl-R
Move one character to right	Right Arrow or Ctrl-D
Previous line	Up Arrow or Ctrl-E

Appendix C
EXERCISES

1. ABOUT THIS BOOK
   a. Why was C designed?
   b. What sequence should be followed to read this book?
   c. What extensions does C++ add to the base C language?
   d. Why are the steps in the Hands-On Activity section numbered?
2. SAMPLE SESSION
   a. What do you type to start Borland C++?
   b. What is the default Borland C++ edit filename?
   c. What is the Programmer's Platform?
   d. What function must every C++ program include?
   e. How is the Main Menu invoked?
   f. Which preprocessor statement causes a header file to be compiled?
   g. What extension do C++ source filenames end with?
3. ≡ MENU
   a. How do you cause the screen to be redrawn?
   b. What happens when Borland Assembler is selected but is not installed on the computer?
4. ARITHMETIC
   a. Name three binary arithmetic operators.
   b. Explain the difference between ++x and x++.
   c. What is the result of 9 / 4? Assume integer division.
5. ARRAYS
   a. Define an array of characters named STRING.
   b. What character marks the end of string for a char array?
   c. Name three data types that may be used in arrays.
6. ASSIGNMENT OPERATORS
   a. What is x += 99 equivalent to?
   b. Is == an assignment operator?
   c. How is a variable initialized in its definition?
7. BITWISE EXPRESSIONS
   a. Name three logical bit operators.
   b. What shift operator is equivalent to dividing by 2?
   c. How do you compute the one's complement of 27?

   d. What bit mask can be used with & to turn off all of the bits in a long integer?

8. BORLAND C++ FUNCTION LIBRARIES
   a. How is a C++ function library referenced?
   b. What system header file is necessary to call BIOS interrupt routines?
9. BREAK
   a. What statements can break be used with?
10. CASE
    a. What other operator is case used with?
    b. What statement causes a branch to the end of the switch?
    c. Is the following case statement valid?

```
case "string":
break;
```

11. CASTS
    a. What is the purpose of casts?
    b. How do you assign a long integer to a floating point variable?
12. CHAR
    a. How many bytes of memory does a char variable occupy?
    b. Give an example of initializing a character string.
    c. What is the form of the character constants that C++ recognizes?
    d. What is the difference between a signed char and an unsigned char?
13. CIN, >>
    a. What I/O stream does >> read from?
    b. Can cin be redirected? How?
    c. >> is an __________ operator.
14. CLASS
    a. Define class.
    b. What are the three protection levels available in a class definition?
    c. Instances of a class are called _______.
15. COMPILE MENU
    a. Large programs should be built from separate modules. The _______ option on the Compile menu compiles just the changed source code module.
    b. A program is generally generated with the Compile after it has been _______.
16. COMPILER DIRECTIVES
    a. Which compiler are command line directives generally used with?
    b. What option selects ANSI C keywords?

17. CONDITIONALS
    a. Why should explicit ( )s be used in complicated conditional statements?
    b. What statement are conditionals used in?
    c. What is the difference between == and =?
18. CONSOLE I/O
    a. What predefined I/O descriptors are automatically opened when a C programs is run?
    b. How is command line I/O redirection accomplished?
    c. What system function reads the next character from stdin?
    d. What system function writes a string to stdout?
19. CONST
    a. What is the naming convention for naming constants?
    b. What is the effect of declaring a function parameter as const?
    c. List the data types that can be declared as const.
20. CONSTANTS
    a. Name two of the three ways to define a constant.
    b. How is const different from #define?
21. CONSTRUCTORS
    a. How many ways are there for implementing a constructor?
    b. What happens if you do not define a constructor for a class?
    c. How do you choose the constructor name?
    d. Are constructors usually public or private?
22. CONTINUE
    a. What looping statements can continue be used with?
    b. What situation is continue used in?
23. COUT, <<
    a. What stream does << write to?
    b. Can cout be redirected? How?
    c. What system file header must be included to use <<?
24. DEBUG MENU
    a. What is a debug watch?
    b. What is the keystroke to add a watch variable?
    c. Which Debug menu option shows the function call hierarchy?
    d. Can the contents of variables be modified from the Debug menu?
25. DEFAULT
    a. What construct is default used with?
    b. What is the purpose of the default statement?
26. #DEFINE, #UNDEF
    a. #define and #undef are ____________ statements.
    b. Define a preprocessor symbol.
    c. Define a preprocessor macro.

d. Define a preprocessor constant.
e. Remove a preprocessor symbol.

27. DELETE
    a. What action does delete perform?
    b. What C function is roughly equivalent to delete?
28. DERIVED CLASSES AND INHERITANCE
    a. What is a derived class?
    b. What are the advantages of using inheritance?
29. DESTRUCTORS
    a. When is a destructor called?
    b. What is the naming convention for destructors?
    c. What reasons are there for defining custom destructors?
30. DEVELOPING LARGE PROGRAMS
    a. What two features does Borland C++ provide to support large program development?
    b. Which compiler is executed by make?
    c. What are the advantages of using make and project files?
31. DO
    a. do is a ______ construct.
    b. Is the exit condition for a do loop tested for at the top or the bottom of the loop?
32. EDIT MENU
    a. You must ____ a block of text before it can be cut.
    b. What commands mark the beginning and ending positions of a text block?
    c. What command pulls down the Edit menu?
33. EDIT WINDOW
    a. What is the purpose of the editing diamond?
    b. What command quickly moves the cursor to the end of the text?
    c. There are two ways to search for a text string. Describe each. Hint: One is a key command and the other is in a menu.
    d. Before copying a group of lines, they must be ________.
    e. How is text marked?
34. ELSE
    a. What statement is else a part of?
    b. Are { } required with else?
    c. Why should { } be used with else?
35. ELSE IF
    a. What is the purpose of else if?
    b. What other statement may be used as an alternative to nested else if statements?

36. ENUM
    a. What is the primary use of enum?
    b. Can the value of an enum set be modified?
37. ERROR HANDLING
    a. What file descriptor is automatically opened when a program starts for writing error messages to?
    b. What system variable is used to hold error values?
38. EXIT( )
    a. Is exit( ) a function or an operator?
    b. When should you use exit( )?
39. FCLOSE( )
    a. What is fclose( ) used for?
    b. What type of parameter is expected by fclose( )?
    c. What is the return value for successful execution of fclose( )?
40. FGETS( )
    a. What parameters are required by fgets( )?
    b. Can stdin be read by fgets( )?
    c. The string read by fgets( ) corresponds to a ____ in the input file.
    d. Does fgets( ) include the newline in the input buffer?
41. FILE I/O
    a. Name four file I/O functions.
42. FILE MENU
    a. What is the shortcut command to save the current file?
    b. What File menu selection edits a new file?
    c. How do you execute a DOS program without exiting Borland C++?
    d. What DOS command restarts Borland C++ after an external program has been run?
43. FOPEN( )
    a. What is the return value from fopen( )?
    b. What mode causes the file to be opened for read only access?
    c. Can a file be opened for both read and write access?
    d. What return value signals an error in the open operation?
44. FOR
    a. for is a ______ construct.
    b. When should for be used?
    c. What action does a continue statement perform in a for loop?
    d. What statement causes an early exit from a for loop?
45. FPUTS( )
    a. What is the purpose of fputs( )?
    b. What other file I/O function should be performed prior to calling fputs( )?

c. What file I/O function should be performed before exiting a program that uses fputs( )?

46. FRIEND FUNCTIONS
    a. What is a friend method?
    b. How do you flag a method or function as a friend?
    c. When should you use friend methods?
    d. What is indicated when a class has large numbers of friend methods?

47. FUNCTIONS
    a. What function must be in every C++ program?
    b. What purpose do function prototypes serve?
    c. How many actions should a function perform?

48. GETC( ), FGETC( )
    a. What is the difference between getc( ) and fgetc( )?
    b. What system I/O function must be called before calling fgetc( )?

49. GETCHAR( )
    a. What does getchar( ) do?
    b. What system header file must be included in order to use getchar( )?
    c. Can getchar( ) be used to read a user specified file? How?
    d. What file does getchar( ) normally read from?

50. GETS( )
    a. Where does gets( ) read its input?
    b. What is the syntax for a gets( ) call?

51. GOTO
    a. Use goto to branch to a _____.
    b. Why is using many gotos bad coding practice?

52. HELP MENU
    a. What command keystroke opens a window containing the help index?
    b. How is the main help menu accessed?

53. IF
    a. The if operator tests a _________.
    b. What value is considered FALSE by if?
    c. What value is considered TRUE by if?
    d. Are { } required in the if statement?
    e. Why should { } be used to group statements?

54. #IF, #ELSE, #ELIF, #ENDIF
    a. #if, #else, #elif, and #elif are _____________ statements.
    b. What is the function of #elif?
    c. What items may be tested by #if and #elif?

55. #IFDEF, #IFNDEF
    a. #ifdef tests for the existence of a preprocessor ______.
    b. What type of compilation are #ifdef and #ifndef used for?
    c. What does #ifdef stand for?
    d. What does #ifndef stand for?
56. #INCLUDE
    a. What is the syntax for including a system header file?
    b. What is the syntax for including a local header file?
    c. What is the most commonly included C++ system header file?
57. INLINE
    a. What is the purpose of inline functions?
    b. When should a function be declared inline?
    c. What is one side effect of using inline functions?
58. INT
    a. int is short for _______.
    b. What are the largest and smallest numbers an int can represent?
    c. What are the smallest and largest numbers that an unsigned int can represent?
59. LOGICAL EXPRESSIONS
    a. Name the three logical expressions.
    b. What are logical expressions used for?
    c. What operator is used with logical expressions?
60. LONG
    a. How many bytes does a long integer use in Borland C++?
    b. What is the largest number a long can represent?
    c. What is the smallest number an unsigned long can represent?
61. MAIN( )
    a. Why is main( ) a special function in C and C++?
    b. What happens at the end of main( )?
62. METHODS
    a. What is a method?
    b. How is a method invoked?
    c. What four modifiers may be used with method definitions?
63. NAMING
    a. How many characters are allowed in a C++ name?
    b. Can a name include the $ character?
    c. Is if a valid name?
64. NEW
    a. What is the purpose of the new operator?
    b. What operator is used to give back memory allocated by new?
    c. What C function is equivalent to new?

65. OBJECTS
    a. An object is an instance of a _____.
    b. The class __________ is called to create an object.
    c. What is the syntax for creating an object?
    d. How is a message sent to an object?
66. OPTION MENU
    a. How is the function of the mouse buttons set?
    b. Does Borland C++ generate programs optimized for speed or size by default?
    c. Which Option menu selection allows you to set up access to external programs?
67. OVERLOADING
    a. What is overloading in C++?
    b. Give two examples of overloaded operators.
    c. Can new be overloaded?
    d. Why are functions sometimes overloaded?
68. PASSING OBJECTS
    a. What are the three ways of passing an object to a function?
    b. What is the default way of passing an object?
69. POINTERS
    a. Does a string pointer allocate memory for the string?
    b. What is the syntax for referring to the fourth byte of string?
    c. What is the syntax to pass a structure to a function?
70. PREPROCESSOR
    a. What is the C/C++ preprocessor?
    b. What is the general format for a preprocessor statement?
    c. Name three commonly used preprocessor statements.
71. PRINTF
    a. Name four variations of the printf( ) function.
    b. What file does printf( ) write to?
    c. Can printf( ) write to a file?
    d. What is the format specifier to cause printf( ) to output a string? A decimal number?
72. PRIVATE
    a. What is the purpose of private?
    b. Why are methods generally not declared private?
73. PROJECT MENU
    a. What is the purpose of a project file?
    b. How is a project file created?
    c. What is the difference between compiling a program with a project file and a make file?
    d. When should a project file be used?

74. PROTECTED
    a. How does protected data differ from private data?
    b. Does class protection apply to derived classes?
75. PUBLIC
    a. Public is a _________ level for class data and methods.
    b. Why are methods usually declared public?
    c. Why are data structures generally not declared public?
76. PUTC( ), FPUTC
    a. What file descriptor does putc( ) write to?
    b. Can putc( ) write to a file?
    c. Can fputc( ) write to stdout?
77. PUTCHAR( )
    a. What action does putchar( ) perform?
    b. How do you cause putchar( ) to write to a file?
78. PUTS( )
    a. What stream does puts( ) write to?
    b. Does puts( ) add a newline character on the end of the string?
    c. How do you cause puts( ) to write to a file?
79. RUN MENU
    a. What is the primary function of the Run selection?
    b. When should you select Program Reset?
    c. How can the arguments to a function be changed without recompiling the program?
    d. What key directs Borland C++ to toggle between the edit window and the user screen?
80. SCANF( ), FSCANF( )
    a. What is the purpose of scanf( )?
    b. What input stream does scanf read from?
    c. Name three of the functions related closely to scanf( ).
81. SEARCH MENU
    a. What is the shortcut command to select the Find... Search option?
    b. The search direction (forward or backward) can be set for what two Search selections?
    c. What command is used to find the next compilation error?
82. SHORT
    a. What is the largest number a short can represent? An unsigned short?
    b. How many bytes of memory does a short integer occupy?
83. STRCAT( ) and STRNCAT( )
    a. What action does strcat( ) perform?
    b. How many arguments does strncat( ) expect?

c. What happens if the destination string in not large enough to hold the concatenated string?

84. STRCHR( )
  a. strchr( ) searches a string for a ________.
  b. What system file header must be included to use strchr( )?
  c. How can strchr( ) be used to find the end of a string?

85. STRCMP( ) and STRNCMP( )
  a. What function is called to compare the first five characters of a string?
  b. What value does strcmp( ) return to indicate the strings match?
  c. Is strcmp( ) case sensitive?

86. STRCPY( ) and STRNCPY( )
  a. What action does strcpy( ) perform? strncpy( )?
  b. What does a return value of 27 from strcpy mean?
  c. Is the contents of the destination string destroyed by a call to strcpy( )?

87. STREAM I/O
  a. Name the four stream file descriptors automatically opened by C++ during program startup.
  b. Which of the streams can be redirected from the command line?
  c. Name three stream classes defined in C++.

88. STRINGS
  a. Character strings are terminated by what character?
  b. A string is an _____ of type char.
  c. The first character of a string is what array element?
  d. How is the address of the second byte of a string referenced?

89. STRLEN( )
  a. What is the purpose of strlen( )?
  b. How does strlen( ) recognize end of string?
  c. What is the return value generated by strlen( )?

90. STRUCT
  a. What is the default protection for a struct?
  b. How is struct different from class?
  c. What is the syntax for referencing a data item within a struct?

91. STRUPR( ) and STRLWR( )
  a. What is the purpose of strupr( ) and strlwr( )?
  b. Is the original value of the string lost when strupr( ) is called?

92. SWITCH
  a. What other operator does the switch replace?
  b. What operators affect control flow in a switch statement?
  c. What operator causes an immediate exit from the switch?
  d. What case executes when the expression does not match any case?

93. TYPEDEF
    a. When should typedef be used?
    b. Define a definition for NUMBERS that defines an int pointer.
94. UNGETC( )
    a. What is the purpose of ungetc( )?
    b. When should ungetc( ) be used?
    c. Can multiple characters be pushed back into the input stream?
95. UNION
    a. How many bytes does a union containing a short and a long occupy?
    b. How are members of a union referenced?
96. VARIABLES
    a. Name three variable data types.
    b. How many bytes are allocated for a long integer variable?
    c. What is the largest number an unsigned integer can represent?
    d. What is the smallest number an unsigned long integer can represent?
97. VIRTUAL FUNCTIONS
    a. What is a virtual function?
    b. Virtual functions must be defined in the ____ class.
    c. How does the compiler know which version of a virtual function to invoke?
98. VOID
    a. What is a VOID pointer?
    b. What is returned by a function of type void?
99. WHILE
    a. What two loops can while be used in?
100. WHILE( ){ }
    a. When should a while( ) loop be used?
    b. Is the exit condition for while( ) tested at the top or bottom of the loop?
    c. What statement can be used to branch back to the top of the loop?
    d. What statement can be used to exit the loop immediately?
101. WINDOW MENU
    a. How is a window closed?
    b. What keystroke makes the next window the current window?
    c. Can a closed window be reopened?
    d. How is a window reopened?
    e. What is the difference between tiled and cascaded windows?
    f. What pointing device can be used to manipulate the Programmer's Platform windows?

Index

ther Books from Wordware Publishing, Inc.

mputer Aided Drafting
strated AutoCAD (Release 11)
strated AutoLISP
strated AutoSketch 2.0

tabase Management
strated dBASE III Plus
strated dBASE IV 1.1
strated Force 2
strated FoxPro 2.0

sktop Publishing
Desktop Studio: Multimedia with the Amiga
strated PageMaker 4.0
strated Ventura 3.0 (Windows Ed.)
strated Ventura 3.0 (DOS/GEM Ed.)
strated Ventura 4.0

eral and Advanced Topics
Clipper Functions
Complete Communications Handbook
ncial Modeling using Lotus 1-2-3
hics User Interface Programming with C
trated CorelDRAW! 3.0
trated DacEasy Accounting 4.2
trated Novell NetWare 2.x/3.x Software
ell NetWare: Adv. Tech. and Applications
erstanding 3COM Networks

grated
rated Enable/OA
rated Framework III
rated Microsoft Works 2.0
rated Q&A 3.0 (2nd Ed.)
rated Q&A 4.0

ramming Languages
rated Borland C++ 3.1
rated C Programming (ANSI) (2nd Ed.)
rated Clipper 5.0 (2nd Ed.)
rated QBasic for MS-DOS 5.0
hics Programming with Turbo Pascal
rated Turbo C++
rated Turbo Debugger 3.0
rated Turbo Pascal 6.0

adsheet
rated Excel 4.0 for Windows
rated Lotus 1-2-3 Rel. 2.1

ems and Operating Guides
rated DR DOS 6.0
ated MS-DOS 5.0
ated UNIX System V
ated Windows 3.1

Processing
ated Microsoft Word 5.0 (PC)
ated WordPerfect 5.1
ated WordPerfect for Windows
ated WordStar 6.0
Perfect Wizardry: Adv. Tech. and Applications

lar Applications Series
Your Own Computer
Control Using Lotus 1-2-3
ng Newsletters with Ventura
ase Publishing with Ventura
op Publishing with Word 2.0 for Windows
op Publishing with WordPerfect for Windows
AmiPro 3.0 in a Day
Learn AutoCAD in a Day
Learn C in Three Days
Learn CorelDRAW! in a Day
Learn DataPerfect in a Day
Learn dBASE IV in a Day
Learn dBASE Programming in a Day
Learn DOS in a Day
Learn DrawPerfect in a Day
Learn Excel for Windows in a Day (Ver. 3.0 & 4.0)
Learn FoxPro 2.0 in a Day
Learn Freelance Graphics for Windows in a Day
Learn Generic CADD 6.0 in a Day
Learn Harvard Graphics 3.0 in a Day
Learn Lotus 1-2-3 in a Day
Learn Lotus 1-2-3 2.4 in a Day
Learn Lotus 1-2-3 for Windows in a Day
Learn Microsoft Works in a Day
Learn Microsoft Assembler in a Day
Learn Norton Utilities in a Day
Learn Novell Netware Software in a Day
Learn Pacioli 2000 Version 2.0 in a Day
Learn PageMaker 4.0 in a Day
Learn PAL in a Day
Learn Paradox in a Day
Learn Paradox for Windows in a Day
Learn PC-Paintbrush in a Day
Learn PC-Tools 8.0 in a Day
Learn PlanPerfect in a Day
Learn Q&A 4.0 in a Day
Learn Quattro Pro 4.0 in a Day
Learn Quicken in a Day
Learn Turbo Assembler Programming in a Day
Learn Ventura 4.0 in a Day
Learn Windows in a Day
Learn Word 2.0 for Windows in a Day
Learn WordPerfect for Windows in a Day
Learn WordPerfect in a Day (2nd Ed.)
Mailing Lists using dBASE
Moving from WordPerfect for DOS to
WordPerfect for Windows
Object-Oriented Programming using Turbo C++
Presentations with Harvard Graphics
Programming On-line Help with C++
Programming Output Drivers using Borland C++
WordPerfect Macros
WordPerfect 6.0 Survival Skills
Write Your Own Programming Language using C++

Regional
Classic Clint: The Laughs and Times of Clint
Murchison, Jr.
Exploring the Alamo Legends
Forget the Alamo
The Great Texas Airship Mystery
100 Days in Texas: The Alamo Letters
Rainy Days in Texas Funbook
San Antonio Uncovered
Texas Highway Humor
Texas Tales Your Teacher Never Told You
Texas Wit and Wisdom
That Cat Won't Flush
They Don't Have to Die
This Dog'll Hunt
To the Tyrants Never Yield
Unsolved Texas Mysteries

Call Wordware Publishing, Inc. for names of the bookstores in your area
(214) 423-0090

